WARRIOR WITHOUT WEAPONS

THE AUTHOR
From a photograph by Howard Coster

WARRIOR WITHOUT WEAPONS

by

MARCEL JUNOD

With a Preface by

MAX HUBER

Sometime President of the International Committee of the Red Cross

Translated from the French (*Le Troisième Combattant*) by

EDWARD FITZGERALD

JONATHAN CAPE
THIRTY BEDFORD SQUARE
LONDON

FIRST PUBLISHED 1951

Dewey Classification
361.506

PRINTED IN GREAT BRITAIN IN THE CITY OF OXFORD
AT THE ALDEN PRESS
BOUND BY A. W. BAIN & CO. LTD., LONDON

CONTENTS

5

CONTENTS

JAPAN

PREFACE

I AM doubly happy to preface this book, in which Dr. Marcel Junod writes so strikingly of his experiences as a delegate of the International Committee of the Red Cross, with a few general observations on the activity of the Red Cross. First of all in order to express my gratitude publicly to Dr. Junod for his long, devoted, efficient and courageous service to the Red Cross, and at the same time to all those who devoted themselves to the great cause, at his side as, so to speak, front-line combatants. And secondly because a book which has been so directly experienced as this gives a much more convincing impression of the nobility and grandeur of Red Cross work, with all its difficulties — and its dangers as well — than any systematic and documentary report possibly could. The two methods of approach complement each other.

Dr. Junod has written *Le Troisième Combattant*[1] on his own initiative and as his personal story, choosing his material from the great mass of his experiences. The choice he has made amongst them and the memories he recalls are not intended in any way to blame or praise particular countries or particular individuals, but in order to show the situations, both general and particular, in which a delegate of the International Committee of the Red Cross can find himself, and to further a general understanding of our problems.

The intention of the book is not to describe the general activities of the Committee, or the conduct of each belligerent; it is rather to serve as an introduction to the particular problems met with by the Red Cross at the very heart and centre of its activities. The diversity and the importance of the missions carried out by Dr. Junod and the length of time he was engaged on them give him every right to say things which must be said.

In accordance with its nature and its particular task the Red Cross aids the victims of war not on account of their particular nationality or because they are fighting for this or that cause, but purely and simply because they are human beings who are suffering and are in

[1] Translated under the title *Warrior without Weapons*.

need of help, and because it strives to assuage all human distress which has no hope of effective aid from other sources. These are the general principles which circumscribe the vast sphere in which the delegates of the International Committee carry on their work.

However, the specific task of the Red Cross is not determined exclusively by the idea of assisting human beings as such, but also by the desire to relieve above all that suffering which is brought about by man, brought about by man's inhumanity to man, and which is still more painful on that account, a circumstance which makes it more difficult to relieve. The most terrible form of man's inhumanity to man is war and that is why the idea of the Red Cross was born on the field of battle, and why it has been given special protection in international law and provided with its own distinctive emblem. However, the Red Cross does not restrict its work to the sphere of international wars; it operates also in civil wars; and in principle it extends its protection to all human beings who are defenceless in the hands of an enemy who persecutes them and threatens to destroy them. There are an infinite number of gradations between the persecution of individuals and wars between peoples, but these are the two extreme forms, and they produce analogous physical and moral distress.

Many governments and independent organizations, including in particular the various national Red Cross Societies, carry on a tremendous amount of splendid work in a great variety of ways to assuage human suffering, and to eliminate its causes by preventive measures. However, we should always bear in mind the essential difference between two situations in which relief work is carried out: it takes place either in time of peace both at home and abroad, or in time of war at home and to the exclusive benefit of the country concerned, or perhaps officially in favour of a belligerent country with which the donors sympathize, or in the interests of prisoners in enemy hands.

Now that relief which is given in the first case is well received everywhere. In the second case, however, the political and psychological tension which arises in time of war between two opposing camps invariably produces hostility towards those whose sufferings need relief and erects a wall of suspicion and distrust against those who seek to bring it, so that first of all this wall must be surmounted. Humanitarian work must at least be tolerated, and if possible it should be encouraged, even when it is primarily directed towards the good of an enemy.

Thus it is our task to form a *third front* above and cutting across the two belligerent fronts, a third front which is directed against neither of them, but which works for the benefit of both. The combatants on this third front are interested only in the suffering of the defenceless human being, irrespective of his nationality, his convictions or his past. They fight wherever they can against all inhumanity, against every degradation of the human personality, against all injustice directed against defenceless human beings. It is for these fighters that Dr. Junod has coined the expression 'the third combatant'.

It is incumbent on neutrals above all to fight on this humanitarian front, because it is much more easy for them to free themselves from the prejudice and hostility which are so natural to men engaged in warfare. At the same time they have a much better opportunity of intervening effectively and carrying out humanitarian work on the territory of a belligerent in favour of the prisoners in his hands. It is in this above all that the importance of an institution of so strictly neutral a character as the International Committee of the Red Cross resides, and this applies equally to its delegates, particularly when they have the energy and the outlook of a Dr. Junod.

However, the spirit of *Le Troisième Combattant* must not in any way be confined to the citizens or the institutions of neutral countries, and, fortunately, it is not. The dominant idea and the essence of the Geneva Convention is equality of treatment for all sick and wounded men irrespective of whether they are friends or enemies. It is the fulfilment of the cry of Solferino: *Siamo tutti fratelli.*

Apart from their purely medical tasks the Red Cross Societies also concern themselves with the care of all prisoners of war no matter what their nationality. However, for a variety of reasons it is clear that this activity pales to some extent by comparison with the assistance given to the national or allied armed forces and civilian populations. At the same time, the Red Cross Societies, and their members as individuals, can greatly assist in securing respect for the Red Cross and ensuring the victory of its ideal by helping to break down the wall of antipathy which surrounds enemy prisoners of war, and to dissipate the suspicion of the authorities against neutrals who seek to aid these men.

Dr. Junod's book gives us an impressive picture of the difficulties which so often beset the work of the Red Cross delegates, and it shows how essential and how comforting it is for them to find moral support from the national Red Cross Societies of the countries in which they have to work. In this respect the independence of the national Red Cross Societies and their members towards the authorities is something very precious.

Where Red Cross work is concerned the question of reciprocity constantly arises. Dr. Junod's book shows the tremendous importance of this principle, particularly in circumstances where it has not been laid down in advance by international agreements such as the Geneva Convention. In practise the reciprocal interests of the belligerents in the fate of their own nationals who have fallen into enemy hands, almost always represents a condition which is to some extent essential for the work of the International Committee of the Red Cross and its delegates. The International Committee seeks to establish this principle wherever circumstances permit and it does so by virtue of its essential quality of impartiality, which impels it to intervene everywhere to the full extent of its power with such aid as it is authorized to provide. However, its work as such is never entirely dependent on the *quid pro quo* principle and it is never the object of political or other bargaining.

In speaking of 'the third combatant', and, in consequence, of a third front, Dr. Junod makes use of the terminology of war and it is above all in time of war that such terms take on their full significance. But despite the points of comparison the ideas themselves are by their very nature profoundly contrary to those of war.

The delegates, who are, so to speak, front line troops of the International Committee or of other neutral organizations, must, like a soldier fighting the enemy, possess certain essential qualities:

moral and physical strength to persevere in difficult and often painful situations, and courage too, not only physical courage in the face of grave and constant danger — several delegates have given their lives in the service of the Red Cross — but also civic courage, because that is indispensable if the cause of those who are hated, despised and defenceless is to be upheld in an atmosphere which is often unsympathetic and sometimes even hostile. And finally, like a military commander, a delegate must possess the necessary ability to take quick decisions, often of the gravest nature, on his own responsibility, because he will often not be in a position to turn to Geneva for special instructions.

Not only the International Committee of the Red Cross in its relations with belligerent governments, but also the delegate himself in his relations with the authorities, the military commanders and the national organizations of the countries in which he has to work, must possess certain diplomatic qualities: tact, discretion, firmness and a sense of proportion. Not, be it remarked, in order to deceive anyone and to obtain advantages by unfair means, but merely in order to make the most of every possible opportunity. The onerous sacrifice which such a reserved and non-committal attitude can mean to the human heart is fully justified by its final aim: to aid the greatest possible number of war victims as effectively as possible. And that is why such an attitude is completely reconcilable with the staunchest fidelity to the cause and the ideals of the Red Cross.

That fidelity is essential and decisive. It is the source from which a delegate draws his courage and obtains that mastery over himself which is so necessary for the performance of his task. It is fidelity to the principle that Red Cross assistance, however vast its developments and ambitious its aspirations, shall be directed above all to the human being defenceless in the hands of his enemy, that it shall protect the human personality and uphold its dignity precisely in cases where no national, party or ideological solidarity is available to afford that assistance and protection. The more difficult, and in a certain sense thankless, a humanitarian task is, the more it demands the renunciation of egocentric impulses and affinities, even where they are sublimated in a national or ideological form, and the more it is in accordance with the spirit of the Red Cross. These ultimate consequences of the Red Cross spirit must animate not only the International Committee itself, but all its delegates, with a sacred fire if the Red Cross is to recognize and perform the tasks for which it exists. Those tasks are determined by humanitarian considerations alone, independent of all separate interests, no matter how legitimate such interests may be in themselves.

It is essential that this aspect of the activity of the Red Cross should not pass unnoticed amidst the enormous amount of work which is carried on within the sphere of national, allied or ideological solidarity, work which, by its nature and despite its humanitarian ends, operates in time of war only in favour of one or the other belligerent front, whereas the Red Cross as a whole draws its spiritual strength and its devotion in the performance of its specific tasks exclusively from its solicitude for the existence and the dignity of the human personality and from the measure of the distress which a defenceless human being can suffer at the hands of his enemy.

I hope that Dr. Junod's book will convey to a wide public a real and lasting impression of the grandeur of the task and the weight of responsibility which devolves on all who work and fight for completely disinterested humanitarian aims.

MAX HUBER
Sometime President of the International
Committee of the Red Cross

OCTOBER 1935

T H E hill of Hasenrain with its green meadows and its crown of dark green firs rises above the grey roofs of Mulhouse. Half way up its side the buildings of the hospital, constructed of the rough and solid stone of the Vosges, are terraced in a park full of shadows, flowers and silence. The road which winds upward through the trees stops, almost at the summit, at an isolated pavilion — the surgical wing.

It was there that in the autumn of 1935 I began the last year of my resident training. Temporarily I was in charge of 270 beds in the absence of the chief surgeon, and the work left me little time to think of anything beyond medical affairs. There were ten assistant doctors to attend to six hundred patients. At the end of our turns of duty we eagerly discussed our own cases and our reading, and we rarely heard anything about the news which was being discussed under great headlines in the newspapers. The outside world ceased at the walls of the hospital and there was nothing to distract us from our essential interests: human suffering, our patients and the risks attendant on an operation to save a human life.

On October 15th I had just made a tour of the wards when an attendant approached me.

'You are wanted on the telephone from Geneva, Doctor.'

On the telephone I recognized the voice of a friend who had helped me, when I was only eighteen, to organize a relief campaign for Russian children. I knew that since the war he had worked ceaselessly and devotedly for the International Committee of the Red Cross.

'It's about a mission we should like to propose to you.'

'A mission?' I exclaimed in surprise. 'What sort of a mission?'

'To go with our delegate to Abyssinia.'

I had to think for a moment before I grasped what he meant. I knew, of course, that war had broken out there, after some dispute about a water source, and that the Negus had appealed to the

League of Nations, from which the Italians had promptly resigned with a great to-do to undertake the conquest of Abyssinia.

Whilst I was doing my best to collect the few notions I had on the subject of a conflict which seemed so completely out of my world, the voice of my friend became more insistent.

'We need a doctor. You're young and you're free. It would be a fine experience for you.'

'Yes, of course, of course,' I said. 'But there's the hospital to think of. You must give me time to consider it.'

'No, my dear chap. You must decide straight away. I shall expect a call from you later on today.'

I hung up the receiver and walked slowly down to meet my chief. Every morning I visited him to report, and to inform him of the state of the patients. As I thought of them the mild temptation I had felt a moment or two before to accept my friend's invitation gradually subsided, and when I went up to the surgical ward with him I had put it out of my mind altogether as impossible.

'Anything of importance?'

'No, sir, nothing special.'

That was true. The nephrectomy and the compound fracture in Ward 12 were doing well. The child in Ward 18 still had fever, but the abscess was draining away satisfactorily. In Ward 23 the fracture of the skull remained restless and the coma continued.

'Do you think we ought to operate?'

'Yes, trepanning. In cases like that we mustn't give up hope.'

The door which had been opened into the outside world for a moment or two by my friend's voice on the telephone closed again. No, the most fascinating adventure of all was here, not in Africa: the battle for human life which kept us bent over the operating table for weary hours, all our senses alert.

Suddenly my chief turned his keen eyes on me.

'Nothing else at all, Junod?'

'Nothing of importance really. I've just had a telephone call from Geneva.'

'Bad news?'

'No. I've been invited to go to Abyssinia.'

'By the Negus or the Italians?'

'Neither. By the International Committee of the Red Cross.'

My chief considered for a moment and seemed to hesitate.

'For how long?' he asked.

'I don't really know; six months perhaps.'

'If I were you I'd go, Junod. Look, I'll give you leave of absence for six months. Go out and see the world. It would be a strange thing if you didn't get something useful out of it.'

The International Committee of the Red Cross . . . At the name I immediately imagined an imposing staff of delegates, secretaries and typists in a ten-storey building. But when I arrived in Geneva ten days later all I found was a smallish house, the 'Villa Moynier', situated in the middle of a splendid park. I don't suppose there are more than a dozen rooms in the place, and half a dozen typists were at work under the instructions of three secretaries.

There was a fine library in which I read up the history and the principles of the Red Cross. I was thinking over some significant words in the Convention of Geneva:

'Members of the armed forces [and other persons mentioned in the article] who are wounded or sick shall be respected and protected in all circumstances.

'They shall be treated humanely and cared for by the party to the conflict in whose power they may be without any adverse distinction founded on sex, race, nationality, religion, political opinion or any other similar criteria. . . .'[1]

when someone addressed me:

'Good morning. Allow me to introduce myself: Sidney Brown. We shall be going together.'

It was said in French with an accent half-English and half Swiss-German which was not disagreeable.

'Oh, I see you're in the middle of mugging it up,' he commented on observing what I was reading. 'I shouldn't do too much of that, if I were you.'

Noticing my look of surprise he smiled.

[1] Article 12 of the 2nd chapter of the 1st Convention.

'Don't misunderstand me. Books are all very well, but when you're on the spot, thousands of miles from Geneva, all on your own, you'll have to fall back on your imagination. There are the official Red Cross texts, of course, but, above all, there's the spirit of the thing.'

'Yes, of course. I understand. What shall we have to do when we get there?'

'I imagine there'll be a good deal of aid to distribute. We shall have to attend to the prisoners of war; see that the Red Cross and the Geneva Convention are respected. . . .'

Brown was a tall fair-haired fellow who seemed to spend most of his life moving about. For seven years he had been visiting Red Cross Societies all over the world, and he had just returned from a mission to China and Japan.

He took me to the President of the International Committee, Max Huber, whom I met for the first time. I put the same question to him.

'What shall we have to do exactly when we get there?'

'You will be our representatives. That is to say you will inform us of the requirements of the Abyssinian Red Cross, which is now being formed. In addition we are being informed from all sides of the sending of ambulances and of foreign assistance. You will have to co-ordinate all that. But remember always that you are neither investigators nor judges, and that your conduct must be dictated above all by the necessity of relieving the distress of the war victims.'

I continued to make myself acquainted with everyone. To every question that I asked I received the same answer:

'You'll see when you get there. Be cautious and, above all, always remain objective.'

I studied the map of Abyssinia with close attention. It was the largest scale map I could discover and was about three feet square. I tried to imagine what the country would be like: four times as big as Italy, with an emperor and twelve million inhabitants made up of various warrior races.

Feverish preparations were going forward for our journey.

Foreign ambulance units were reported to be arriving from Sweden, Great Britain, Egypt and Holland.

Adowa had just suffered its first bombardment from the air. There were hundreds of victims and no doctors. Assistance was urgently required. At the last moment thirty cases of material for the Abyssinian Red Cross were entrusted to our care.

At length we were ready to leave.

The farewells of my friends on that evening at Cornavin Station and a certain anxiety aroused by such words as 'volleys', 'bombardments' and 'ambushes' almost made me feel that I was going off to war myself.

I did not realize then that the war would continue for me long after the conquest of Abyssinia by the Italians, and that it would take me to Spain, Germany, England, Poland, Greece and to the Far East — including Hiroshima.

A strange kind of soldier whose only arms were two conventions. Two conventions and something else besides. . . .

'The spirit of the thing' as Brown had put it.

To the Memory of my Father

There are never more than two adversaries engaged in battle. But these adversaries are apt to find that suddenly in their midst is a third combatant — a warrior without weapons.

ABYSSINIA

CHAPTER I

'KAY MASCAL'

Suez was the sluice-gate of the war. Its closure would have made it easier for the Negus to defend his country; free passage for Italy meant the toleration in practice of a conflict condemned in words.

When we left Marseilles fruitless diplomatic discussions were still proceeding. Would they impose the sanctions provided for in 'Article XVI'? The League of Nations Pact had been invoked for the first time in its short history. The chancellories were getting together. Governments exchanged confidential notes which the press immediately made public. Eden was in favour of enforcing the Pact. Laval was in favour of an arrangement. Mussolini trumpeted threatening proclamations from the balcony of the Palazzo Venezia.

The wireless of the *Chantilly* brought us nothing but contradictory information.

Passing through the Straits of Messina we had already heard the rumbling preparations of a nation entirely bent on African conquest. Every ton which passed through the Suez Canal cost the Italians a gold franc. The jewels of the House of Savoy were sacrificed to pay that exorbitant tribute, and throughout the peninsula women enthusiastically took their wedding rings to the local town halls as contributions to the national cause.

When we arrived at Port Said we found dozens of vessels anchored in the roads. They were crowded with Italian troops, their holds full of tanks, guns and arms. On all the decks the soldiers were singing the 'Giovinezza' and roaring at the tops of their voices from time to time: 'A chi la vittoria?' And answering themselves: 'A noi.'

The vessels weighed anchor and slid slowly towards the south. The sluice-gate was open. It was war.

On the quaysides the crowd watched the scene with indifference.

Someone standing next to me murmured audibly: 'The Suez betrayal.'

I said nothing. I was in the service of the International Red Cross, and I recalled the instructions given to me by Max Huber: 'Be objective.' I quite understood why the President of the International Committee was so insistent on that. It was difficult, but I knew that a single word could compromise our whole mission.

Five days later we arrived at Jibuti. Once we had landed the lethargy of the voyage was replaced by an indescribable activity. In this arid corner of the world friends and enemies, suspects, speculators and spies of all sorts rubbed shoulders.

Jibuti had become the common ante-room of the belligerents and their secret allies. It was the terminus of the only railway line which connected Addis-Abbaba with the outside world. All the war material that the Abyssinian Government had been able to purchase abroad passed through Jibuti; there was an airfield where Italian planes landed to maintain connections between Eritrea and Somaliland; and numerous vessels put into the port coming from Massowa or Mogadishu.

An atmosphere of war made itself felt everywhere. The Italian and Abyssinian Consulates, the advanced posts of the belligerents, kept a watchful eye on each other's movements. Fantastic bargains were being struck in the sordid little bars along the waterfront.

Our stay in Jibuti was short, and November 6th saw us leave the town by the Franco-Abyssinian express, on which the beds of the Emperor and his Empress had been reserved for us in the special coach of the Negus.

Once we had left Jibuti we were in the desert. Then the land rises towards the Abyssinian frontier and we passed through an area of volcanic rocks without a trace of vegetation, a sort of lunar landscape reminiscent of Spain in the neighbourhood of Almeria. It was easy to picture the difficulties which had had to be surmounted in order to build these 500 miles of railroad: bridges carried away by sudden floods; torrential rains which sometimes raised the surface of the rivers by as much as twenty feet within a few hours; buildings and erections destroyed a dozen times and built up again;

the workshops and camps attacked almost every night by bandits. Each sleeper had cost a human life it was said.

Suddenly on emerging from a defile the train came to a halt at the frontier. Our papers were examined by Abyssinian soldiers in good khaki uniforms, but without boots. The puttees wound round their calves ended at their ankles and left their feet bare.

We went on through the Abyssinian lowlands to Diredawa. The countryside had become delightful. Streams were everywhere and the vegetation was luxuriant. From the windows of our carriage I observed graceful antelopes which fled at our approach. Everything was calm and peaceful. Peasants were at work in the fields and they hardly turned their heads as we passed. Then night fell and the next morning, after a journey of nineteen hours, we awoke in Addis-Abbaba.

Clinging to the slope of a hill the town is a collection of low and rounded Abyssinian houses, miserable huts with thatched roofs pointed like a dunce's cap, cheap buildings, hotels, garages and sumptuous residences, partly concealed amidst bottle-green eucalyptus trees, fragrant and peaceful.

The only big street of Addis-Abbaba is the endless, winding Boulevard Makonnen, which is asphalted. The houses stand side by side uninterruptedly, though some are situated in large gardens or uncultivated fields. There is great activity in the town throughout the day. Greeks and Armenians, mostly tailors, grocers and photographers, provide the main shopkeeper contingent. Their role here is the same as in Cairo, that of the indispensable intermediary. In front of their shops are always colourful and gesticulating crowds. The Abyssinians in their white chammas are like flakes of snow whirling slowly around amidst motor cars, lorries and ox carts, and their shouts mingle with a horrible din of motors and klaxon horns.

Above the town, around the palace of the King of Kings, it is quiet. It was here that the Emperor was anxiously preparing to defend his country. His government consisted only of a few intimate counsellors. Sometimes a Ras, or Governor of a province, having raised troops, would come to visit the Emperor and pay him homage, and then the Makonnen would see files of strange barefooted warriors loping silently along to the muffled rhythm of great drums borne by mules. Their hair, dressed in close pointed tufts, gave them the appearance of an army of hedgehogs.

'Glory to the King of Kings! Death to his enemies!' On one shoulder they carried a lance or an ancient musket; from the other depended a bundle containing pimentos and flour. Sometimes they carried great curved sabres and wound around their waists were innumerable cartridge belts. They were the front-line troops, the transport service and the catering corps all in one.

They made me think of the other soldiers I had seen three weeks earlier steaming through the Suez Canal with their planes, tanks and artillery: well equipped, well organized, and very sure of victory.

In their residences, lost in the depths of immense gardens, foreign diplomats carefully watched the course of events. Code messages were broadcast from Addis-Abbaba to capitals all over the world. A detachment of 120 Sikhs, fine big fellows with impassive faces under their neat turbans, were encamped in the grounds of the British Legation. The representatives of His Britannic Majesty were well protected.

Many leading foreign correspondents of Europe and America could be met with in the bars, but it was not often that they had anything exciting to cable back to their papers. The Emperor had forbidden them to go more than twenty-five miles outside Addis-Abbaba. There was no interesting news to be had, and many of them left the capital at week-ends to go to Bichoftu, a little distance away. A place kept there by a couple of Germans offered all the comfort of a Swiss hotel on the banks of a lovely little lake where the duck shooting was good.

On waste ground off the Makonnen was a long low building which looked as though it might have been a primitive barracks. On the door was a wooden signboard on which were the words 'Kay Mascal' in Arabic and Amharic. Over the roof flew a very clean flag, obviously quite new. On a white ground were two bands of scarlet forming a cross. No further translation of the two words 'Kay Mascal' on the door was necessary. The building was the headquarters of the Abyssinian Red Cross.

Inside almost the only furniture was a big table of unvarnished wood and a few chairs. So far there was not even a typewriter, but a local printer had delivered a stack of notepaper headed with the insignia of the Abyssinian Red Cross Society.

When Brown and I entered we were a little shocked by the barn-like atmosphere, but we took our places at the table to attend one of the first meetings of the National Committee of this new Red Cross organization, which made up in enthusiasm and good will what it lacked in equipment. The President, Gueta Herrouy, an Abyssinian notable with a greying beard, dressed in a black chamma, made a speech of welcome. With him were three or four other Abyssinians. An American missionary, Dr. Lambie, was General Secretary. Dr. Hanner, a Swede, and Herr Abel, an Austrian, were the Vice-Presidents. A Greek doctor, Colonel Argyropolus, represented the medical service of the Abyssinian Army.

It was to this colonel that Brown addressed his first question.

'Would you tell us, Colonel, what the medical service of the Negus actually consists of?'

Colonel Argyropolus gave a disillusioned smile.

'At the moment it doesn't exist at all,' he answered frankly. 'The troops of His Majesty have gone to the front without any doctors, without any nurses and without even bandages.'

'Incredible. And who is going to see to it all now?'

'The Red Cross, I suppose. We can provide a certain amount of medical supplies which we have been able to purchase on behalf of the Abyssinian Government. I have enough so far to equip ten ambulances modestly.'

Gueta Herrouy intervened.

'Haven't we been informed that a Swedish ambulance unit has arrived at Jibuti?'

'It has,' said Brown, 'and I can also inform you of the arrival of other units from Great Britain, Egypt, Holland, Norway and Finland. They are all first-class units and well equipped. But what seems to me more difficult is to form purely Abyssinian ambulance units.'

Dr. Lambie spoke.

'We have already organized two ambulances each with a doctor and ten assistants. One of them is already at the front, south of Harrar. The doctor is one of the missionaries of our hospital. The second is about to leave for Sidamo. We are in a position to organize five others, and we should be very glad of the advice and assistance of Dr. Junod.'

All eyes turned on me, including Brown's.

'My advice and assistance are completely at your disposal, of course,' I declared, 'but first of all you must give me information and help. May I ask a preliminary question: are there any Abyssinian doctors?'

The Swede Hanner showed his teeth in a broad smile.

'Well, there are the *Hakims*, a sort of native sorcerer. They have inherited certain traditional practices based on the curative action of herbs, and their remedies are extremely curious and closely guarded secrets. I think it would be difficult to make M.O.s of them. If my information is correct there is only one Abyssinian medical man in the whole of the country, and his degree comes from an American Negro faculty. In Addis-Abbaba and the bigger towns like Harrar and Dessie, there are a few hospitals, all in charge of foreign missionaries, and these are staffed with doctors like myself in the service of the Emperor. The fact is that if you want doctors for your ambulances you will have to appeal to foreign doctors already in Abyssinia, or get them from Europe. I have a list here of all the doctors I know in the country and they are all prepared to work for the Red Cross. I can give you a copy if you like.'

A few days later I made the acquaintance of our future ambulance staffs. The first unit which presented itself was in charge of a young Greek surgeon, Dr. Dassios. He was assisted by a German medical officer, Dr. Loeb, whose breast was smothered with medal ribbons won on the French front in the first World War.

I put Dr. Schupler in charge of the second ambulance. He was a man of about thirty, an Austrian who had had to flee from Austria after the Nazi putsch which cost the Austrian Chancellor, Dr. Dollfuss, his life. His anti-Italian sentiments — this was the period of the 'Watch on the Brenner' — had led him to support the Abyssinian cause.

His assistant was a Hindu doctor, a Dr. Ashmed, whose services had been placed at the disposal of the Emperor by the rich Hindu merchants of Addis-Abbaba. He was a thin, bearded little man, and I often noticed him exchanging Bibles for Korans with the American missionaries. His chief subsequently informed me that he had the awkward habit of leaving his patients to look after themselves, and even abandoning the operating table, when the moment arrived for his religious devotions.

The third ambulance was placed in charge of two Poles, Dr. Belau and a medical student named Medinsky.

The fourth ambulance was given to a Jewish doctor who had been in practice in Addis-Abbaba for thirteen years. This was Dr. Mezarosh, a charming man of about fifty, an amateur poet and musician. His chief anxiety when the caravan departed was to make quite sure that his violin had been included in his personal baggage.

An Englishman, Major Burgoyne, was in charge of the transport unit.

These made up the very disparate elements we had at our disposal. Medical orderlies we obtained from amongst Abyssinians who had received a certain amount of training in the missionary hospitals. The men and supplies were carried in lorries as far towards the northern and southern fronts as the roads allowed. After that each unit had its mule train to bring it through the scrub and over the mountains to the scene of hostilities.

I was not too happy about the efficiency of ambulances put together in this fashion, but we had no alternative, and it was clear that we should have to accustom ourselves as quickly as possible to the strange conditions of existence in a country suddenly dragged out of its age-old traditions to make the acquaintance of 'progress' as the modern world understands it in the roar of exploding bombs.

Brown and I had the honour of being received by the Negus.
Palace ceremonial was strictly adhered to. Tail coat and top hat.
Three bows were prescribed: one on the threshold of the throne
room, which was draped with red velvet; one in the middle of the
great Smyrna carpet; and the third about a yard from the Emperor.

However, our reception by His Majesty was very simple and
most affable. The interpreter retired, because the Negus spoke
fluent French. We held a brief conversation during which two
lovely dogs played around our feet. I stooped to stroke one of them
and the Emperor smiled. He looked very much like the pictures I
had seen of him. The expression on his face was agreeable but
melancholy.

He asked us whether we were in touch with the League of Nations
and if we had any important information for him.

'The Pact of Geneva. . . .'

'No, Your Majesty, the Geneva Convention. . . .'

He could hardly be reproached for confusing those two solemn
engagements of a civilization so far removed from his own: the one,
so easily broken, intended to prevent war; and the other, so difficult
to observe, intended to assuage human misery.

The chiefs of State were wise indeed when they agreed that the
flag of the Red Cross should always float, like a supreme hope, over
the battlefields which they had not succeeded in abolishing.

When we reminded the King of Kings of the difference his face
clouded over.

CHAPTER II

THE BOMBING OF DESSIE

Nᴇᴡѕ from the front began to come in at the beginning of December. The battle of Makale was fought in the extreme north. A preliminary Abyssinian success soon changed into disaster, and the Italians penetrated about sixty miles inland towards the south. There was no one on the spot to attend to the numerous wounded, and I heard that our ambulances were held up at Dessie, a small town half way between Addis-Abbaba and Makale, owing to the lack of mules to carry their personnel and supplies forward. The roads had become impassable for lorries.

On December 6th I received a telegram informing me that Dessie had been bombed. Some of our ambulances had been destroyed and the hospital of the American Mission hit.

'But Dessie is an open town,' I exclaimed in horror, 'and the hospital and our ambulances are clearly marked.'

'Fascist airmen don't take any notice of that,' was the laconic reply.

Up to that time our only idea of the ravages of the air arm had been provided by one or two sinister prophets. From now on, they had told us, the towns in the rear will be just as much in danger as the arena of hostilities. Nothing will henceforth be safe. Everyone will be in danger: women and children, and even the wounded in hospital. Were they right after all?

The Emperor himself was at Dessie, and Brown and I decided that I should leave for Dessie the next day to see to what extent our ambulances had suffered.

The one road which goes from Addis-Abbaba to the north extends for about 250 miles. It first traverses high plateau land which is relatively fertile and cultivated by the robust peasants of the Galla tribe, whose rounded huts are dotted on the sides of hills in the shade of majestic trees. Then the clumps of acacia and the fields of

maize become rarer and rarer until finally the road winds into a
barren desert area where herbage can be seen only during the rainy
season.

Our convoy of six lorries made its way towards the mountains
visible in the distance. Two of them were loaded with supplies
which I was taking to replace those which had been destroyed in
the bombing of our ambulances. On the third lorry was the British
military attaché. The others were taking the medical unit of Dr.
Mezarosh as near to the fighting line as possible. ·

About sixty miles from the capital our convoy entered into a
series of valleys between high steep walls. Bearded shepherds in
brown cloaks leaned on their staffs amidst their flocks and made an
impressively biblical picture as we passed.

At Terma-Ber, which is over 11,000 feet above sea level, we saw
the broken chaotic countryside of central Abyssinia. Towards the
north was an abyss dominated by inaccessible terraces. It seemed
to me that such a barrier could easily be rendered impassable, but
there were no signs of any military works. Five months later the
Italian forces were to pass along this very route without being
harassed by a single ambush.

During our descent the lorries behaved erratically. In places the
path had crumbled away and sloped dangerously towards the abyss.
A few days before, our driver told me, a car had side-slipped and
fallen over the precipice to crash nearly a thousand feet below.

On the plain, which was traversed by a number of rivers, some
of them perhaps 150 feet wide, the vegetation became tropical
again. The lorries forded the rivers at top speed, the water splashing
up above the motors. We had covered about 125 miles when the
approach of night obliged us to make a halt. We knew that darkness succeeds daylight in these parts almost without transition.

We were in a forest and I chose a clearing in which to camp.
Hastily we erected our tents and started fires. Monkeys were
chattering in the branches. There was a stream near by and clouds
of mosquitoes danced merrily round our lamps.

Above my head the branches formed a tracery of black against
the starlit sky. It was my first night up country.

I was preparing to sleep when I thought I heard a sound of scratching at the entrance to my tent, and at the same time a disagreeable smell came to my nostrils. I shone my torch out into the night. It illuminated a hyena, which gave its strange laughing howl in the light and then turned tail and bolted.

I was awakened early by shouts from the other side of our encampment. I ran out to see what was happening. One of my transport officers was quarrelling furiously with an Abyssinian. The Abyssinian gesticulated with a dagger, and the transport officer was armed with a carbine. With one hand I seized the dagger and with the other the barrel of the carbine and ordered the two men to hand them over, which they did unwillingly, abusing each other vigorously. It appeared that my officer had lost some money which he believed the other had stolen. I searched his tent myself and found the money without difficulty in quite a different place from the one he indicated.

Order having been restored we got away at about seven, hoping to be in Dessie before nightfall.

When we left the forest we came through marshy plains in the middle of which was a large village. At its entrance stood a number of soldiers at a wooden barrier on which was the inscription in large Amharic letters: 'Military Control Point.'

As soon as they learned I was on my way to see the Emperor I was paid a thousand flattering attentions. A soldier led me to a small building of stone which was the headquarters of the Abyssinian chief of the district. We exchanged courteous salutations and he offered me a drink.

'Don't drink,' whispered my interpreter.

Why not? I thought. It was a sort of mead made of fermented honey and it was very agreeable to drink. In face of so much kindness I could hardly refuse, and so I drank to the health of the Abyssinian chief, a courtesy which made him show his strong white teeth in a broad smile. As a precaution against possible dysentery germs in the mead I then took a tablet of stovarsol.

All our names were written down in a big book, which was

covered with ink blots, and when we remounted our lorries, the barrier was solemnly opened for us and we drove through.

The morning had been fresh, but now the torrid heat of the day was stifling. Muddy stagnant water covered the ground and in order to avoid it we drove along the foot of the hills.

'This part of the country isn't very safe,' my driver informed me, and he added the one word 'Chiftas', which meant bandits.

I shall have occasion to refer to them again, but I was already sufficiently well informed of the danger to take every possible precaution. I kept the convoy well together and placed guards on the roofs of the lorries. I squatted on top of the leading lorry myself with my Winchester between my knees. Everything seemed quiet. Their metalwork shining in the sun, the lorries rolled on, bumping over the dusty path and raising clouds of dust behind them.

At midday we made a halt for lunch. The atmosphere was becoming heavier and heavier and great clouds had formed in a sombre sky. The drivers gave me something else to worry about: we must press forward as quickly as possible in order to reach the firmer road in the hills of Dessie before we were caught in the rain, because a heavy storm would turn the dusty path into mud and make it impossible for the wheels to get a grip.

Big drops were already falling heavily on to the bonnets. We got under way. A few minutes later torrential rain poured down. Our lorry began to slip and slide dangerously; so much so that we were obliged to halt, and for an hour the rain poured down on to the path, opening up gulleys everywhere. Our wheels were already up to the hubs in water.

Gradually the rain ceased and the sun came out again, but when we got down we were up to our ankles in thick, sticky mud. We tried to get started, but the wheels turned round without gripping, the gear boxes began to screech, and the engines revved uselessly. We tried half a dozen times and then had to give up. There was nothing for it: we had to wait until the mud dried hard enough for the tyres to get a grip.

'How long is that likely to be?' I asked my driver.

'A few hours or a few days,' he said. 'It all depends on whether we get any more rain.'

There was no chance of starting in the afternoon and we had to camp out again for the night. We put up our tents along the side of the path and set guards. Fortunately the sky remained clear and by the next morning the mud had hardened sufficiently to allow us to get the lorries out of the ruts into which they had sunk.

We travelled across vast plains covered with scrub towards the high mountains in the distance. Near a village a rudimentary air field had been prepared, and what looked like a great grey bird was perched there behind a screen of reeds. It was the personal plane of the Emperor.

The road climbed rapidly. It was cut out in the rock and it skirted a dizzy precipice to debouch on high terraces encircled by jagged summits. Once again we smelt green pastures and the odour of eucalyptus, and amidst the trees we saw the first yellow walls and collapsed huts of Dessie.

The arrival of our caravan in the grounds of the Mission, where the tents of our ambulance unit and those of the journalists had been set up, produced an outburst of joy. Everyone welcomed us with obvious delight.

'We have been waiting for you with impatience,' said the Greek surgeon who was in charge of our first ambulance unit. We have carried out about fifty operations — laparotomy, trepanning, compound fractures and so on. Our supplies have been greatly reduced; not to mention what was destroyed in the bombing.'

It was too late to make a tour of the town and inspect the damage, and I accepted the offer of a bed from the American missionaries of the hospital. We dined all together that evening and the head of the Mission, Dr. Bergman, told us about the bombing.

'On December 6th at about a quarter to eight in the morning twelve Italian planes approached Dessie from the south and gave us a regular pounding which lasted for an hour. The first bombs hit our hospital. The corrugated-iron roof wasn't much protection. One of them exploded in a ward, but by a miracle no one was hurt, though all the equipment was destroyed. Others fell on the tents, smashing up our boxes of supplies. Our operation room is in ruins.'

'Could the planes have made a mistake?'

'I don't see how it's possible. They might not have seen the Red Cross flags over the tents, but the big red cross painted on the hospital roof is certainly easily visible at 6000 feet up. Assuming they didn't deliberately try to turn us into a sieve the only explanation is that they were after the old Italian Consulate where the Emperor is staying at the moment. Its grounds abut on ours. But in that case their aim must have been very bad, because not a bomb fell anywhere near it.'

'What about the town?'

'Pretty bad. They dropped over 800 incendiary bombs, and the thatched huts went up like torches and the roofs fell in. You can imagine the effect on the inhabitants: shrieks of terror went up and then there was a mad stampede out into the country-side.'

'And the Emperor?'

'He rushed at once to his machine-gun and began to fire at the planes, but that only increased the general panic and his men began to blaze away wildly in all directions and their bullets ricochetted amongst the fleeing inhabitants. They had never seen planes before and thought they could bring them down with rifles.'

'Many casualties?'

'Two hundred and fifty killed and wounded. Our doctors worked for two days without relaxation. They were splendid, and so were our transport men, who went out to bring in the wounded amidst the smoke and flames.'

The next day one of the counsellors of the Emperor conducted me on a tour through the ruins of Dessie. The acrid odour of burning still rose from the rubble. All that was left of the stone houses were the scorched walls. The thatched huts were just heaps of charred cinders.

This was only a poor little town of mud huts and thatched roofs lost in the Abyssinian scrub, but it was the first time in history that airmen had carried out a mass raid to destroy hearths, homes and families. Today it is easy to understand the anguish we felt then at the thought that perhaps our own towns and villages would one day suffer the same fate.

All the doctors signed a message of protest against the barbarity and sent it to the League of Nations.

It was a prophetic message. After Dessie, Guernica was to follow. Then a little later Warsaw, and in quick succession Rotterdam, London, Coventry, then Aix-la-Chapelle and Berlin — and finally Hiroshima.

His Majesty invited me to dine with him together with the officers and doctors of the British ambulance unit which had just arrived.

The dining-room was quite small. The table was in the form of a cross, which is a tradition with the Copts, and it was covered with a white cloth. Around the table in front of our places was a yellow and green garland — the Abyssinian colours. In the centre was a cross of red roses, a delicate compliment to His Majesty's guests.

During the course of the dinner the Emperor turned to me.

'The doctors of the Abyssinian Red Cross were heroic under the bombs,' he said.

No other mention was made of the raid. I felt that he was very sad, and perhaps more upset than he would ever have admitted. Was it fear at being forced to recognize the ridiculous inadequacy of his means of defence against an enemy supplied with such engines of destruction? Was he already horrified at the magnitude of the sacrifice he was asking of his people in a war whose outcome must appear almost certain to him?

'Where are your ambulances stationed?' he asked.

I explained the difficulties we were having in getting the ambulances to the front at all. For instance, the road from Waldia to Kworam would not be passable for lorries for another three weeks at least.

'I will send a thousand men to speed up the work,' he said.

'Because of lack of transport the Abyssinian ambulances are still being held up here,' I went on.

'I will give the necessary orders. Two hundred mules and their drivers will be placed at your disposal within three days.'

The Emperor had to attend even to details in person, and I admired the calmness and methodical persistence with which he carried out such a thankless task.

During the course of the evening I was able to get to know the head of the British ambulance unit, Dr. Melly. Despite the recent warning issued by the Italian Air Force, he had decided to play the game according to the rules and to give his men the protection of the Red Cross flag. He would travel by day and the tops of his lorries would be painted with a big red cross, and at halts a big Red Cross flag would be spread out on the ground.

When I was about to leave, little Prince Makkonnen, the youngest son of the Emperor, told me sadly that his wireless no longer worked. I had a look at it and saw that the accumulators were dry. With a glass of rainwater I was able to bring life back into them again and I left the set working and the little prince thinking what a wonderful man I was to be able to repair it so quickly.

Dr. Melly took me back to his place to have a final drink. His tent was ingeniously arranged to provide as many home comforts as possible. There was a work table, a small library and comfortable canvas arm-chairs. His wireless carried us thousands of miles away to where a dance band was playing in the Savoy.

Returning to the mission house I passed between the tents of the journalists. They were making a good deal of noise despite the advanced hour, drinking and playing cards around their camp beds, transformed into bridge and poker tables.

A few days later the Abyssinian ambulances left for the north with the mules the Emperor had provided. They were soon followed by the British ambulance unit. At the same time I learned that the Dutch ambulance unit had left Addis-Abbaba.

Just before Christmas I decided to visit the ambulance stations on the northern front and I left for Waldia.

It was there, about 100 miles from Dessie, that the Imperial Guard was quartered. It consisted of 10,000 picked men who

37

were being held in reserve by the Emperor for decisive battles. They were dressed in good khaki uniforms, but they marched barefooted like all other Abyssinian warriors. They were equipped with modern rifles and they even had a small number of machine-guns.

Dr. Dassio's Abyssinian ambulance unit was encamped on a little hill outside the soldiers' quarters. I arrived early in the morning and was pleased to see that the unit was already at work dealing with a certain number of lightly wounded men and some cases of dysentery.

From the hill on which the unit was situated we could see over the great camp of the Imperial Guard, whose little Abyssinian tents, round and rising to a point, were symmetrically disposed and looked like haystacks.

Shortly after I arrived bugle calls sounded. The ambulance attendants immediately began to scurry around, taking down the tents and folding them up, collecting the supplies and covering them with brushwood.

'What's happening, Dr. Dassios?' I asked.

'We have to do that several times a day now, my dear fellow,' he replied. 'Since a fascist plane paid us a visit and dropped its bombs all around us. In the circumstances I don't feel like taking risks with the lives of my patients or my staff.'

And he added with some bitterness:

'Have you already forgotten the bombing of Dessie?'

In the plain below us the camp of the Imperial Guard had disappeared as though a fairy wand had been waved. I marvelled at the rapidity and the skill of the Abyssinians in the art of camouflage. But over on the right I saw a line of tents in a semi-circle.

'What about those?' I asked.

'Made of straw,' one of the boys said, 'a blind.'

The bugles sounded a second time to indicate that the planes were in sight. Immediately afterwards three planes flew towards us. It was a disagreeable feeling to watch them approaching. They made straight for the dummy tents, swooped round and dropped a stick of bombs. The explosions as they hit the ground produced vivid violet flashes. Around me all the Abyssinian boys were laughing heartily at the successful trick played on the Italians.

The 'All Clear' sounded and I took leave of my friends to visit the British ambulance unit, which had established itself on the other side of the hill about a mile and a half from the camp. On crossing the brow of the hill I had to admire the perfect alignment of the fifty tents set up in the plain below and the twenty lorries drawn up around the great Red Cross flag spread out on the ground.

I went down the hill and was welcomed by Dr. Melly. He laughed when I told him the story of the Abyssinian ambulance which hurriedly camouflaged itself at every air-raid warning. He was still determined to do nothing of the kind and to put his confidence in the protection offered by the Red Cross. Incidentally his English temperament forbade him to display the slightest sign of doubt, and his assurance filled me with admiration.

A few hours later when I visited the tents I was presented to the mascot of the camp: a big tortoise on whose shell a red cross had been painted as an amulet against bombing.

At that moment we heard the drumming of a plane again. The English glanced up impassively at the tiny speck flying towards us.

'Those airmen are as inquisitive as monkeys,' observed Dr. Melly. 'They come to see us every day, and sometimes several times a day.'

Suddenly we heard the whistle of falling bombs. The English watched them fall without moving.

'Total damage a few holes in the ground,' said Dr. Melly contemptuously.

CHAPTER III

THE DESTRUCTION OF THE SWEDISH AMBULANCE

I SPENT nearly a month inspecting medical arrangements on the northern front, where seven ambulances were stationed at suitable intervals over a distance of about 125 miles.

The situation on the southern front was very much less favourable; there we had only one real ambulance unit, the Swedish, supported by elements of an Abyssinian unit.

On December 31st in the morning I received an urgent request from the Emperor to come to Dessie.

On my arrival I was received by His Majesty's private secretary. I could see at once from his face that something serious had happened.

'Read this,' he said, and he handed me a telegram.

It was a message from Ras Desta, the commander of all the Abyssinian forces on the Sidamo front.

'Swedish ambulance completely destroyed by bombing stop doctor in charge seriously wounded. . . .'

It looked very much as though the bombing of Dessie hospital, the bombing of the ambulance of the Greek surgeon and the bombs dropped near the British ambulance had not been accidents. Were the Italians deliberately bombing the Red Cross? It was my duty to find out whether there was any excuse for them this time, and whether the Swedish ambulance unit had itself observed all the rules laid down by the Convention; if the tents had been sufficiently far removed from any military objective; and if they had been made clearly recognizable.

When I was received by the Emperor I told him that I proposed to go immediately to the spot and find out these things for myself.

'It's a long way,' His Majesty said doubtfully. 'You would have to pass through the whole country from north to south. . . .'

However, I insisted that it was necessary that I should go, and

I asked for the necessary safe-conduct. The Emperor signed the papers required for my journey and in addition he gave me a personal letter for Ras Desta, who was his son-in-law. And finally he placed a civil plane at my disposal, a single-engined Fokker piloted by a young Swedish Red Cross volunteer, the twenty-four-year-old Count Rosen.

On January 1st, 1936, I was again in Addis-Abbaba, where we were to pick up the Swedish Consul, who was at the same time the chief doctor of the Imperial Hospital. One of the hospital boys was attached to us as an interpreter. I gave him one or two things to do in connection with our departure and after a while he returned with the assurance:

'Ichi naga . . . All in order for tomorrow.' I had already been in the country long enough to know what that popular Abyssinian expression really meant: 'Some day; don't know exactly when.'

The next morning, having got up at five o'clock in order to make a good start, I found myself faced with a definite refusal on the part of the aerodrome commandant to let us set off.

'Impossible to leave today,' he declared, 'but ichi naga.'

The next day it was the same, and the day after that. This time, in despair of ever getting anything done, I went to wake the American counsellor of the government, and the two of us set off for the palace. It was too early when we arrived; all the doors were closed, and we had to kick our heels under the eucalyptus trees for an hour.

When the business of the day finally began in the palace we were received by a number of Abyssinian notables who seemed to know nothing about my journey. It was in vain that I pointed out that the chief of the Swedish ambulance unit was seriously wounded and that perhaps his life depended on quick transport to Addis-Abbaba hospital where he could be given proper medical attention. I showed the safe-conduct signed by the Emperor and his personal letter of introduction to Ras Desta.

I had the impression that they were unwilling to let me go for two reasons. For one thing they were afraid that our plane might be intercepted and shot down by the Italians despite its Red Cross markings, and for another they were not sure that we should not be brought down by Abyssinian troops, who might mistake our plane for an Italian. I learned later that the only means of communication with Addis-Abbaba at Ras Desta's disposal was a small field-broadcasting station, and that the day after the bombing it had broken down. Thus the General Staff was completely cut off from the commander of the southern front and was unable to tell him that we should be coming.

After a discussion lasting two hours I finally succeeded in obtaining permission to continue my journey — at my own risk.

My companion and I were well aware of the dangers of the journey. There was an air field at Irga Alem, the last point towards the south which was still in telephonic communication with the capital, but after that there was nothing and we should have to land in the bush at the best place we could find.

The only precaution we could take was to cable the approximate course of our journey to Geneva so that the International Red Cross Committee could inform the Italians in order to obviate any 'misunderstandings'. This step seemed to allay the misgivings of our Abyssinian friends somewhat and we took off from the Addis-Abbaba air field at midday on January 4th.

Far below, sombre undulating stretches of forest alternated with grey expanses of volcanic desert. Clumps of acacias, spurge and jujube trees crowded around the blue splashes of lakes. In the distance the water flashed in the sun like burnished steel.

From the temperate highlands of Addis-Abbaba we passed into the seething torrids of the tropical zone, and its heat rose up to us in damp and shining vapour.

Our only guide was the winding ribbon of river below us and we realized what it might mean to fly off our course, or run into even a small barrier of cloud. After about two hours flying we spotted a village of small brown huts clustered along the banks of the river. Count Rosen circled round and then touched down with complete and confident mastery on the air field of Irga Alem.

Princess Desta sent us an Abyssinian lunch which consisted of a piquant sauce in which eggs and pieces of chicken were floating succulently. In order that we should not be embarrassed by the natives a table was set for us in a corner of the air field and four Abyssinians stood around holding up a large white sheet, thus creating a sort of private dining-room in the open air.

Whilst we were eating the food prepared for us the personnel of the air field filled up our tank and stowed away extra cans of petrol so that we should be able to make the journey there and back without refuelling. The southern front was about 180 miles from Irga Alem, and we had to be supplied with sufficient petrol to fly something over 400 miles if we were to have a margin of safety.

For our guidance we had only a primitive small scale map of Abyssinia and a compass. We had no means of blind flying should it prove necessary and we had no wireless. The best way of estimating our position was by consideration of the time taken, the speed flown and the distance to be covered.

The latest information concerning the Swedish ambulance unit placed it at about 175 miles north of the village of Melka-Dida, where it had been bombed. We calculated that after about two hours flight we ought to be approximately in the neighbourhood.

We took off at three o'clock in the afternoon. This time I was less sensible of the magic of the soil and the countryside and I kept my eyes fixed on my watch, the map and the compass. Count Rosen flew low and followed the course of the river closely. When we had been flying for about two hours I passed him a scrap of paper on which I had written: 'Anything in sight?' He shook his head. He began to fly round in wide circles whilst we anxiously scanned the ground beneath for some sign of the Red Cross flag or any other indication that the Swedish ambulance unit was in the vicinity. We were beginning to get anxious because the oil level was dropping dangerously and we had no means of replenishing the tank in flight.

At a quarter past five I spotted a village at the end of a great plain and I proposed that we should land there and see if we could get any information from the natives.

Count Rosen brought the plane down rapidly and we looked around for a suitable landing place. As far as we could see there was high scrub all around. Up to the last moment I feared that we should crash, or perhaps collide with the herds of antelopes fleeing madly before us, but Count Rosen made a perfect landing.

We had come down some distance away from the village, and we decided that Rosen and I should make for it, taking the 'boy' with us as interpreter, whilst the Swedish Consul remained behind to look after the machine. After a quarter-of-an-hour's march through scrub and brambles which tore our knees we came face to face with four black shadows grasping assegais in their hands. We immediately unfurled a small Abyssinian flag and shouted:

'Denestiligne (Greetings)! Kay Mascal.'

Their reaction was not altogether reassuring, and I went closer shouting:

'Haile Selassie.'

But there was no change of expression on the immobile faces of these woolly headed savages.

Suddenly by inspiration I let off a prolonged yodel in the best style of the Swiss herdsmen. At that the four faces opened out in broad grins and they advanced towards us, their white teeth flashing amiably. At the same time scores of other natives bobbed up all around from hiding places in the scrub. We had certainly not suspected that so many eyes had been regarding us.

Our Abyssinian interpreter found it impossible to make himself understood or to understand these natives, who spoke a totally different dialect. It was by means of gestures and imitating the noise of a motor car that I had to ask them for news about the Swedish lorries. Their faces remained blank. In the end one of them, who seemed to be their chief, grasped what I wanted and pointed in the direction of Nagale, as the spot where the ambulance was to be found. I invited him by gestures to go back with us to the plane.

On the way I noticed a baby antelope which could not yet walk properly and which had been abandoned by its mother, who had probably forgotten her maternal instincts in the panic created by our landing. One of the natives picked it up and carried it in his arms. I was reminded forcibly of the Good Shepherd and the lost sheep. I found a piece of sugar in my jacket pocket and the baby antelope raised its beautiful muzzle towards it, which brought fresh smiles to the faces of these savages, who were truly behaving very well towards their unexpected and strange visitors.

I offered a 'Lucky Strike' to their chief. He looked at it, smelt it and then ate it, paper and all, and asked for another one. From cigarette to cigarette we arrived at where the plane was waiting and I persuaded him to come with us to show us the general direction.

Count Rosen started up the engine and just before I closed the door of the cabin the native who had been carrying the baby antelope deposited it at my feet. The Fokker rose into the air with two extra passengers.

Our guide appeared quite at his ease. He passed his hand over his forehead probably to indicate a slight headache, but he was otherwise not in the least distressed by the height and in a calm and authoritative manner he showed us by gestures which way we were to fly.

In about ten minutes we were above Nagale and we could already see our Swedish friends, who had heard the noise of our engine and were waving Red Cross flags. It was high time — another ten minutes and we should have been lost in the night.

Our Abyssinian friend seemed disappointed that we did not drop straight down at once to where our friends were waving, but Count Rosen sought out a spot more favourable for landing than the tree tops and the rocks scattered around. Happily only a mile or so away we discovered a clearing which seemed to be free of obstacles and there we landed.

By the time the propellor had ceased to turn the darkness was complete. We made a fire of grass and brushwood to indicate our position to the Swedes who were no doubt looking for our landing place. As the hours passed and no one came to find us we became increasingly anxious. Although we had dropped Red Cross and Abyssinian flags on the last village we had flown over, the appearance of further natives would have filled us with some apprehension.

We had an interpreter with us it was true, but our last experience in that respect had not been altogether comforting.

From what I had been told at Addis-Abbaba the country around here must be full of soldiers, since the total strength of Ras Desta's armies was estimated at half a million, though, of course, we were still quite a long way from the front.

At about ten o'clock two headlights appeared on the crest of the hill followed immediately by two others. One of Ras Desta's lieutenants was in the first lorry, and the second belonged to the Swedes. Stretched out on a mattress, hollow eyed and with his teeth clenched, to conceal the pain, lay the chief of the Swedish ambulance unit, Major Hylander. He had been badly wounded in the right thigh by an Italian bomb fragment.

The Swedes were very depressed by the ruthlessness of the Italian airmen, and they said very little. We decided to leave Major Hylander with the plane, which would take him to Addis-Abbaba the next morning, whilst I went with the lorry to the Swedish camp in the centre of the forest.

The next day I looked in vain for any sign of a Red Cross flag — all confidence in the protection offered by the Geneva Convention had disappeared.

Sitting around the fire the same evening I heard the story of the bombing from the survivors.

'We experienced incredible difficulties in crossing the mountainous region of Sidamo, but by the middle of December we managed to reach the scene of hostilities and we established our ambulance station about five miles away from the headquarters of Ras Desta, which was itself about twenty miles behind the front line. Our tents were set out in a square partly in a clump of palm trees along the River Ganale and partly in a clearing surrounded by more palm trees. Two tall bare trees carried the three flags in accordance with the regulations: the Red Cross flag, the Abyssinian flag and the Swedish flag. Other Red Cross flags were spread out on the ground, easily visible from the air.

'On the morning of December 22nd a number of Italian planes flew over the camp and machine-gunned the tents. Fortunately no one was hit and we thought there had been a mistake. We had then been at work for about a week, attending to about 600 sick men and 130 wounded. Our cars were going up to the front line and bringing back the seriously wounded.

'On December 30th at about seven in the morning Italian planes flew along the river dropping leaflets printed in Amharic. Then they turned and ten of them flew towards our camp at about 2000 feet and dropped a rain of explosive and incendiary bombs.'

A Swede went away and returned with one of the leaflets. He translated it for me haltingly:

'You have violated international law. You captured one of our pilots and cut off his head. By international law prisoners should be well treated. For that you will get what you deserve.'

The leaflet was signed 'Graziani'.

'What does it refer to?' I asked.

'An Italian airman had to make a forced landing somewhere behind the Abyssinian lines and the natives killed him.'

'And so in return they machine-gun and bomb the Swedish Red Cross!'

'The chief of our unit badly wounded, a Swedish driver with part of his jaw blown away, another driver hit in the head, twenty-eight Abyssinian patients killed in their beds, and fifty others, including attendants, more or less seriously wounded.'

I saw the effects of the bombing on the equipment of the unit. The tents were riddled with bullet holes, the lorries had been badly knocked about by blast, the big sterilizer was out of action, and there were holes right through the cases of instruments and medicaments.

There was only one lorry left sufficiently serviceable to take me to the scene of the disaster at Melka-Dida.

We had to go first to Ras Desta's headquarters. The Swedish doctor who went with me prepared me to some extent for what I was to see, but even so I did not imagine that the first rays of the morning sun would reveal quite such a heart-rending spectacle. . . .

The plain which extends between the Rivers Davo and Ganale is a desert in which for a distance of about 125 miles it is impossible to find any water at all. Along the way were numerous deserters, sick and dying men tortured with hunger and thirst. They were nothing but walking skeletons staggering along in the dust. Some of them had their faces smeared with whitish mud. Hardly liquid, it was all that their 'Korkoro', the water bottle of metal which is the most precious of all their belongings, contained.

We arrived too late at Ras Desta's headquarters to be received by him, but a Belgian officer attached to the Abyssinian General Staff attended to us and told me of the terrible conditions in which the last warriors on the southern front were fighting and dying. Contrary to what had been told me in Addis-Abbaba the Sidamo army had never been more than 15,000 strong, and now there were between 4000 and 5000 left for whom three bullocks a day were killed. The Abyssinian commissariat was able to give the men only a cup of flour a week, and even that was not distributed when the two miserable vans, which were all there was to maintain supplies for the whole army, broke down or were plundered *en route*.

The half-starved soldiery offered little or no resistance to the scourges which decimated their ranks: malaria, dysentery. . . .

An atmosphere of despair weighed heavily on the whole region, which is one of grand beauty. From the promontory on which we set up our tent we could see one of the bends of the Ganale. The river at this point is about 1000 feet wide. On each bank there is a thick curtain of palm trees and about 1500 feet of luxuriant vegetation. Beyond that is barren land swept night and day by the burning wind of the desert.

In the middle of the sufferings endured by his troops we did not expect the reception which Ras Desta had prepared for us at midday the following day.

He invited us to lunch with him in his tent, and the meal he set before us was an excellent one with most savoury dishes and a variety of wines. After lunch he opened two bottles of champagne and ceremoniously raised his glass to the health of his guests.

In all his gestures he showed an extreme feeling for nobility and elegance. He was a small man, and he had changed the black chamma for a beautifully cut khaki uniform. Under his sun-helmet sparkled bright intelligent eyes with long black lashes.

Upon reading my letter of introduction from the Emperor he prostrated himself and kissed the ground at my feet.

After lunch he led me to the bank of the river and caused a splendid carpet to be spread out. Offering me his own carbine he indicated a number of crocodiles which were sunning themselves on the opposite bank some 150 feet away from us.

Three shots from the Remington were sufficient to make them slide lazily back into the water. The Ras lolled back, fanned gently by a 'Panka'. The relaxation of a prince in the ante-room of hell. . . .

Despite the overpowering heat I tore myself away from this oasis of ease to go and inspect the place where the Swedish ambulance unit had been bombed.

I skirted the edge of the forest of palm trees which grows along the banks of the river there, following its every winding turn. I drove several miles and then suddenly I came across bomb craters, uprooted trees and general signs of catastrophe.

I pulled up. All around were pieces of smashed equipment, damaged materials, stretchers, burst cases, fragments of canvas. Here and there were traces of blood. And in the middle of the clearing were the two tall dead trees from which the flags had flown in accordance with the Geneva Convention.

What struck me forcibly was that nowhere along the whole route had I seen any spot which had been bombed with such concentrated fury. It was obvious that the Swedish ambulance unit — the only source of any assistance for that whole unfortunate southern army — had been deliberately destroyed.

A package of bandages was half buried in the sand near a bomb crater. On its torn paper I could still read the words 'Stockholm 1935' and on each side a red cross. The sight moved me more than a great deal of talk. Men had travelled with that package of bandages all the way from Sweden to Abyssinia and made their way into the heart of the desert and the scrub to help their fellow men. I recalled what the Swede had said to me: ' We experienced incredible difficulties in crossing the mountainous region of Sidamo.'

At Dessie after the bombing of our ambulances we had at least had the assistance of an army in sorting ourselves out again and all the resources of an accessible area had been at our disposal. And there had been plenty of water to quench the thirst of men in delirium.

Here there was nothing.

Nowhere did I realize more clearly the value of the things they had brought than in this desert solitude.

I hardly heard the advice of the Belgian officer that we should leave as quickly as possible.

'The Italians are about to attack. They are less than three miles away now.'

I thought of that long line of human skeletons I was going to meet again on the track, and their pleading eyes as they looked after us through the dust of our lorry.

CHAPTER IV

'ABIET...ABIET...'

FROM February 1936 on events followed each other with great
rapidity. Everywhere our ambulances fled from the Italian
bombing, fell into the hands of the enemy or escaped only in
the nick of time.

First of all there were the survivors of the Swedish ambulance
unit. Badly informed by Ras Desta's staff they had to beat a pre-
cipitate retreat and make their own way to Irga Alem in order not
to fall into Italian hands. They had to leave all their equipment
behind, including their lorries, and they covered 125 miles on foot
in the path of the rapid advance of Graziani, who had completely
routed the southern Abyssinian Army under Ras Desta.

I received a telegram from the Austrian doctor's unit informing
me that as repeated bombings had demonstrated that the Red Cross
insignia offered no protection whatever he had removed all obvious
signs from his tents, etc., and now worked under cover.

The two Poles attached to the Abyssinian unit on the northern
front had been captured by the Italians. I was to meet both of
them again later on: the one as a prisoner of war in Germany and
the other in a Swiss sanatorium dying of consumption.

It was the latter, Dr. Belau, who described the dramatic end of
their mission in Abyssinia.

'On January 15th,' he told me, 'we were informed by Abyssinian
soldiers that the first Italian patrols had already succeeded in reaching
the nearest mountain. There was no possibility of withdrawal
because our mules were tethered about six miles away from the
camp, and also, in order to retreat more expeditiously, Abyssinians
had stolen a great number of them.

'When the fighting came closer I went into our shelter with my
patients and two native attendants. My assistant Dr. Medinsky
joined me there with the information that all our stretcher-bearers
had fled, disregarding his instructions. The rearguard of Ras

Muluetta's army was now nothing but a horde of pillagers and the only thing left for us to do was to await the arrival of the Italians.

'The first Italian who came into our shelter was a young lieutenant. He was astonished to find two white men there and he treated us very brusquely, and tried to obtain military information from us about Muluetta's retreat. As I refused to give him any information he contented himself with taking away our personal effects, including a carbine to which I attached some importance, and which he slung from the pommel of his saddle.

'Towards the end of the afternoon we were taken to the divisional staff where we were again questioned most brutally. They reproached us in particular as whites who had taken service with the Negus and signed the protest against the bombing of Dessie.

'The days that followed were terrible. Every two or three hours soldiers came and took us out of our cell and put us up against the wall to be executed. It became a form of distraction for them, and each time the farce was renewed they laughed heartily at our distress.

'When I was transferred to Adowa I thought the torture was at an end, but it began again as soon as I arrived. They talked all the time about Dessie. They had it very much on their consciences and our crime was to have made it known to the world. You can hardly imagine how desperately hard they tried to get me to make even a vague retraction. They hit the backs of my hands with the butts of their rifles, and when I was too ill to be capable of a will of my own and delirious with fever I must admit that I ended up by signing whatever they put before me.'

The ambulance unit in the charge of the two Poles was the fourth we had lost. There were now no ambulance units at all on the southern front and only three in the north.

Under a barrage of reports which I was unable to check and a wealth of rumours, true or false, the atmosphere in Addis-Abbaba became more and more tense, and more and more pessimistic.

When I confided my fears to the British Minister he declared confidently:

'There's no need to worry. I've known this country for years.

The Abyssinians won't run away from the Italians. The apparent rout is only a ruse.'

He went over to a large map of Abyssinia and pointed out the chain of mountains which covered both the north and south of the country.

'That's where they'll conceal themselves. They will attack the Italian flank and cut off their supplies. It will all end in guerilla warfare which will be fatal to the Duce's men.'

Alas, Sir Sidney was the only optimist left in Addis-Abbaba, and on March 4th even he was to suffer a rude shock.

On that day we received a short telegram. This time it was the turn of the British ambulance unit. The telegram informed us that it had been bombed and more or less destroyed by Italian planes.

Later on I met a strange lad named Dobinson, who had been appointed transport officer by my good friend Dr. Melly, and he told me the whole story. Incidentally I must point out that Dobinson had been made transport officer on account of his great ingenuity and his extraordinary adaptability, and many fantastic stories were current about his adventures.

One day, annoyed at not having been invited to a dinner given by the French Minister he had turned up at dessert amongst the delegations of Abyssinian chiefs, disguised as an Abyssinian notable. His fluent command of the Amharic tongue and his knowledge of Amharic customs allowed him to play his role perfectly. But the demon drink betrayed him in the end. Having drunk a good deal he was unable to resist the temptation to sit down at the piano and play a wild American rag to the astonishment of everybody not in the joke.

He was also famous for his inventiveness. He had produced a multi-purpose soap. Apart from using it for washing it was excellent for cleaning boots. Smeared on the face it gave protection from sunburn, and if fat happened to be short there was no reason why a lump shouldn't be put in the pan for frying eggs.

Needless to say, the career of Dobinson did not end with the war in Abyssinia. When I heard the whole story of the bombing of the British ambulance unit from him he was bored to tears at the enforced inactivity which resulted from the fact that he was a prisoner of Franco in a San Sebastian jail.

But let us return to the disaster which marked the end of our illusions about the humanity of Italy's airmen.

'We had arrived near Amalata,' Dobinson informed me. 'That is at the foot of a big mountain situated to the south of the Kworam plain. A high Abyssinian officer advised us not to set up our camp in the plain but near the road, because the place was infested with Chiftas.

'In the evening of March 2nd the British ambulance unit made a simple bivouac, its lorries drawn up one behind the other, and all of them marked with large red crosses easily visible from the air. Night fell and we were not aware that the neighbouring forest was full of Abyssinian soldiers.

'The next morning an Italian reconnaissance plane flew low over our camp. The Abyssinians in the forest began to blaze away at it, and, according to the subsequent Italian version, it returned to its base riddled with bullets, its pilot firmly believing that the firing had come from the British Red Cross camp, which was the only sign of life visible from above.

'In the afternoon of the same day we rapidly shifted our camp out into the great Kworam plain in order to get well away from any military objective.

'The morning after that, March 4th, the unit was ready to start work. The flags had been spread out on the ground and the wounded were beginning to come in. In the operation tent Dr. Melly was putting on his gloves to make the first amputation when an S.62 plane flew over. Without warning it dropped a heavy bomb which fell right in the middle of the Red Cross flag stretched out on the ground about 60 feet from the tents.

' "It must be a mistake," said Dr. Melly, imperturbable as usual, but he had hardly closed his mouth when a second bomb fell to one side of the tent riddling it with fragments. The next bomb, one of small calibre, fell on the tent itself, killing the patient on the operating table and blowing doctors and attendants in all directions, fortunately without injuring them.

'The plane dropped ten large bombs, twenty smaller bombs and a number of incendiaries. Three patients were killed outright in their beds and four others mortally wounded. Several tents and lorries were completely destroyed.'

When we received Dr. Melly's telegram in Addis-Abbaba reporting the bombing we knew nothing about these details, but we soon learned that the British ambulance unit had been compelled to withdraw from the plain into the neighbouring mountainous region. The doctors and their attendants, assisted by a few Abyssinian soldiers, must have worked like demons to move the remnants of their unit, particularly as the move had to be carried out in pouring rain. From that time on the British unit followed the example of the other units and worked camouflaged and under cover as far as possible.

There was more alarming news. One of the officers of the Dutch ambulance unit had disappeared, and Dassios, the Greek surgeon in charge of our third Abyssinian unit, was dead or missing.

All these reports began to cause me very serious misgivings and I decided to leave for the northern front.

This time I went north by plane, leaving Addis-Abbaba around March 18th.

When we were approaching Dessie our plane suddenly dived and I made my way hurriedly forward, to ask the pilot what had happened. 'Italians,' he replied laconically and pointed out of the window to two planes which were weaving in and out in the sky. It was an unpleasant moment. Our plane was clearly marked with red crosses on the wings and fuselage, but I already had reason to know how much that protection was worth. If we were spotted it would mean almost certain death.

My pilot went in for a series of acrobatics, flying through a narrow valley to escape the view of the Italians and climbing from time to time to observe their movements. This went on for about half an hour, but fortunately the position of the sun was in our favour: the two Italian planes showed up clearly in the sun whilst for them we were in the shade. In the end to our relief they turned north and disappeared.

We landed safely on the Dessie air field where we found the U.S. military attaché and the chief of the Dutch ambulance unit waiting for me. The latter informed me that one of his transport officers, van Schelven, had been attacked by Chiftas between Kworam and Waldia and seriously wounded in the chest. For several days he had been in the hands of the British ambulance unit. I was asked to arrange for his transport to Addis-Abbaba as soon as possible.

It was then five p.m. Kworam was about twenty miles from the Italian lines and it was subjected to bombing from the air all day long. In order to avoid unpleasant encounters we should have to arrive just before nightfall, too late to be caught by Italian planes and yet early enough to be able to make a landing whilst there was still enough light. Night fell at six o'clock.

We left Dessie again at 5.20, having calculated a quarter of an hour's flying time for the first stage of the journey. By good fortune all went well and at a quarter to six we landed and taxied over to the side of the Emperor's plane.

When I descended I was surprised to find that His Majesty had sent one of his own mules to carry me to his headquarters, and there was also a mule for my pilot. So there we were making our way astride our mules along the mountain paths towards the famous caves which formed the refuge of the Emperor and his General Staff.

The whole time I noticed a certain persistent smell, something like horse-radish, and I asked an Abyssinian officer what it was.

'What, you don't know!' he exclaimed. 'That's mustard gas. Every day Italian planes sprinkle it over the whole sector.'

So the rumours that I had heard repeatedly in Addis-Abbaba that the Italians were using poison gas were well founded.

'They are using it in two ways,' my informant went on. 'By gas bombs which scatter the liquid in all directions up to about a couple of hundred yards or more, and by direct diffusion from low-flying planes which spread a cloud of very fine particles. They are using it in a consistency which doesn't stifle but causes bad burns. They know our soldiers go bare-footed and in that way they contract terrible burns. In addition our mules die from nibbling grass and leaves contaminated with the liquid.'

For about two hours we had been making our way along an out-of-the-way track, and suddenly as we came beyond the shoulder of a hill we saw thousands of fires glowing amidst the trees. They were the camp fires of the Imperial Guard who were encamped around the Emperor's shelter. The sight was unforgettable. It was like a well-lighted town under a sparkling heaven of stars.

We had to dismount. The path now rose so steeply and became so narrow that it was impassable for mules. Climbing up we came to a sort of terrace before a steep rocky face.

Towards the edge of the terrace I saw the menacing shape of an Oerlikon anti-aircraft gun, and I knew that we were near to the Emperor. That gun was famous. It was said that the Emperor himself rushed to serve it whenever an Italian plane attempted to attack the cave.

I was received with deference by the Chief of the General Staff. 'His Majesty is expecting you,' he said. 'He wishes to see you at once.'

We went into the cave. The floor was covered with a thick carpet, and the cave itself was divided into a number of chambers by heavy hangings. A curtain was raised and I entered a large space furnished only with two small garden chairs facing each other. The Emperor was already sitting on one of them and motioned me to occupy the other. His expression was sad and he seemed depressed.

'Have you any news?' he asked. 'Is there any message from the League of Nations?'

I had to remind him again that I was a delegate of the International Red Cross and not of the League of Nations.

'Yes, I know,' he replied, 'but I thought you might nevertheless have a message for me.'

From the opening of hostilities the Emperor had never ceased to hope that one day the member States of the League of Nations would send him the assistance provided for in the Pact to assist the victims of aggression.

In a few words I informed him of the terrible situation of our ambulance units and asked him to provide me in good time, before dawn the next day, with a company of soldiers to help camouflage my plane on the Kworam air field. I also told him that I intended to leave as soon as possible taking the wounded Dutch officer with me.

I took my leave of His Majesty, and for that evening and the subsequent night I was the guest of his officers.

At four o'clock in the morning when the dawn was just breaking 200 Abyssinian soldiers lined up near my tent. Silent and motionless each man carried a large leafy branch in his hand. It was a strange procession which set off for the air field. I sat astride my mule at the head of the procession and behind me marched the 200 men with their foliage. One might have thought that, as in *Macbeth*, Great Birnam Wood was on the march.

At about half-past five we arrived at the air field and hastily camouflaged the planes, then we turned towards the mountains to join the British ambulance unit.

After a climb of about an hour and a half we turned and looked back towards the plain and there we saw the shapes of our plane and the Emperor's clearly outlined by the greenery on the yellow air field. I looked at my pilot, who grinned. The camouflage was a waste of time.

Whilst we were still looking down at the air field we heard the drumming of aeroplane engines, and three Caproni bombers flew over towards the air field. One of the first stick fell squarely on the Emperor's plane, which flared up like a torch. We looked at each other again and then decided to hurry back to the air field and remove the camouflage from our plane if we could, and to chance once again the slender protection of the Red Cross.

We made our way down to the plain as fast as we could, constantly stumbling in our haste, still protected to some extent by a few trees. The Capronis were still circling round. One of them was obviously trying to hit our plane, a second was dropping bombs round the air field and the third was bombing the surrounding hills. We had to keep an eye on them and throw ourselves to the ground whenever they flew over us.

When we got to the foot of the hill the ground was terribly open, not a spot of cover anywhere. I proposed that one of us should run a hundred yards or so whilst the other kept watch and shouted a warning when the planes came near, and that the roles should then be reversed, and that we should get to the air field by such stages.

After progressing for about 600 yards I became aware of an acrid odour and at the same time my eyes began to smart. There was no doubt that the Italians were dropping mustard-gas bombs.

We took a rather longer way round which skirted the shoulder of a little hill and kept us above the level of the gas. Having no doubt exhausted their bomb loads the Italian planes now turned away and soon they had vanished over the horizon.

When we got to our plane we found that, as though by a miracle, it was undamaged. We removed the camouflage hurriedly and no sooner had we finished than three Italian Fiat fighters roared over. We ran for about 300 yards or so to the shelter of a rock. The fighters dived one after the other for about a quarter of an hour, machine-gunning as they dived. But to our astonishment our plane did not catch fire.

When the Fiats had gone we returned to our plane full of hope, only to find that our tank and all our petrol containers had been riddled with bullet holes and that the petrol had run out. Almost at once a new drumming in the sky announced the approach of further danger and once again we retreated hurriedly. This time we ran for about 500 yards and took cover on a little hill from which we had a good view of the scene. It was comic and tragic at the same time. The Italian airmen dropped scores of incendiaries in an effort to destroy our plane. They fell all around it, behind, in front and on either side, and not one hit it. It began to look as though our little plane was immune.

Once again the Italian bombers made off and I decided to return as quickly as possible to the headquarters of the Emperor to see if I could find someone capable of repairing our petrol tank. I was successful in doing so and I went back with the man in all haste to the air field to see what could be done. But on reaching the brow of the last hill which gave us a view of the air field I observed with a sinking heart that our plane was now a heap of charred wreckage from which smoke was curling into the air. My pilot told me when I came up to him that two Italian fighters had finally finished it off with incendiary bullets.

We were now over 600 miles from Addis-Abbaba without means of transport — and about twenty miles from the Italian lines.

Whilst we were still exchanging bitter reflections a small group of men approached us. Amongst the Abyssinians there were two Europeans, one of them riding on a mule and being supported by the other, who was walking at his side. The man on the mule was the wounded Dutch transport officer, van Schelven, who was being brought to us for the flight back to Addis-Abbaba. He was very exhausted and found it hard to conceal his disappointment that his last hope had now gone.

We were not far from the little town of Kworam and about three hours' journey from the Emperor's headquarters. We were discussing what best to do when the sound of planes was heard again and for the fifth time the Italians returned to the attack. We sent the Abyssinians and the mules off as quickly as possible, and the four of us, the pilot and I and the two Dutchmen, took cover at full length behind a large rock.

The bombing which followed seemed to have us as its objective. Looking at the Italian planes I could see the bombs leaving the racks and whistling down towards our hiding place. We lay face down with our hands behind our heads as the bombs fell. On all sides there was an uninterrupted series of explosions, and several times stones and earth thrown up by the bombs fell on to us. The Italian planes flew round in wide circles, and every time they flew over us they released further sticks of bombs. But at last it was over and they flew off. We had escaped again. We sat up and lit cigarettes — magnificent cigarettes marked ironically with the red cross, offered to us by the Dutch Red Cross men —and felt that we had earned them.

By this time I had only one idea: to get as far away from this exploding hell as I could as quickly as possible. I proposed to return to the Emperor's headquarters and to ask him for some means of conveyance for the wounded Dutch officer, whilst my pilot and the other two remained behind to await my return.

I went back along the path to the Emperor's shelter alone. The slopes through the mountain were slippery with dried grass and pine needles. Sometimes on the way I came across Abyssinian soldiers, their faces bloodless under their colour, their features drawn and suffering. I had no time to stop.

As I came to the last hill, whose outline stood out clear-cut against a shining limpid sky, I became aware of a strange chant-like plaint in the distance, an uncanny sound which made me shudder. It was a heart-rending chant which came and went in a slow but persistent rhythm.

I hurried on breathlessly, eager to find out what it was. And suddenly when I came out into the narrow space between the brow of the hill and the Emperor's refuge the sound swelled larger.

'Abiet . . . Abiet . . . Abiet. . . .'

Have pity . . . Have pity. . . .

Men were stretched out everywhere beneath the trees. There must have been thousands of them. As I came closer, my heart in my mouth, I could see horrible suppurating burns on their feet and on their emaciated limbs. Life was already leaving bodies burned with mustard gas.

'Abiet . . . Abiet . . . .'

The monotonous chant rose towards the refuge of the Emperor. But who was to have pity? Who was to help them in their suffering? There were no doctors available and our ambulances had been destroyed. There was no longer any material means of going to the assistance and succour of these unfortunates. Those who turned their faces towards me no longer saw me. I had nothing to assuage their distress.

Throughout the night which soon fell the endless and hopeless plaint continued to rise to the lonely and helpless Emperor.

'Abiet . . . Abiet. . . .'

CHAPTER V

'THE CHIFTAS'

Wɛ finally left Kworam in the Emperor's car. When he offered me its use His Majesty said only:

'Take care.'

'Of the Italian planes?'

'No, of the Chiftas.'

Chiftas were, as I have said previously, bandits.

Abyssinian bandits are of a particularly dangerous kind. They come primarily from amongst the nomadic Galla tribesmen in the neighbourhood of the Eritrean frontier. Armed from some mysterious source with good Italian rifles they operated behind the Abyssinian lines in innumerable bands, harrying and pillaging the countryside along the northern route between the mountains and the desert.

It was at the hands of these bandits that Dr. van Schelven had suffered his wound when he was in charge of a convoy of the Dutch ambulance unit. He was now with me in the last means which offered itself of regaining the capital, and it was with considerable relief that we took our places in the splendid V8 which His Majesty had placed at our disposal.

I had decided to do the driving, for the Abyssinian chauffeur struck me as more dangerous to our well-being than the Italians and the Chiftas combined. I was also taking along a British doctor, sick and much weakened from dysentery. Thus there were five of us in the car; Count Rosen, the pilot of the destroyed Red Cross plane, who sat beside me in the driving seat, the wounded Dutchman, the sick Englishman, and the Abyssinian driver who sat behind.

Before leaving I had made sure that each man had a revolver and ammunition, and in addition I took two rifles and a supply of cartridges.

At the end of the plain of Kworam, rather daunted at the idea of pressing on into the mountainous area after dark without an escort, we decided to wait for daylight before proceeding.

As soon as the first light of the dawn became visible we drove on and I assigned a special task to each man. I kept to the steering wheel, and that was no easy task on a winding road laid out in haste only a few weeks previously without proper metalling or embankments and sloping steeply into the Gobbo plain. All my attention had to be directed to the driving and steering in order to avoid sliding and slipping. Theoretically the driver, who was in the back seat on the right, was supposed to assist me with advice and at the same time to keep a look-out towards the precipice side. It was Count Rosen's job to keep an eye open for Italian planes and give warning at once. The wounded Dutchman and the sick Englishman were armed with Winchesters, which they held in their laps ready for instant use. Their instructions were to open fire at once on any Chifta who might menace us.

However, everything went well and we reached the plain without untoward incident. At eleven o'clock in the morning we arrived in Gobbo, the former capital. The village was deserted. The abandoned huts were half concealed by spurge, whose thick foliage was higher than their roofs.

The silence was oppressive. It was here that all the caravans were attacked.

'Italian plane to the right,' the pilot suddenly called out.

We were then in the village itself. Without hesitation I turned the car to the right and drove at full speed into a clump of spurge. It cracked and splintered as we drove through, but falling over the roof it formed a perfect camouflage from the air. I pulled up and we all got out. The Dutchman, himself too weak to go far, advised us to get outside the village. We left him under a large tree with his Winchester, and the rest of us dispersed as rapidly as possible.

The pilot and I had just time to fling ourselves into the cover of a small hedge of brambles. The plane was almost over our head. Explosions sounded. The plane had dropped three or four bombs on the village. Gradually the noise of its engines diminished until finally it could be heard no more. We had the impression that the plane had come down very low. My pilot listened intently with some excitement.

'His motor was misfiring,' he said. 'He's had to come down. Perhaps we shall be able to get hold of an Italian plane to replace the one they destroyed.'

He drew his revolver and stood up above the hedge, but suddenly a terrible roar of an engine starting up caused him to dive back again hurriedly. The Italian had played us a trick. It roared directly over us hedge-hopping and machine-gunning all around the village where he thought people might be hiding.

I don't know whether he had actually seen us. It was possible. In any case a hail of bullets thrashed the field to the left of us, throwing up little spurts of dust and stones which fell around like rain. This time the noise of his engines did die away in the distance and the plane disappeared as it had come. Once again we had escaped without injury.

I called our party together and hastily we climbed into the car.

We were driving at full speed along dry and dusty brown paths as flat as a motor-road. Herds of wild horses often galloped parallel to us for miles and then fell away exhausted.

We came up to the last hill which lay between us and Waldia, but first there was a large river to cross before we could enter the town.

We came to the ford and I sent the driver on ahead to reconnoitre. The water rose half way up his thigh. It would just about do. I put the car into first gear and went forward into the water, turning a little upstream in order not to be carried away by the current. Suddenly it gave a violent jerk and the engine stopped. I tried to get it going again, but in vain. I got out and asked the Englishman to take the wheel whilst the pilot, the driver and myself pushed with all our might. It was no good. We were stuck about half way across. Rapidly stones and sand carried along by the swift current began to collect against the wheels and robbed us of all hope of ever getting the car out again.

We took out our things and our weapons and carried them to

the shade of a clump of acacias. I was very much disturbed by our misfortune, particularly on account of the possibility of an attack by Chiftas. I communicated my misgivings to the pilot.

'Ask van Schelven to tell us how it happened to him,' he suggested.

In a restrained voice and with some difficulty in breathing van Schelven, his face still pale and drawn, told us his story.

'You see that hill? The way goes round there and drops down into Waldia. It was there, at the last bend, that we were attacked.

'I was going up towards Kworam with a caravan of about a hundred mules. I had been told that it was dangerous to attempt to get through without an escort, but I'm used to scaremongering of that sort. I lived for twelve years in Malaya and I heard the same sort of stories about the head-hunters, but I never took any notice of them. I know that sort of thing, I said to my friends. All you have to do is to stand firm and kill one or two of them and the rest fly for their lives.

'I left Waldia at about three in the morning without the slightest misgiving. As we reached the foot of the hill a brilliant sun appeared over the horizon. Walking with an attendant at the end of the caravan I could see a long line of magnificent white cases, all marked with the red cross, dangling from the pack saddles of my mules.

'Suddenly without the slightest warning shots sounded quite near me, but before I could even draw my revolver I felt a blow full in the chest and I knew that I had been hit. I dropped to my knees but fortunately I didn't lose consciousness immediately. A great black devil jumped at me, seized my rifle and ran after the mules. I began crawling towards the bushes which lined the path, but the effort quickly exhausted me. I could hardly breathe, my heart was banging away and then I fainted.'

Van Schelven was silent for a while. He passed his emaciated hands over his face. When he began to talk again his voice was so hoarse and low that we had difficulty in distinguishing what he said above the bubbling of the river and the murmur of the forest behind us.

'I don't know how long I remained unconscious,' he continued, 'but I woke up with a pricking sensation in the stomach. Opening my eyes I saw another bandit standing over me calmly sticking his spear into my stomach. I thought it was all over for me. A stupid end, far from anywhere and for no good reason. However, the villain did not jab me violently. Apparently he was chiefly interested in my watch whose chain was depending from my fob pocket. With some effort I went to draw my watch out to give it to him when to my surprise he turned tail and fled. I think he must have thought I was drawing a revolver.

'I profited from my consciousness to crawl into the bushes and conceal myself in the undergrowth. After lying quite still for about an hour during which there was no sound or sign of life I decided to discover just what had happened to me. I pulled up my tunic and found two wounds, still bleeding, the entry and exit of the bullet. The entry was between my ribs to the right and the opening was a little to the left of the sternum. The bullet had gone through the lungs. That accounted for my feeling of suffocation. I undid my belt and buckled a pad as tightly as possible across the wounds. It made me faint again, but it very likely saved my life.'

Van Schelven paused again, this time to light a cigarette, then he continued.

'When I came to myself again it was night and pitch dark. The silence too was absolute. There wasn't the slightest indication of any human life anywhere, but I kept on the alert, because I knew there were hyenas about. By daybreak I was desperately thirsty and the walls of my throat seemed stuck together. I plucked leaves from the bushes and chewed them for their sap, spitting them out afterwards. I managed to stagger to my feet in order to look up and down the path to see if there was any sign of life, but there wasn't. The day passed and the second night came and I was still there. The following morning I was half dead with hunger and thirst. I've had it, I thought. All I've got to do now is die. However, I wasn't very keen on the idea and I fought against it. The morning of the third day found me still there amongst the bushes.

'And then just as dawn was breaking I heard a thin sound in the distance, a very familiar sound. It was a cock crowing. A cock in the scrub? Not likely, I thought. Where there's a cock there's men not far away. There must be a village somewhere near. I felt hope returning and summoning up my remaining strength and taking what observations I could in order not to lose my way I made towards the sound. After a step or two everything began to turn round and round, but I kept at it. Stumbling, falling, picking myself up again a dozen times, I covered less than two miles in eight hours. But the village was there, all right. I came in sight of the huts and staggered forward. It was a village of Chiftas.

'Never mind. It was my one chance. I tried to cry out. The natives spotted me and one or two of them began to draw a bead on me. I had nothing more to lose and I held myself up and went forward like a drunken man. In my mind I kept thinking that it was death I was looking for. Impressed by the strange phantom wandering in the scrub the Chiftas let me approach. I pushed them aside to fall into the first hut I came to. I knew that I was saved as soon as I fell over the threshold because, just as in the east, a man mustn't be killed under your roof even if he's your worst enemy. Drink, I gasped, drink. But no one took any further notice of me. I had been there in agonies for about two hours when finally the village witch doctor arrived in a very imposing rig-out. He looked me over, stretched me out on a sort of mattress and then made me drink turbid water which was terribly salty. After that he forced me to eat an egg which was so rotten that there was already a half-formed chick in it. It was his supreme recipe and I wasn't in a position to argue.'

Van Schelven's stomach turned over again at the very thought.

'I got it down,' he said, 'and then I went off to sleep and I spent a peaceful night. The next day, with all the Amharic words I could remember, I managed to explain to them who I was and they immediately showed themselves more friendly. They had heard about my disappearance and they knew that the Emperor was offering a very attractive reward for news about me. In the afternoon they hoisted me into the pack saddle of a mule and off we set for Kworam.'

Van Schelven cleared his throat before concluding his story.

'After about twenty miles of agony, constantly falling off because the saddle kept slipping, we came up with a British lorry. I don't think I could have lasted another mile.'

That was what we were hoping for too, a lorry which would get us out of the mess we were in.

We waited all day without result until the evening, and then, with my eyes glued on the path, I thought I could detect a cloud of brown dust approaching. I was right; gradually it became more distinct. It turned out to be a lorry driven by Abyssinians out searching for food.

We fixed a rope between the two and after having dug away the silt and stones round the wheels of our car the lorry managed to pull it out on to the other side of the river. But nothing we could do could persuade the motor to start up again. It was sad, but we had to leave the Emperor's superb V8 where it was.

We all piled into the lorry and an hour later we arrived in Waldia.

There we had a double piece of good fortune; first of all we found a detachment of the British ambulance unit which offered us hospitality, and secondly we found the only three-engined plane of the Abyssinian Army on the airfield as though it were waiting there expressly to take us to Addis-Abbaba the next day.

In the evening I began to inquire about my Greek surgeon Dr. Dassios, whose fate had caused me a good deal of anxiety, and I was delighted to hear that he was camped in the neighbourhood. I visited him and explained the situation on the northern front, advising him to return to the capital at the first sign of danger.

'Go back before it's too late,' I begged.

He looked at me with a smile.

'The war won't be over as soon as all that,' he replied, 'and the Chiftas aren't so very terrible.'

I was not to see him again in Abyssinia. The next time I met him was in Paris a year later. The war in Abyssinia had been over for some time and I had good reason to believe that he had changed his views as to the harmlessness of Chiftas.

When we touched glasses in the Champs-Élysées bar where we had arranged to meet, the smile on his lips was just as optimistic as when he had listened sceptically to my good advice about the necessity for prudence a year before. But now his face and his body bore indelible scars to remind him of those strange days.

'Do you remember our last meeting in Waldia?' he asked.

'Indeed I do,' I replied. 'What happened to you after that?'

Dr. Dassios looked idly at the long stream of splendid cars moving along the Champs-Élysées towards the Arc de Triomphe. I doubt if he really saw them, and what he had to say caused them to recede for me and conjured up at once the wild background of the Abyssinian bush. Once again we were back there far away from all this reassuring civilization and luxury, surrounded by the treachery and relentless savagery of the jungle. He spoke slowly, interrupting himself from time to time to take a sip of whisky.

'A few days after you left, having waited in vain for two lorries which were supposed to bring me supplies, I decided to move on — not towards the south, but north. I took advantage of a convoy under the command of Blaten Tessama with an escort of 300 men. But we had hardly passed Gobbo when we were attacked by hordes of Chiftas. The fighting lasted all night, but they were finally driven off. After that Tessama refused to let me go on to Kworam and made me go back with him to Waldia.

'Whilst we were there the situation got steadily worse. On April 10th a soldier came to me and reported that the Chiftas were about to attack again; not only did they intend to plunder the town but also to seize my ambulance. I went to the Governor and asked for protection, but he said he hadn't sufficient forces to defend my ambulance as well and so I was left to my own devices. I guarded my shelter as well as I could with the ten men of my personal guard. My attendants and stretcher-bearers had to content themselves with scalpels and other surgical instruments for arms. Then we awaited events.

'At midnight about 150 Chiftas came towards our shelter. We immediately opened fire and prevented them from getting close. The firing went on all night and when they retired at dawn, they left about thirty bodies behind them. We realized that they would return to the attack at night, and probably night after night. Obviously we shouldn't be able to hold out indefinitely. So I decided to make a get-away if I could persuade any of those damned village headmen to offer us sanctuary. I did find one, Graziamatch Negatou, who was willing to offer my small band shelter. Hardly had we arrived when the Chiftas sent a delegation demanding that he should hand over the white medicine man who had managed to escape them and whom they regarded as their prey. The gallant old Negatou refused and in the night the bother started up again.'

The Greek turned a twinkling eye on me.

'You know, Junod, I often thought of you. It would have been wiser on my part to take your advice. However, I didn't lose faith in my star, and, in fact, the situation gradually improved. After two or three days Italian planes began to fly over the village dropping leaflets in Amharic calling for the surrender of the whole country-side. I obediently signed a surrender for myself and the ambulance and sent my interpreter Yonna Nathalie with it to the Italian lines.

'You didn't know Yonna Nathalie, did you? A pity; because I don't believe there was a more devoted fellow anywhere in the world. I'll tell you in a minute what he did for me.'

'He brought you back a safe-conduct, I suppose?'

'No, and I waited for days in vain for his return. I thought that either he had fled on his own account or that the Italians were hold-ing him as a prisoner. His failure to return began to demoralize my party. One by one the guards, attendants and stretcher-bearers dis-appeared until finally I was left alone with my personal servant, who seemed to have more courage than the rest. Seeing what had happened old Negatou must have come to the conclusion that we were embarrassing guests, because he disarmed us both and put us in his jail. I think his chief aim was to get hold of our baggage. When he had carefully deprived us of everything he lodged us in a hut about three hours' march from the village. Two days after, he had us taken out and marched off into the mountains where we were turned loose and left to our own devices.

'However, my "boy" found a path leading to another village. He found out that its chief was named Desta, an honest and peaceable fellow, and he advised me to go to the village and ask for his protection. Well, there was nothing much else for me to do so after a painful march through the night over rocky, thorny country I found myself the next morning knocking at the door of the honest and peaceable Desta.'

A certain twitching at the corners of his mouth made me realize that Desta had not been as good as his reputation.

'He turned out to be a brutal, cowardly fellow,' he continued. 'The idea of giving me shelter and provoking the reprisals of the Chiftas put him into a blue funk. Of course, I wasn't a very desirable guest. Anybody who gave me shelter risked being massacred. However, when I went off to the village I was cheerful enough and quite confident.'

Dassios paused. What came afterwards seemed difficult to talk about. He looked away and then continued.

'I had to go down on my knees,' he said slowly. 'Round my neck was a heavy stone and I had to murmur a prayer, which my "boy" taught me, to that black-visaged black-hearted savage. It's an old Abyssinian custom; a suppliant abandons his freedom in this fashion in order to save his life. It works both ways: whoever hears the prayer may not reject it. I was allowed to take up my residence in a stable and my "boy" brought me food — food, did I say? It was hardly fit for dogs.'

'What were the Italians doing in the meantime?'

'The devil knows. I don't. The first news I got of them came through my faithful interpreter, Yonna Nathalie. He had been prevented from reaching their lines, but he had never ceased trying to get into touch with me, in defiance of the Chiftas sent out in pursuit of him, to let me know their approximate position. For days he had searched for me, following my tracks, casting around in the mountains, until one fine morning he appeared from nowhere and threw himself down at my feet. Do you know why? To ask me to forgive him for being so late in returning.

'Unfortunately the Chiftas had followed him and now they knew my whereabouts. My friend Desta realized that too, and so he turned me out at once and told me to make myself scarce. Nothing loath I set off before dawn accompanied by Yonna Nathalie and my "boy". But we were out of luck. We hadn't been on our way more than an hour when we were suddenly attacked by a band of Chiftas flourishing swords and spears. My "boy" managed to escape, but Yonna and I were seized, hurled to the ground and thoroughly beaten. Then all our clothes were ripped off and we were dragged along the ground. I thought my last hour had come, and no doubt it would have but at that moment another band of savages, having heard the noise and thinking there was some interesting pillage proceeding, rushed up and demanded their share of the booty. In the ensuing explanations I managed to fly into the surrounding bushes despite a wounded leg.

'Incidently, it wasn't only my leg, I had spear wounds everywhere, particularly in the knees and the right shoulder. I felt as though there wasn't a square inch of my skin that hadn't been gouged, scratched or otherwise abraised. Eight days after that . . .'

'Eight days!' I exclaimed in astonishment.

'Yes, eight days. I remained in the forest for over a week, living on nothing but wild roots. You know how cold the nights can be in Abyssinia, and you must remember I was naked. Naked in the torrential rains. After eight days of that I was in such a state of moral and physical exhaustion that I was at the end of my tether.'

'How did you manage to save yourself?'

'I owe my life to the devotion of Yonna Nathalie. He, too, had succeeded in getting away in the brawl. Half-carrying me, half-supporting me he managed to get me to a village where he knew there was a man who would not refuse to help me. His name was Ato Foutigues and I had tended him when our unit was still working. He did, in fact, show himself grateful, but this time it was his own people who wanted to kill me. He watched over me night and day until I had recuperated a little, then he and Yonna led me to the Italian camp. We arrived twenty days after I had left Waldia.'

'And was that the end of your misfortunes?' I asked.

'No.' He laughed. 'At first I was received amiably enough, but then they sent me to Dessie where I was handed over to the "Questura". I was bitterly reproached in particular for having signed the protest against the bombing of Dessie, and when I said it contained nothing but the bare truth I was insulted, beaten and thrown into prison.

'The prison was a sort of dirty basement. The window was barred but it had no glass or covering of any sort so that the wind and the rain blew in on us. I had about a score of chained Abyssinians as fellow prisoners. Although it was bitterly cold I had no mattress and no covering. Once a day only I received a plate of very bad food. I should certainly have perished of cold and hunger but for the fact that the carabinieri took pity on me and gave me some of the bread from their rations, whilst at night one of them covered me up with his greatcoat. I began to shake with fever, but it was ten days before they consented to send me to hospital. My temperature was 104 degrees and my pulse was 150.

'As soon as I could stand on my feet I was sent by lorry to Asmara. It was a terrible journey which lasted five days exposed to the broiling sun during the day and lying directly on the frozen ground at night. The jolting of the lorry, the fever and the despair made me delirious and I tried to fling myself under the wheels. In the end the Italian police escort manacled me. I was in such a state when we finally arrived in Asmara that they didn't dare to put me into prison. I was given a room in the former Abyssinian Consulate, and I found a number of Englishmen there who were in much the same case as myself. After a few days' peace the interrogations of the "Questura", the insults and the ill-treatment began all over again.'

Dr. Dassios's face clouded over and his fist clenched.

'I'll never forgive them for what they did to me then.'

'They tortured you?'

'Not specifically, but they robbed me, and in such a dirty fashion.'

'But had you got anything left at all by that time?'

'No, but I had managed to get into touch with the head of the Greek colony in Asmara, and he asked permission from the Italian authorities to hand over a sum of money sufficient to pay the expense of my repatriation. They agreed and the authorization was given to him in due official form, note that. But the day before I was to leave Italian police searched my room and took the money on the pretext that I had concealed it for dishonest ends. All I was left with was sufficient to pay my ticket, and the ticket of the policeman who escorted me, to the Sudanese frontier. And there I was turned loose, on the edge of the desert at a village called Tesleni.

'There I was, without papers and without money. In order to get food I had to work for a compatriot who kept the local café. Through another compatriot, who was a traveller in the Sudan, I managed to get news of my plight through to the Greek colony in Kassala, and they obtained the authorization of the British authorities for my repatriation.

'I disembarked at Piraeus towards the middle of July. The Chiftas had kept me a prisoner for twenty days; the Italians for three months.'

Dr. Dassios rapped nervously on the bar counter and called for another whisky. As he lifted his glass the brilliant spectacle offered by the most beautiful avenue in the world was reflected in it.

'And what are you going to do now?' I asked.

'I've only one idea, my friend,' he answered without hesitation, 'to get back there as quickly as possible.'

CHAPTER VI

THE ABANDONED CAPITAL

T H E Emperor had the greatest difficulty in getting back to Addis-Abbaba. Fifty officers and men who had remained faithful escorted him through country infested with Chiftas, through bands of deserters and pillagers, and through the human debris of his army.

When he finally arrived on April 29th his capital was like a sinking ship whose passengers were all anxious to leave it before it finally submerged. The train to Jibuti was besieged by Abyssinian notables and by foreigners who judged it prudent not to await the arrival of the Italians.

My original companion Sidney Brown had been in Geneva again for two months and I received a telegram from him which read:

LEFT TO YOUR JUDGMENT TO REMAIN IN ADDIS-ABBABA OR GO BACK TO JIBUTI.

I remained in Addis-Abbaba in an effort to regroup the remnants of our ambulance units which succeeded, often under incredible difficulties, in getting back to the capital. The British arrived first with one or two lorries and some of their material. All the way back to the capital what was left of the Dutch unit had been harassed constantly by Chiftas. Schupler, the Austrian surgeon, had covered more than 500 miles on foot and he was in a deplorable state. What had happened to all the others? According to the Dutch, the French attendant Gingold had remained behind with the American missionaries in Dessie.

As I had done before on a number of occasions, I requested information from the Foreign Affairs Department of the Emperor's Government as to the number of Italians who had been taken prisoner since the beginning of the war.

'Five,' was the answer.

It was quite true, and what it meant was only too clear.

For months the Italians had been informing the International Committee of the Red Cross at Geneva of the names and particulars of their soldiers who had fallen into Abyssinian hands. All the steps we had taken to discover their whereabouts or their fate, and all the vehement protests we had transmitted to the Emperor had been useless. It was the savage custom of the Abyssinians not to take prisoners.

The five Italian prisoners of the Abyssinian war, a tank crew, owed their survival to a sudden inspiration on the part of their commander. Their tank broke down, and they were soon surrounded by deliriously triumphant natives dancing and brandishing their spears and rapping from time to time on the steel hulk of the tank to demand the surrender of the crew. Suddenly the turret opened and the tank commander appeared shouting in Amharic:

'Long live Haile Selassie. Christ is arisen!'

The enthusiasm of the natives at these words was so tremendous that they led their captives off to the Emperor himself instead of putting them to death at once.

The five men were now lodged in the prison of Addis-Abbaba. Fearing that they would be massacred I approached the French Ambassador on their behalf and he took charge of their safety.

On all sides foreigners, Hindus, Greeks and Armenians, were seeking refuge in the legations against the coming storm. Every diplomatic building became a little autonomous town, and tents for fugitives were erected by the hundred in the grounds of the legations. France had no less than 3000 refugees. Germany had a hundred. The Americans had barricaded themselves in their Consulate. A thousand British nationals had sought safety behind the bayonets of the Sikhs.

An oppressive atmosphere of anxiety weighed down on the town. At first it was a sort of stupor, the precursor of the panic to come. The Makonnen boulevard was now crowded with soldiers in rags begging with menaces from the passers. In the evenings the streets were deserted.

The Zabanias deserted their posts. The Belgian officers who were relied upon to take over the policing of the town failed at the last moment. No one knew who was supposed to maintain order.

Capronis appeared in the sky over the capital for the first time. The Italians were now only fifty miles away.

On May 1st the Emperor left by special train for Jibuti.

Who would formally surrender the abandoned capital?

As soon as the news spread that the Emperor had left the town a shouting mob made its way towards the palace. All its buildings were sacked. Abyssinians and Gallas, ex-soldiers, fought bitterly for the treasures they believed were amassed there. In the absence of treasure they seized arms.

I left my house, but not wishing to take refuge in any of the embassies I installed myself with a French journalist in a little apartment overlooking the Makonnen. From its window I could not have been better placed to observe what happened when the Italians arrived, but I soon realized that it was not going to be easy to remain a peaceful observer.

Shots began to be heard. At first they were isolated, but before long they developed into fusillades. At various points the smoke of fires began to rise.

'Don't worry,' said a doctor who had been resident in the country for ten years. 'The Abyssinians like firing into the air when they're excited. It doesn't mean a thing.'

That was on May 2nd. In the night he was driven from his hospital, leaving it and his house in flames.

From my balcony I observed the first cases of plundering. The shop opposite was a travel agency, and a group of Abyssinians machine-gunned its iron shutters. They forced open the door and then, disappointed at finding nothing worth stealing, set fire to the building.

After that shop after shop in the Makonnen was plundered and set alight. The journalist and I had collected all our personal effects and papers in his apartment and we decided to stay on there, defending ourselves if we were attacked.

In the afternoon I was sitting at a table writing when I was disturbed by a great noise below. Looters had broken into the tailor's shop. Their entry was accompanied by a succession of shots, and I saw the floor splinter around me as bullets came up through the ceiling below.

I sprang to the door and saw my friend the journalist hurrying with a large case in the direction of the small house in the courtyard behind our own which was inhabited by Greeks. I had no time to follow him because the Chiftas were already surging up and levelling their rifles at my chest.

'Berr, berr, berr,' they shouted. It was money they wanted.

'Yelem berr,' I shouted back. 'No money here.'

They began to break open the cupboards, and in the meantime I had snatched up my most important papers and fled to the Greeks in the rear.

Once there I was seized with rage, and revolver in hand I returned to the apartment. Only six Abyssinians were left of the original assailants, and they were quite drunk and in a threatening mood. Two of them were quarrelling over my clothing which they had emptied out of the drawers and the wardrobe on to the floor. I collected one or two photographs which were of sentimental value to me and pushing two soldiers aside who were standing at the door I made my escape a second time. Turning my head I saw a rifle aimed at me. Without hesitation I vaulted over the balustrade and dropped about fifteen feet into the courtyard below. I heard the sound of shots, but I arrived safely at the house of the Greeks a second time.

The foundations of the house were of stone, but the upper part was of dried mud and plaster, and a hail of shots went through and through it and forced us to take refuge in the cellar.

My 'boy' joined me and begged me to leave. My car was parked just opposite. From the yard we had only to open a great wooden door and cross the street. I convinced the French journalist and the Greeks that they had better come with me. My 'boy' set about opening the wooden door to the street. All the surrounding houses were already burning, but perhaps I should have time to get the car out before they collapsed.

I looked behind. The Frenchman and the Greeks were ready to

follow me. The door opened and I ran into the street. Immediately my heart fell. I was surrounded by a gang of plundering soldiers who were firing wildly into the windows of the burning houses. They surged around me at once. I was unarmed because I had dropped my revolver in my jump over the balustrade. My 'boy' who tried to defend me was swept away in a mêlée. I felt that my end had come.

At that moment one of the looters snatched at my camera which I carried slung round my neck. Quite spontaneously I gave him a heavy blow in the face which made him stagger back, and I seized advantage of the momentary diversion to rush back through the wooden door to the house of the Greeks.

I escaped without injury but I was furious that the Frenchman and the Greeks had left me in the lurch. Their attitude did not encourage me to make a second attempt.

By six o'clock night had fallen and we could see nothing but the light of fires. The whole Makonnen was burning, and a rain of sparks and ashes fell over the thatched roofs all around.

We had again taken refuge in the cellar, and I posted myself near the door with a heavy club to hand, determined to brain the first aggressor and make my way out in case of an attack.

But I had forgotten that Abyssinians went barefooted, and that their arrival was not heralded by any noise of footsteps. At seven o'clock a group of maddened looters irrupted into the cellar. One of them had an electric torch in whose light we could see rifles aimed at us. For the third time that day chance came to my assistance. One of the group sprang forward, fell on my neck and showed me signs of the greatest affection and regard, exclaiming 'Kay Mascal . . . Kay Mascal . . .' It was a soldier to whom I had attended in the ambulance unit at Waldia.

He succeeded in persuading the rest of the band to go and leave us in peace, and then he led us all to the house of one of his friends not far away. It was a round building with thick stone walls surrounded by an enclosed garden. He left three soldiers armed with rifles to guard us and we promised to speak in their favour if they protected us until the Italians arrived.

The night passed in great anxiety. Outside the firing was almost continuous. The light of a candle showed me that we were in some sort of a stable. Apart from myself there were three Greeks, the French journalist, two Abyssinian women, two half-breed children who cried all night, a mule and two dogs. There were also myriads of fleas, but I felt rather than saw them. They bit me all over. In the end I preferred to go outside and risk a stray bullet rather than stand their attentions any longer. Our three guardians were constantly firing at imaginary enemies. I urged them to economize ammunition and not to fire unnecessarily, but they obviously did not understand a single word I said.

Just before the dawn of May 3rd a certain calm descended on the town. The Greeks, who understood Abyssinian, declared that the Italians were at the gates. All the Chiftas and the looters disappeared gradually, but the Lebbas stayed behind. They were ordinary footpads, some of them now armed with rifles, and the rest with clubs. They looted what the others had missed. They were certainly not so dangerous, but far from harmless for all that.

The news spread in the neighbourhood that there was a *hakim*, or doctor, in our house, and people began to knock on the iron door which gave on to the street. They were wounded and they asked for treatment. Many of them had probably been damaged by our wildly firing guardians in the night. I agreed to treat them but I established a strict control and let them in only if they surrendered their arms and ammunition, a circumstance which greatly strengthened the defensive capacity of our small garrison.

I lined my patients up against the wall and gave them very rudimentary attention. I had a certain quantity of an Abyssinian cloth known as *aboujedid* for bandages and a bottle of American oil of peppermint as a medicament. A drop or two of the oil of peppermint and a turn or two of the cloth and my patients were greatly comforted.

We began to feel hungry. After all, it was twenty-four hours since we had eaten. It was no use standing on ceremony and I went over to the attack. Placing my men along the wall I stopped all the groups of looters passing through the street and forced them to disgorge at the rifle point. After an hour or so of this I observed with satisfaction that our booty was rapidly increasing. It was very varied: there was flour, whisky, champagne, biscuits, Rhine wines, mirrors, braces, perfumes, typewriters, etc. Nicholau, one of the Greeks, was already quite drunk.

However, we were by no means out of the wood, and during the following night we repulsed a strong attack made on the house by the last of the Chiftas in retreat.

Quite apart from that, the second night was terrible. There was no air, the babies went on crying, the dogs growled and barked, and the Greeks never failed to start a loud discussion whenever we wanted silence to hear what was going on outside. But even all that was as nothing compared to the fleas. In the morning I was covered with their bites and I feared spotted typhus more than I feared Lebbas.

On the third day one of the Abyssinian women agreed to take a message to the British Legation. In a few lines I indicated our position and explained our situation. Then I gave the message to the woman and instructed her to hand it to the first European in a car or lorry she saw.

At about four o'clock in the afternoon I heard the sound of a motor car and then my name was shouted. I made a cautious sortie and found several of my French friends perched on a lorry and armed with four machine guns. We were saved. I invited the companions of my terrifying experience to come with me, but to my astonishment the Greeks refused. When I asked them why, they pointed to the pile of booty which had accumulated in the hut. Apart from typewriters there were now gramophones and umbrellas. They were not going to let all that go so easily.

'And what about our business?' they asked. 'If we go there'll be nothing left when we return.'

I made no further attempt to persuade them, and I went off with the French reporter to the French Embassy.

The journey through Addis-Abbaba gave us some idea of the extent of the disaster which had overtaken the capital. Almost all the European houses had been destroyed by fire. Some of them were still burning. Hundreds of tradesmen were ruined and without stock or homes.

I was greeted at the Embassy with pleased surprise. I had, it appeared, already been numbered amongst the dead. For days numerous lorries carrying volunteers had searched through the streets in the hope of picking up surviving Europeans. At the same time it had been necessary to organize the defence of the Embassy itself, which had often been attacked. A number of the defenders had been wounded and I arrived opportunely to organize a sick-bay.

On May 5th Addis-Abbaba awoke to find its streets silent and deserted. Smoke was still rising here and there from devastated buildings. All the natives had fled or were hiding in their huts. The Italians must be very close now.

Corpses could be seen here and there amongst the ruins. Most of the dead were Abyssinians, but there were also the bodies of Europeans, usually Greeks and Armenians, who had been killed when their premises were plundered.

Scattered around in the gardens of the Imperial Palace were carpets, torn hangings and other debris of furniture.

Even the hospitals were empty. The wards had been ransacked and the dispensaries rifled. The patients had all disappeared taking material and medicaments with them. The Menelik hospital, the French hospital, the Italian hospital and the Filoa hospital had all suffered in the same way.

All the shop windows in the Makonnen had been smashed and pillaged and the street was littered with boxes and charred beams. The building which had flown the proud flag of the Kay Mascal was gutted. Where the tragically deceived hopes of the new-born Abyssinian Red Cross had been housed for seven months was now a heap of charred rubble.

In the afternoon I learned that my friend Dr. Melly of the British ambulance unit was dying in the British Legation. The head of that splendid body of men who had saved so many lives by their fine work on the northern front had ended his mission in the streets of Addis-Abbaba. He had gone out with his lorries to aid the victims of the wild shooting. Straightening himself after having examined a wounded woman a drunken Chifta had discharged a rifle point blank at his chest.

When I arrived at the British Legation I found the Minister and his wife standing on the steps of the residence. From that vantage point one could see far out into the country through which the famous road to the north passed.

A cloud of dust was already visible on it. We watched it eagerly.

It came closer and closer and finally resolved itself into the advance guard of the Italian Army arriving in a great din of motors, sirens and trumpets.

A cheer went up in the grounds of the Legation. For the refugees gathered there, but for them alone, the aggressors came as liberators.

I hastened towards the hospital room, but I was too late. Dr. Melly breathed his last as the armies of Mussolini entered the capital.

That evening — Marshal Badoglio had just arrived at the Italian Embassy — I was present at the official ceremony of the taking over of Addis-Abbaba by the Italians. It marked the last act of the Italo-Abyssinian War.

The Italian flag, now both royal and imperial, fluttered up to the masthead. Trumpets sounded and the assembled Italian troops shouted the slogans I had already heard in Port Said:

'Viva il Duce! A chi la vittoria? A noi.'

I was received by Marshal Badoglio who greeted me coldly when I was presented as the delegate of the International Red Cross.

'The International Red Cross would have done better not to interfere,' he said reproachfully.

I made no reply.

SPAIN

CHAPTER I

'CAMARADAS AND CABALLEROS'

IT was the end of July 1936. The headlines of the newspapers were full of the happenings in Spain. The name of an obscure Spanish general named Franco had suddenly become known to the whole world.

He had set out from Spanish Morocco to conquer Spain, and his supporters were rallying in Navarre and Castile. His rebellion against the government of the Spanish Republic was growing more and more serious. The people in the big towns were behind the government. Both sides took hostages. The prisons were over-crowded. Everywhere the blood of summary executions seeped down into the earth.

In Geneva the leaders of the International Committee of the Red Cross began to pore over the map of Spain: Burgos, Bilbao, Salamanca, Almeria, etc. Where exactly were all those places which had so suddenly emerged from the background? Where were the Reds? And where the Whites? There was no front line.

The International Committee of the Red Cross was meeting once again in that same Villa Moynier which I had left nine months before for Abyssinia. Now I was back there again to give the Committee a full report of my mission. But it was no longer Abyssinia which chiefly interested them. . . .

'All postal communication with Spain has been cut,' declared Max Huber, the President of the International Red Cross. 'We must do something. The Red Cross cannot remain indifferent when men, women and children are in need of assistance anywhere in the world. We must find someone to go there as quickly as possible and find out what can be done.'

All eyes turned on me.

I made a gesture of protest. I was beginning to think that it was high time I went back to my sanatorium in Mulhouse, and the white coat of the surgeon attracted me more than the grip of the globe-trotter. The leave of absence I had been given so generously was long up. But they had words of consolation and encouragement.

'Do agree to go. It won't be long. Three weeks at the most. It's only to find out exactly what's happening.'

Those three weeks lasted three years.

In August 1936 I was in Paris at the Spanish Embassy. Albornoz, the Spanish Ambassador, received me. He had remained loyal to the Republic, but he seemed to know little more than we had already known in Geneva. All the assistance he could give me was a general recommendation on the notepaper of the Embassy which read:

'The Spanish Ambassador in Paris recommends Dr. Marcel Junod, delegate of the International Committee of the Red Cross, to the good offices of all Spanish anti-fascist militiamen.'

At the French Air Ministry I was informed that all air traffic with Spain had been suspended. A plump little man sitting at his desk looked at me coldly through his glasses:

'Frankly, I don't recommend you to go by a French plane. Owing to an error some of our planes were used by the Republicans to bomb Franco's men whilst our insignia was still on their wings. But the German plane service from Stuttgart is still operating. You might get that at Marseilles.'

The next day I was on board a German plane flying to Spain and wondering who would receive me in Barcelona, the anti-fascist militiamen or the supporters of Franco.

No sooner had the plane landed at the Pratt airfield than I knew. Hundreds of militiamen, rifle in hand, surrounded the place. The Spanish officials examined my Swiss passport with sympathy. On leaving the customs I was fortunate enough to meet our consul who drove me away in his car. Hardly were we alone than I saw him glance with misgiving at my collar and tie. He was wearing neither. I took mine off and put them in my pocket.

On the way to Barcelona we were stopped several times by controls. They were all dressed in the same fashion in workmen's dungarees with an army forage cap perched on the side of the head —

and the hair seemed rather long for soldiers. But the Swiss flag on the bonnet of our car acted as a passport every time.

'Consulado de Suiza. Siga hombre!'

The consul did not know where the headquarters of the Red Cross were and he advised me to ask at one of the hospitals.

We were now in the city. The streets were full of life. The trams and motor buses seemed to be plying normally, but here and there at the side of the road were the remains of overturned cars. These were the traces of the first few days' fighting. Along the streets and in the squares were great placards in many colours with propaganda of the celebrated F.A.I., the Anarchist Federation of Iberia.

We passed an open car flying the Red Cross flag in which were four 'senores' in white coats. Doctors, I thought. I stopped at a little distance and made a sign to them, raising my clenched fist. To have raised my open hand might have produced a burst from the tommy-guns of the militiamen who were prowling around everywhere.

One of the occupants of the car spoke French. He was delighted at my arrival and proposed to take me at once to the hospital of the Spanish Red Cross.

When we arrived I was immediately surrounded by doctors of all sorts. To my astonishment there were both monarchists and liberals amongst them, and I was given a preliminary course of political instruction. It is a fact that many doctors known as reactionaries, but known also to be devoted to their poor patients, remained in Barcelona and were left at liberty. The same was true also of certain employers who were known to have treated their workers fairly. One of the striking features of the attitude of the anarchist F.A.I., which was now the master of the situation in Catalonia, was a certain tolerance towards elements who were opposed to its policy but which in the past had shown definite signs of a social conscience.

I soon learned how different Catalonia, like the Basque country, was from Spain proper. A Basque was to say to me later:

'The Ebro, which cuts Spain in two from the west to the east parallel to the Pyrenees, is not merely a geographical dividing line.

To our way of thinking it marks the extreme southern limit of Europe. Everything to the south of it has an African strain.'

That may be a rather summary judgment, but it has an element of truth in it. Both Catalans and Basques are separatists. They both fear the Castilian military caste and the curly-headed Andalusian. As the Spanish Republic granted a certain degree of autonomy to these two provinces in a central federal administration the majority of the Catalans and Basques were against Franco from the beginning despite the fact that they are profoundly Catholic. However, these separatist elements played no very important role in the events of the day because the real holders of power were the unions, the C.N.T. and the F.A.I., etc.

'We are legal Spain,' they declared with pride. Yes, it was a legal Spain certainly, but a Spain completely broken up by local gangs and with doubtful elements prowling everywhere. In Barcelona the anarchists were guilty of brutal killings but they were also capable of acts of great generosity. On principle they detested any form of government.

Whilst the head doctor was showing me round the hospital he drew my attention to recent posters put up everywhere by the F.A.I. announcing: 'We are out to disorganize organization, and to organize disorganization!' The shrug of his shoulders when I looked at him questioningly was eloquent.

When I told him of the mission with which the International Committee of the Red Cross had entrusted me he advised me to get into touch with the Catalonian Government — in the hope that all administration there had not yet been disorganized. . . .

However, the atmosphere of order and normality which prevailed at the Generalidad was encouraging. Alert guards were at the door and within were no milling crowds. My name and my particulars were taken expeditiously and five minutes later I was led through a succession of magnificent rooms decorated with paintings of the Spanish masters illustrating the great moments of royal history. The chairs were gilt and the fireplaces were of marble. Finally I was led into a large room and my feet sank into a deep carpet. Before a great window stood an authentic caballero, well dressed and very much the man of the world. He came towards me smiling, dressed in a light grey suit. It was the Governor himself.

My astonished eyes stared at his clean collar and his neat tie. In accordance with the prudent advice given me by my consul I never wore a collar or tie, and I must confess that my half-open shirt caused me a little embarrassment. With a muttered excuse I produced my own collar and tie from my pocket and proceeded to put them on again. They were a trifle creased, but good enough. The Governor was highly amused.

'Yes,' he admitted, 'of course we are passing through an awkward stage at the moment, but never fear, things will get back to normal in time.'

I sensed the dealer in high politics, the man who makes revolutions within four walls. He listened politely to what I had to say, based on the scrappy information I had been able to gather during my short period in Barcelona. My one idea was to try to end the shooting of hostages on both sides. That seemed to me to be the most urgent problem, and the future was to show how right I was. It was the most horrible aspect of the drama which was to go on before our eyes for three long years.

I spoke of the Republicans who had been executed by Franco's men in Malaga and Seville, and I got him to admit that in Barcelona too men and women were being taken out of their houses merely on account of their names and an anonymous denunciation, to disappear without trace. Since the same thing was happening in both camps why not put a stop to the whole thing by effecting an exchange of the condemned men and women through the intermediary of the International Committee of the Red Cross? It would mean so many Spanish lives saved....

But the attitude of the Governor remained reserved and cautious. To save his people in Malaga meant practically to forgive his enemies in Barcelona. How was that blind and passionate justice of the people to be prevented? He did not say as much to me, but I could read it in his attitude. He advised me to go to Madrid and discuss the matter with the central government.

I took my leave with some disappointment, but I was determined to continue my efforts.

It was 500 miles to Madrid. There were no passenger planes and the railway service was at a standstill, but chance stood me in good stead again. One of the assistants of the Red Cross in Barcelona owned a motor car and he offered to drive me there. His name was Andres and he turned out to be a popular motoring ace who had taken part in many international events. He was to be my faithful companion throughout the time I spent in Republican Spain. Born of a French mother and a Spanish father he spoke French and at the same time he knew the countryside well. He had never belonged to any political party, but his irrepressible optimism was a political programme in itself. His favourite expression, which recurred invariably whenever the situation was at all emotionally charged, was: 'Todo farsa' — it's all nothing but a farce. But that rather airy scepticism covered a great deal of very real courage.

'When do we go?' he asked simply.

'At once.'

But we had to have some documents for the route. I showed him the letter of the Spanish Ambassador to France recommending me to the good offices of all anti-fascist militiamen.

'Splendid,' he said. 'Give me just enough time to get two safe-conducts signed and I'll be ready.'

One hour later we pulled up at the first control point on our way out of Barcelona. It was early afternoon, but the heat seemed to have no effect on the militiamen whatever as they carefully examined our papers. The letter of the Ambassador impressed them visibly.

'Siga, camarada,' said their leader to me clenching his raised fist.

Andres and I answered in kind: 'Puno alto.'

The road skirted the coast between the sea and the pine woods, and the drive was beautiful. The reddish rocks and the sudden bends reminded me of Estérel and of holidays spent in the Midi of France. Andres was an excellent driver and the revolution was temporarily forgotten.

But then we approached a village. From afar we could see the blue uniforms of the militiamen. They had felled a tree on the left and another one on the right so that all traffic had to thread a way between them. The control here was much more strict; at least it was to judge from the suspicious, almost menacing, looks of the controlling militiamen. Their leader, a short stocky man with a shock of hair flopping down over his forehead, rested the barrel of his rifle on the door of our car and took our *salvo conducto* for examination. After a moment or two I noticed that he was holding them upside down. I had some difficulty in keeping a straight face. When he turned the page and saw my photo he returned them at once. He grinned and observed to his companion.

'That's a good photo.'

Apparently he wasn't so terrible after all.

'Siga, camarada!'

We passed through scores of such control points. When the militiamen were so illiterate that the examination became prolonged we had our own little trick.

'Have you heard about the fascist car which has just passed?' we would ask innocently.

'A fascist car? No.'

'What! You haven't heard? They told us about it at the last control point.'

The militiaman in charge would then usually let us go on so that he could rush off to the telephone.

Towards evening we approached Valencia. A lorry full of men was drawn up sideways, and there seemed to be something in our path. There was a sudden braking. We had almost run into bodies. There were four or five of them sprawled across the roadway. Those in the lorry who had executed them were looking at them calmly, seemingly proud of their handiwork.

I got down and drew two or three bodies to the side of the road so that we could pass without running over them. Who were they? Where did they come from? I thought of their families waiting for their return and remaining without news of them for ever. We exchanged no word with the occupants of the lorry.

Valencia was lit up and the streets were full of life. Swarms of badly dressed and dirty people were everywhere. We had to go to the Town Hall to obtain further *salvo conducto* to permit us to go on to Madrid.

We took a meal at the Hôtel Inglès and then pressed on again along the hilly route which led to Castile. Night seems to favour confidences and Andres told me something of his life.

Since the beginning of the troubles he had been attached to the Red Cross. He had collected both dead and wounded in the streets of Barcelona. One day he had been seized by a band of anarchists who had mistaken him for someone else. Despite his protestations he was taken in their lorry for the famous *paseo*, the promenade of those condemned to die. Just before his execution he was recognized by an enthusiastic frequenter of motor races. Instead of being shot he was then acclaimed and put at the wheel for the drive back into town.

'Todo farsa' was his comment.

About every quarter of an hour now we came up with a lamp swinging in the middle of the road and were compelled to halt for another examination. The nearer we approached to the capital the more numerous the road blocks became.

At the break of day as we drove into Madrid I totted up the number of times that we had been stopped by patrols or road blocks since we had left Barcelona; the grand total was 148.

A great fair, noisy and populous, was going on in the Puerta del Sol. Militiamen on leave from the Somotiera front strolled around puffing at their pipes, their rifles slung over their shoulders to the great terror of the señoritas. Everyone was drinking to forget for a while. Tomorrow the men would have to go back to the line, and people already knew what that could mean.

At the headquarters of the Spanish Red Cross everyone was very interested to hear what people in Switzerland thought of the war in Spain. Their committee consisted chiefly of doctors and politicians. One of the latter offered me a suit of brown dungarees.

'They're reserved for officers,' he explained.

The blue overalls were for militiamen it appeared.

The next day a doctor took me near to the front line at the Escurial. On the doors of the palace of the Kings of Spain was affixed a piece of paper on which these words were typed:

CLOSED BY ORDER OF THE MUNICIPALITY.

The library had been turned into a hospital. I arrived just in time to witness a furious quarrel between the doctor in charge and a captain of militia. The captain had come with a squad of men to look for four wounded enemies in order to take them out into the near-by wood and shoot them without trial or process. For a doctor a wounded man is sacred. No one has a right to lay hands on him. I joined in and supported the doctor with all my might, but I realized how difficult it was in the first days of violent conflict to obtain respect for an idea which appears so natural to us.

After a while I was received by the Minister for Foreign Affairs, José Giral, a moderate who belonged to the Republican Left. When he heard my suggestion for an exchange of hostages he agreed immediately and promised to do his best to win over the other members of the government in its favour. He even gave me an official document declaring that women and children should be allowed to leave republican territory freely if they so desired.

I was overwhelmed by my unexpected success after the disappointment I had suffered in Barcelona and I had just one aim: to get over to the other side as quickly as possible to obtain the same success there.

Franco was not far away; only about sixty miles separated me from Salamanca. But in order to get there I should have to make the journey back again to Barcelona — passing through the 148 road blocks and controls — go from there to France, travel along the Pyrenees and enter Spain once again, this time through St. Jean-de-Luz. Just a little journey of about 1000 miles, chiefly through clenched fists, revolutionary songs and blue dungarees, in order to go sixty miles.

Irun was on fire. The sound of firing could be heard. Houses were burning everywhere. It was impossible to pass. A Carlist whom I met in Hendaye and to whom I communicated my mission agreed to take me in his car. We came to a little frontier post, Dancharinea. The Red Cross Society in Franco's Spain had been informed of my coming.

Instead of militiamen in blue dungarees saluting with the clenched fist there were 'Requetes' with red berets saluting by raising their arms with the palm open and the fingers extended, and shouting 'Arriba España.'

The representatives of Franco's Red Cross were authentic caballeros, tight mouthed and lantern jawed. My Carlist presented me to Count Vallelliano, a big fellow with a condescending air, who was flanked by two very stout ladies, one a countess and the other a marquise. Hands were kissed and courtesies exchanged.

'Spain is honoured to receive a delegate of the International Committee of the Red Cross,' I was informed. 'We will take you straight to Vittoria, where Monseigneur the Bishop is expecting you.'

I took my place in a magnificent car next to the countess, whilst Vallelliano sat in front with the driver.

'You have just come from Madrid!' exclaimed the countess in astonishment. 'How terrible! And what courage to have gone amongst the Reds! You were certainly very lucky to have escaped with your life.'

What could I say to that? For me they were all Spaniards.

On the way the count revealed himself as an historian of talent and he regaled me with descriptions of all the battles which had taken place in the neighbourhood, including those fought against the French.

The countess was an intelligent woman. She had lived for a long time in Paris and spoke French very well. When I mentioned the object of my visit, the exchange of hostages, she dampened my enthusiasm a little with an enigmatic smile as though to warn me to walk circumspectly. Spain was touchy. To exchange a caballero for a Red!

In Madrid I had been asked whether I was a Freemason, and when I said no my reply had astonished everyone. Here I was asked whether I was a Catholic, and when I replied that I was a Protestant my answer seemed to embarrass everyone a little. I almost found it necessary to correct a bad impression by pointing out that I was first and foremost the representative of the International Committee of the Red Cross.

In Vittoria an immense seminary had been turned into a hospital thanks to the generosity of Monseigneur the Bishop, the Primate of Spain. When we entered into the reception hall a hundred pairs of dark eyes were turned on me from a sea of white robes broken by a brilliant splash of scarlet, the robes of Monseigneur the Bishop himself. The hundred hospital nurses all in white intimidated me more than the pointed rifles of the Madrid militiamen. They seemed the prettiest girls in all Spain.

When I bowed to the bishop but made no attempt to kiss his ring the astonishment was obvious. However, Monseigneur the Bishop was himself a man of engaging simplicity, and he immediately put me at my ease. I suggested that we should visit the wounded.

What a difference there was compared with the hospitals in Madrid! Everything here was clean and well organized. But medicaments were short, Monseigneur informed me. The stock of them available in Navarre was almost exhausted. There were 200 patients in the hospital and there were new arrivals daily from the Irun front.

My journey continued. Pamplona, a charming, lively city, had not been damaged at all because the town had immediately declared itself for Franco; its entire population seemed Carlist to a man. Everywhere, in public places and from balconies flew the colourful red and gold flag of old Spain.

Whilst I was there came news of the fall of Irun and the rapid advance of the Requetes on San Sebastian. Enthusiasm was at its height, and the optimists could already see the war ending in six weeks. 'Spain, united, great and free!' But in fact Franco had not yet made his junction with the armies of the north and he needed time before being in a position to wage the horrible battle of Badajoz.

During lunch I was informed that I would be received that evening by the Nationalist Junta of Burgos. The car drove across the Guipuzcoa, the richest province of the Basque country, where the storeyed houses have flat roofs and Gothic windows.

'That's Red Miranda,' the count informed me. 'I'm afraid we had to put the whole town in prison and execute very many people.'

Then came the plains of Castile. From afar the cathedral spire announced that we were approaching Burgos. In Burgos all the flags of Franco's supporters were flying together: the red and gold of the Monarchists, the black and red of the Phalange — which reminded me of the flag of the F.A.I. — and the purple banner of the Requetes. Everywhere the walls were covered with inscriptions: 'Arriba España . . . Viva Franco!'

Old houses huddled up against the sides of the immense cathedral. 'The very stones are nationalist here,' the countess informed me with a smile.

At six o'clock that evening I found myself in the presence of the leaders of the insurrection, including General Cabanellas with his great white beard, and his second-in-command, General Mola, a tall man whose cold eyes were half hidden behind thick-lensed glasses.

As soon as I began to talk of my proposal, the exchange of hostages, lips tightened and looks grew harder. General Mola expressed the general feeling:

'How can you expect us to exchange a caballero for a red dog?'
There was no doubt about it, that was the official view here.

'If I let the prisoners go my own people would regard me as a traitor. Once the Reds believed that we were willing to exchange hostages they would massacre the last remaining prisoners. You have arrived too late, Monsieur, those dogs have already destroyed the most glorious spiritual values of our country.'

I did not allow myself to lose heart at General Mola's words, and I asked only for what the Republican Government in Madrid had already accepted: that women and children should be allowed to move freely from one camp into the other if they wished.

After a discussion which lasted two hours I at last obtained the precious paper signed by General Cabanellas in the name of the Nationalist Junta. They were also prepared to assure me that the proposition for the exchange of hostages either as individuals or by lists through the intermediary of the International Committee of the Red Cross would not be rejected *a priori*.

Before leaving Burgos I visited the Red Cross organization of the Nationalists and made a note of what they needed in respect of medicaments, surgical instruments, bandages and so on. Then I returned to St. Jean-de-Luz where I got through to Geneva to report the result of my efforts.

The success I had achieved seemed enormous: women and children were to be allowed to leave the territory of one camp to join their friends and relatives in the territory of the other. The agreement signed by both parties was in my pocket. Alas, the future was to show how much reliance could be placed on it!

The first delegation I received in St. Jean-de-Luz requested that I should organize the exchange of two men. The one was a well-known Carlist deputy named Don Esteban Bilbao. He was now in Bilbao, a prisoner of the Basques. The other was an old man named Ercoreca, the socialist mayor of Bilbao, who was a prisoner in the hands of the Carlist Requetes at Pamplona.

I sent a telegram to the Nationalists to secure their agreement to the exchange and somewhat to my surprise their consent arrived promptly.

The difficulty was that neither side was prepared to let its prisoner go first. After ten days of discussion I persuaded the Basques to consent to release Don Esteban Bilbao provided that I personally came to fetch him and that he gave me his word of honour to remain in France until I had succeeded in extricating Ercoreca from Navarre.

The French Ambassador M. Herbette proposed to accompany me on board the light cruiser *Alcyon*, and on September 24th, 1936, we arrived at the little Basque port of Bermeo.

We travelled the twenty-five miles which separated us from

Bilbao by car and had an interview with one of the Basque separatist leaders, who, on hearing what I had to say, arranged that I should be received the same evening by the Basque Nationalist Junta.

Within a few hours he succeeded in collecting the dozen members of the Provisional Government and our conference began at once.

We were in the middle of our discussion and the Basques appeared to be quite favourably disposed towards my proposals when a secretary entered the conference room with a copy of a message being broadcast by the Burgos wireless. It read:

'Attention! Attention! If Dr. Junod values his life he is requested to leave Bilbao tomorrow not later than one o'clock in the morning.'

The Basques looked at me in astonishment. What did that strange message mean? It seemed to threaten a bombardment of the town for the following day. The Basques were deeply disturbed and the session was interrupted at once. I tried to mend matters by assuring them that I had nothing whatever to do with the hostilities, but my explanations seemed vain.

However, the Basque President, José Antonio Aguirre, came up to me and assured me that his confidence in the Red Cross had not been shaken in the least by the incident, but that obviously the moment was not propitious to discuss the question of an exchange of hostages because if Bilbao were bombarded the reaction of the people towards the prisoners would be terrible. He advised me to return as quickly as possible to San Sebastian and try to persuade the Nationalists not to bombard the Basque capital. He also gave me permission to take Don Esteban Bilbao with me, as the exchange had already been agreed upon.

I at once took him at his word.

We waited until nightfall and then we took off Don Esteban Bilbao in a taxi, carefully hidden between the French Ambassador and me. The poor man was more dead than alive and I had to reassure him constantly, because he was convinced that his last hour had come. When I explained the position he immediately gave me his word to remain in France until I had succeeded in securing the release of Ercoreca.

At nine o'clock in the evening we arrived back at the little port of Bermeo where the French light cruiser was waiting for us. It was not until we were on board that Don Esteban finally realized that I had not been lying to him. He promptly abandoned himself to a fit of hysteria, because he had previously given up all hope.

As for me, my heart was overflowing with gratitude towards the Basques for trusting me and nobly being the first to show a little humanity.

At St. Jean-du-Luz I took Don Esteban to a hotel and instructed him to wait there for my return from Pamplona, and then I immediately set off to secure the release of his opposite number Ercoreca.

My reception by the Nationalists was very different. Although I had the document of the Nationalist Junta signed by General Mola, which I produced to the Governor of the prison in Pamplona, and although all my documents were in order, the man refused to hand over Ercoreca, declaring that a more recent order issued by General Mola forbade the release of any political prisoner under any pretext whatever.

I got into touch by telephone with the military Commandacia in Valladolid where I met with the same refusal.

I was unable to suppress my anxiety. If Ercoreca was not surrendered to me for exchange I should be unable to present myself to the Basques again with any further proposals.

I then telephoned to the Nationalist Junta in Burgos and requested the prison Governor to listen in to the reply.

The reply from Burgos was satisfactory, but the Governor remained obstinate and demanded to speak to General Mola in person. General Mola, it appeared, was not available and I had to wait as patiently as I could. By this time my anxiety had turned to indignation and anger, but all I obtained in return was insult. They refused to understand that the Basques had been generous enough to make the first move and that their own deputy, Don Esteban Bilbao, was already safe on French territory.

The whole day passed and it was not until six o'clock in the evening that a personal order signed by General Mola arrived instructing the Governor to hand over Ercoreca to me. Ercoreca proved to be a calm and tranquil old man. He knew nothing about what was going on around him. In the car I explained the situation to him and the conditions on which he was being released and he immediately thanked me again and again for my good offices. I asked him as a matter of interest whether he knew the man with whom he was being exchanged, and when he told me that he did I decided to bring them together in St. Jean-de-Luz.

We arrived at the hotel at about ten in the evening. Don Esteban was in the hotel lounge when we came in. As soon as the two men who had been condemned to death by the opposing camps came face to face they embraced each other like old friends.

'Hombre! Hombre!'

They both swore solemnly that each would do his utmost to persuade his own party to put an end to the killings.

'We shall be your best allies,' they both assured me.

I never heard of the Basque again, but Don Esteban Bilbao later became Franco's Minister of Justice, and quickly forgot the International Red Cross and his fervid promise.

The threat broadcast by the Burgos wireless had not been an empty one and on September 25th, 1936, Bilbao suffered its first bombardment.

The next day I went to San Sebastian. The successful exchange of Don Esteban Bilbao for Ercoreca was already known to everyone. Hundreds of people came to me and begged me to continue my efforts. There were, it appeared, 130 women and young girls, all of whom belonged to the Spanish aristocracy, now imprisoned in Bilbao, and the immediate task was to secure their release. They had been on holiday in San Sebastian at the outbreak of the civil war, and the Basques had seized them as hostages and taken them with them when they retreated. Amongst them were a number of marquises, countesses and wives of high Nationalist officials and officers.

I must say that I felt some bitterness at the eagerness of their relatives when I thought of the difficulties the Nationalists had made before I could get Ercoreca out of Pamplona prison.

'I am very willing to try again,' I said, 'but this time your people

must not make any difficulties. Franco must liberate an equal number of Basque women he is now holding in prison in Pamplona,
Vittoria and San Sebastian.'

'But of course, of course,' they assured me. 'We are quite in
agreement.'

'That's all very well and good,' I replied, 'but I must have an
official guarantee.'

Count Vallelliano intervened sharply.

'Our word is good enough,' he declared.

I accepted it. All I had to do now was to return to France and find
a boat to take me back to the Basques again.

At St. Jean-de-Luz I was fortunate enough to fall in with the
British consul in Bilbao, who had just arrived. He invited me to
pay a visit to a squadron of British destroyers anchored in the harbour. I accepted his invitation and we went on board H.M.S.
Exmouth where I made the acquaintance of the man who was to
be my most valuable ally throughout the whole Spanish civil war:
Commander Burrough.

Burrough was a very big man with broad shoulders and a ruddy
complexion, weather-beaten by wind and spray. Later on his
name was to figure in a famous communiqué: promoted admiral it
was he who opened the Rhine for the armies of Montgomery.

We liked each other at once. When I explained to him what I
was trying to do he laughed good humouredly.

'You're a bit like Mickey Mouse,' he said. 'You keep your eye
on the Spanish scales: one side white and the other side red. When
one side tips down you immediately hop on to the other to restore
the balance.'

'That's more or less it,' I replied. 'When ten people are condemned to death on one side I try to find ten on the other and
arrange an exchange. In that way I succeed in saving twenty lives.'

'Marvellous!' he exclaimed. 'Well, when are we going?'

'Tomorrow, for Bilbao.'

We arrived there safely the next day and first of all I obtained
permission from the Basques — a reward for my services in securing
the liberation of Ercoreca — to visit their political prisoners.

There were three small cargo-boats anchored in the harbour and used as floating prisons, and it was here that many of the hostages were held. There were hundreds of them and they were kept in the holds in frightful conditions and the only light and air which came to them was through the port-holes. Their misery was terrible to behold. It was as great as the hatred which separates the Basque from the Carlist, the socialist from the officer, the communist from the proud Castilian.

'We are doing our best to prevent a massacre,' the Chief of Police said to me, 'but after the last bombardment our people dug out 200 corpses of women and children from the ruins, and crowds surged to the prison ships, which are attached to the quay by gangways as you see, and no police in the world could have done anything in the face of their fury. We just had to hand over some of the more notorious amongst the hostages in order to prevent the slaughter of them all. I know that's terrible. I should have liked to prevent it, but as God is my witness I was unable to.'

And he added: 'If you want to take them all I will willingly hand them over to you, but you must bring me the same number of Basques. Although, alas, many have already been executed there are still plenty in the prisons of Navarre and Burgos.'

Unfortunately the agreement I had with the Nationalists was strictly limited and it applied only to 130 women and young girls.

We went to the Los Angelos Custodios convent where they were detained. My Red Cross armlet and the idea that perhaps an exchange could be arranged had excited the women and they surrounded me eagerly as soon as I entered. They went in terror of being sent like so many others to the dirty holds of the prison ships. They told me how after the bombardment a mob had demonstrated in front of the convent. Only the vigorous intervention of the police had saved their lives; they would all have been massacred.

'The Basques are brutes,' they screamed.

But I knew that at San Sebastian their friends had executed a woman for no greater crime than that her son was a communist.

And once again it was the Basques who made the first move.

The Provisional Government agreed to let these 130 women and girls leave on board H.M.S. *Exmouth* that very evening. In order to avoid transporting the precious hostages through the town under the eyes of the inhabitants we decided to take them after dark by car to the little port of Plencia about ten miles away. The *Exmouth* would be cruising around in the neighbourhood and would send us four of her boats to pick them up and take them on board.

The operation was carried out quietly at ten o'clock at night without the slightest difficulty. The police were efficient and everything went off without a hitch, though the women were half dead with fright.

At Plencia the cars avoided the port itself, and the women had to walk in the dark over the rocks for the few hundred yards which separated the road from a little creek where it had been arranged that the boats should pick them up. The British sailors came to their assistance, helping them along and sometimes carrying them like children to the boats.

By eleven o'clock everyone was on board. I took leave of my Basque friends. Above the noise of the oars I heard a cordial farewell:

'Salud camarada, buena suerte.'

And then in particular the confident shout:

'Now bring us back our women.'

The *Exmouth* received her passengers with open arms and the next morning they all disembarked at St. Jean-de-Luz. French cars then drove them immediately towards Irun, and they were met at the frontier by the Nationalist authorities. San Sebastian had hung out flags and bunting in their honour.

In the great hall of the Governor's Palace these women and girls found their parents and relatives awaiting them. The scenes of joy at the reunion can be imagined. A Nationalist colonel made them officially welcome.

'Greetings to you all in Nationalist Spain. Our heartiest congratulations on having escaped from the clutches of the foul Reds . . .' etc. etc.

'Arriba España! Viva Franco!'

They all joined in and thrust up their arms in salute. I alone remained silent and kept my hands to my side. I saw the colonel looking at me suspiciously.

'What is your business, señor? And, first of all, who are you?' The question disconcerted me a little.

'I am the delegate of the International Committee of the Red Cross,' I replied. 'It was I who brought back all these women.'

'Oh, very good. I didn't know. You're Swiss, aren't you?'

'Yes.'

'And what do you want?'

'I want you to hand over to me 130 Basque women, the exact number in exchange.'

'What, this is an exchange?'

'Yes, colonel. Didn't you know?'

'No, I didn't,' he replied stiffly. 'But you must know that we have already released many Basque women. None of them wanted to go back. And incidentally,' he added with an ironical smile, 'they're better off here than they would be in Bilbao.'

I wondered immediately whether that meant a new bombardment.

'The Basques were promised the same number of their women in exchange,' I repeated. 'They must be handed over to me.'

'Well, well,' he replied, 'we'll see about that with the Spanish Red Cross.'

Two days later I was invited to a grand dinner given by the Count of Castifole, whose house was one of the most splendid in Burgos. It was several hundred years old and its walls abutted directly on to the Cathedral. I was told that the subject of hostages and exchanges was to be discussed. Many Spanish aristocrats were present and I was congratulated on all hands and thanked for my services. But I was filled with misgiving. I could not forget that my mission was as yet only half performed. At the end of the meal I could contain myself no longer.

'Will you please tell me when I can reckon on receiving the Basque women in exchange?' I asked.

The faces around the table showed obvious embarrassment.

'But Monsieur,' replied Count Vallelliano, 'we have already released your Basque women and none of them has the least desire to leave Nationalist territory.'

'I'm sorry,' I declared, 'but I know that quite a number of them are still in prison.'

'Who are they?'

I had no difficulty in providing him with names. First of all there were several relatives of the Basque Minister Irujo.

'Oh no, they don't come into question for an exchange. They are close relatives of a Minister don't forget.'

'What!' I exclaimed. 'What about the women I brought back to you, don't they all belong to your aristocracy? Weren't many of them closely related to your high officials and your leading military commanders?'

In the embarrassment caused by that indignant reply I produced the list given me by the Basque Government.

'These are the women who must now be liberated in exchange,' I declared. 'All of them,' and I stressed the word 'all'.

'No, Monsieur, that is quite impossible.' The tone became icy. 'General Franco would never permit that.'

'Am I to understand that you have no word of honour?' I demanded.

'We have,' replied the count, 'but the Reds haven't.'

I looked at them calmly and spoke deliberately.

'I am beginning to believe that the real caballeros are at Bilbao and not at Burgos.'

It was a bombshell. They sprang up from the table and I rose too. I was probably a little pale, but I was certainly tired of their overweening vanity.

'I see that it would be better if I left now. We can discuss the matter again later.'

The negotiations went on for several weeks. I never obtained the 130 Basque women prisoners in exchange and I had to content myself with the relatives of the Basque Minister Irujo and one or two other women who had been condemned to death in San Sebastian.

But I did obtain a promise that I should be allowed to repatriate forty Basque children who had been on holiday not far from Burgos.

The mothers of Bilbao had never hoped to see their children again. The most fantastic rumours were in circulation, one of which was that they had been eaten by cannibal Moors. As soon as I had obtained the promise that they would be returned I sent a telegram to the Basque Government. The joy the news caused in Bilbao can be imagined.

They were to arrive at St. Jean-de-Luz on October 25th where the *Exmouth* was to take them on board and return them to Bilbao that same evening.

But on the morning of the 25th I waited in vain for the arrival of the children. At eleven o'clock a message arrived for me from the frontier that the arrangements had been countermanded and that the whole project was now called into question. Perhaps if I went to Burgos . . . But I had promised the Basques that I would bring their children back that very day. I decided to go to Bilbao at once to explain the situation.

The atmosphere on board the *Exmouth* was depressed. Burrough was furious and so was I.

It was a terrible situation. When the *Exmouth* entered the Bilbao roads at five o'clock in the afternoon we could already see the crowds swarming along the quayside waiting to welcome back the children. All the church bells were ringing and sirens were howling. They all believed that the returning children would be on board. I was beside myself with grief and anger.

When I went down the gangway the mothers surrounded me at once.

'Los ninos? Los ninos?'

The look on my face and the gesture of my arms was enough to tell them that their hopes were dashed. The disappointment was too great and a surge of anger went through the crowd. The women began to show resentment towards me. The Red Cross was blamed for the atrocious deception. Insults began to be hurled and there were even shouts of: 'Down with the Red Cross!'

Distracted women spat in my face and the Basque police had to intervene to protect me. One or two Englishmen who had disembarked with me tried to explain that the Nationalists were alone responsible for what had happened, but they could hardly make themselves heard. I made my way to the Town Hall amidst shouts of anger and abuse and clenched fists — and not in salute this time — and only there was I able to speak calmly to the distraught mothers. For an hour, with all the resources of my poor Spanish, I did my best to comfort them and to restore their hope, and in the end I swore a solemn oath to them:

'I will return in ten days, and I swear to you that I shall return with the children.'

Should I be able to fulfil my oath?

I had to fight every inch of the way at Burgos before I finally secured a favourable decision. Fortunately, some good friends of mine who were Carlists supported me with all their influence, and on the appointed day I led all the Basque children towards St. Jean-de-Luz.

Once they were on board the *Exmouth* seemed to skim over the waves with joy as she made her way along the Cantabrian coast.

At Bilbao the bells were again ringing out in welcome and in the indescribable joy which awaited our disembarkation the memory of the horrible experience of our first journey was effaced.

The children were reunited with their parents. I had managed to keep my word.

I mentioned above that I also succeeded in securing the release of a number of Basque women who had been condemned to death in San Sebastian. To do so I needed all the good will of the mayor of the town and what amounted to his complicity. He was a monarchist, and an honest and upright man. For so much generosity he soon got his reward: his dismissal. But by that time the condemned women were safely over the French frontier.

Amongst the group were three or four young girls. I remember one of them in particular; her name was Maria Olazabal. She had been seized by the Nationalists on board the steamer which makes the return run between Bayonne and Bilbao. She had been in charge of a group of children, most of them orphans, whom she was taking to a holiday camp in France. When she was arrested they found a membership card of the International Red Aid in her bag, and this was considered sufficient of a crime to justify a death sentence.

It was towards the end of October when I managed to get her out of prison. I drove her towards the French frontier in my own car.

During the whole journey to the frontier she did not speak once. In the half light of the evening I could see her pale face. She was obviously unable to believe that she was saved.

Once the frontier was passed she turned to me and said simply: 'Muchas gracias, señor.'

'Where do you want to go now, Maria?' I asked.

'To the children at Biarritz,' she replied. 'They'll be waiting for me.'

I set off for Biarritz.

She was a little nervous on the way. She crossed and uncrossed her legs and bent forward to look where we were going through the car window.

'Take the first road on the right,' she said suddenly. 'That's the way.'

I turned into the road she had indicated and we came to a big villa. A flight of steps led up to a balustrade. Then there was a great wrought-iron grille and beyond it a huge brilliantly lighted hall full of children playing and shouting. Suddenly one of them spotted her.

'Maria! Maria!'

And all the children rushed towards us and dozens of small hands were stretched out to us through the iron tracery.

CHAPTER II

THE EXCHANGE OF LIVES

'AMONGST those people who claim that the Basques . . . have occasionally shown a little humanity . . . is a renegade and miserable idiot. . . .'

There was no need for me to read any more. I was the 'renegade and miserable idiot'. The newspaper which brought me that delicate compliment was the organ of the Phalange in San Sebastian. It concluded a long communiqué on the exchange of hostages.

For a month I had been doing everything possible to make the Nationalists keep their word. The prisoners handed over in exchange for the aristocrats released by the Bilbao authorities had not by any means represented a fair exchange, and I was determined not to condone such an act of injustice. On my last visit to Salamanca I had insistently demanded to be told officially whether the few measures of grace parsimoniously accorded by the Nationalist authorities were to be regarded as the final settlement of account as against the 130 prisoners promised to the Basques. The contemptuous communiqué was apparently the reply of the Nationalist Government.

Since my credit with the Nationalists seemed to be completely exhausted I thought it better to leave the field to other delegates who might be better received. However, I was not in the least discouraged. After this partial defeat I realized better than ever the magnitude of the task which the International Committee of the Red Cross had to perform amidst all the horrors of civil war.

Incidentally, we were not alone in occupying ourselves with the fate of the hostages. Our intervention had produced generous co-operation and suggestions from many other quarters. The Legations, the Diplomatic Corps — the British in particular — had worked to set up 'exchange committees' in many places. Their chief weakness was that they acted only too often without cohesion. But vanities became involved too: each stressed its good relations with both camps and insisted on its ability to achieve the impossible.

Representatives from all groups came to see me at St. Jean-de-Luz: Basques, Carlists, Republicans and even, though without the official knowedge of their government, Nationalists. All of them begged me to continue elsewhere the efforts which the insolent vanity of a few 'caballeros' had rendered impossible in the north.

'If you can't work any longer with the Whites go and work with the Reds.'

But as far as I was concerned there were neither Whites nor Reds but only human beings, and I pointed out that if I went to 'work with the Reds' it would only be to save the lives of 'White' prisoners in their hands. However, what did it matter? There were suffering human beings in need of assistance everywhere, and that was all that concerned me.

In the spring of 1937 instructions arrived for me from Geneva to go to Valencia, to which town the Spanish Republican Government had then retired. Along the Catalonian roads I met with the same experiences of the early days of the troubles: innumerable controls, the militiamen in their blue dungarees, somewhat soiled after a hard winter, the streamers of the F.A.I., the songs and the clenched fists.

The gardens of Valencia were already bright with masses of roses and orange blossom, but the town itself was in indescribable confusion. Two hundred thousand people had fled there for refuge from besieged Madrid and from the ruins of Malaga, which had fallen into the hands of Franco a few days before.

Together with Dr. Roland Marti, another delegate of the International Committee of the Red Cross, we installed ourselves in the vast rooms of the Calle Ciscar. I immediately got into touch with José Giral, who had been appointed President of the Exchange Committee of the Republican Government, and his second-in-command, Manolo Irujo, the Minister for Justice. For months I begged them, prayed them, persuaded them to give me lists of names whilst in exchange I gave them other lists. The exchange routes went via Gibraltar or Marseilles, thanks to the faithful ships of the British Navy, whose very presence often did much to diminish our difficulties. But our difficulties were often almost as great as those previously experienced in the north. As soon as an exchange was agreed to by Valencia it was Salamanca who said 'no' or refused to reply at all. And sometimes it was the other way about.

Our delegation soon became very important. From morning to night people were coming and going. The *Cruz Roja Internacional* became known everywhere. Almost illimitable power was attributed to it and that was distinctly embarrassing because successful exchanges were unfortunately rare.

'His name is on the list. I'm quite sure. . . .'

Because a man's name was on the list his relatives were inclined to regard him as already saved. That was far from certain, and yet there was something in it. Many, many cases were 'reserved' in this way for day after day and month after month until the final deliverance.

We never ceased to harass the police or the War Ministry with our demands for the names of prisoners. It was a delicate task because orders for internment or imprisonment were always surrounded with mystery and secrecy. Generally speaking we knew the names of those who had been condemned; they served their sentences in the 'Carcel Modelo' or in the various internment camps, which we had authority to visit. But there was also a long list of *incommunicados*. Such people had been arrested as suspects on some vague denunciation. Some of them were really spies in process of examination and, clearly, the authorities refused to give us their names. Whoever intervened to make inquiries about them came under suspicion himself. The result was that their relatives came to us. Usually the inquirers were women: a father or a brother had disappeared one fine day, had perhaps failed to return from work. And sometimes the friend who had last been with him had disappeared too.

And then there was the other category; those whose relatives were prisoners of 'the other side' and held in Franco's jails. They came to us to fill up a questionnaire giving the name and address of the missing man and whatever details were known about his fate, usually very vague.

In this way friends and enemies rubbed shoulders in our offices, irreconcilable for ever. Those they came to inquire about had fought on opposing sides. They all knew it, both the one and the other, and each believed in his brand of truth. And each hated the other side who imprisoned and maltreated a loved one. And yet they were all Spaniards, all experiencing the same human suffering.

One example amongst a thousand others: Isabella.

She bore the name of a Spanish grandee, and she was a fierce monarchist and a very great lady. Her father had been killed before her eyes at the beginning of the troubles. On behalf of her brother Juan I had pestered the prison officials of the Spanish Republic every day for three months.

Every week Isabella came to see me and every time I had to listen to the same plea:

'If they would only tell me at least what has become of him . . . I would sooner know that he was dead than live in this uncertainty. . . .'

And at last the reply came: 'Executed with ten others. Names follow. Buried in a common grave. No . . . in the . . . cemetery.'

Isabella left my office tearless but pale as death, slim in her close fitting black dress. On her way out she passed Carlita who was coming in to me to ask for news of her fiancé who was missing 'on the other side', perhaps a prisoner in Salamanca.

Each knew the story of the other. They had seen each other, and they understood at once. With the same movement of contempt and hatred they avoided each other as they passed.

There was a strange light in Carlita's eyes as she came in to me, and I heard her murmur:

'At least she can visit his grave, but I shall never know, never. . . .'

That sort of tragedy was a daily affair. An insurmountable wall separated the two camps. No one crossed it. Only insults and bullets went from one side to the other. And above all there was silence, silence on one side and silence on the other. Someone was on the other side of the line and his nearest did not even know whether he was alive or dead.

For a long time I had realized that this uncertainty was the greatest agony of all. I had seen too many trembling hands stretched out for the sheet of paper that we had at last succeeded in getting from one side to the other: the Red Cross card.

There was not much on it: a name and address and a message which was not allowed to exceed twenty-five words. Often when it came back the censor had left only the signature on it, but at least it was proof that a loved one was still alive. And then the eyes which read the name and the signature would fill with tears of joy.

During the Spanish civil war the International Red Cross succeeded in exchanging no less than 5 million of these messages between the two Spains, Burgos and Barcelona, Madrid and Saragossa.

On 5 million occasions the Red Cross accomplished the same miracle: gave a little hope or dissipated an uncertainty.

Every Saturday I escaped from Valencia and took refuge in a little place on the coast.

The big villas of Las Arenas had been invaded by the Diplomatic Corps, and I preferred to go down to the creek where there were a few huts near to the boats rocking on the water.

On the beach was an old fisherman mending his nets. As I came near him he raised his wrinkled sun-tanned face and looked up at me.

'They tell me you're from the Red Cross,' he said.

I hardly needed to be told what he wanted.

'Who is it that's missing?' I asked.

'José,' he muttered. 'My son José.'

José was twenty years old. Six months before he had joined the militia, and then he had been reported missing on the Madrid front. I made a note of his number and the name of his regiment.

José and his father were, I learned, the best fishermen on the coast. All Las Arenas said it: the two men were more like good friends than father and son. Together they had fished along the whole coast, exploring all the banks and rocks. Every evening together they had drawn in their nets.

'They were happy men, señor, happy men.'

The old woman who had spoken mumbled under her black scarf:

'Without his José he won't live long.'

The message form was filled in and despatched to Burgos. I waited. Weeks passed.

Every week-end when I returned to Las Arenas the old man was there waiting for me. As soon as he saw me he would drop his nets and run up.

'Cuales son las noticias?'

And five times I had to answer.

'Nada.'

The visit to Las Arenas was becoming painful. I knew always that the old man would be there, his trembling lips muttering eagerly:

'Cuales son. . . .'

Then one day on going through the messages which had returned from Burgos I read: 'Las Arenas.' The old man's name and the Christian name 'José'. The lad was alive.

I got into my car at once and drove as quickly as I could to Las Arenas. This time the old fisherman was not expecting me and I had to find him. As soon as I saw him I began to shout:

'Oyé, oyé . . . Buenas noticias.'

And when I came up to him I put the message-form into his gnarled hands. He was unable to read, but he recognized the signature of his son. José was a prisoner, but still alive. Then he turned to me and said simply.

'No tengo nada, señor, solo mi barco. Toma le. (I have nothing but my boat, señor. Take it.)'

Everywhere throughout Spain, with the Whites and with the Reds, in Burgos and in Madrid, in Valencia and in Barcelona, the delegates of the International Committee of the Red Cross were doing the same kind of work. The web we weaved endlessly over a torn and divided nation was a network of misery and suffering, of despairing appeals and heart-breaking tragedies.

Not only the relatives of the missing and the mothers and wives of the executed came to us, but the prisoners themselves wrote. Terrible revelations and heart-rending plaints came to us from the dungeons in which so many men were cut off from the outside world.

What could we do? We had no authority and no right to intervene. It needed a lot of courage to say to those men who were holding on to the reins of government in the general chaos:

'This and that atrocity is being committed in your prisons. . . .'

However, one day I decided to go to see the Minister of Justice, Manolo Iruja. I knew him to be an honest man. He was a Basque and earlier on I had succeeded in getting some of his family out of the jails of Navarre. Perhaps he would not have forgotten.

'Your Excellency,' I began, 'will you please take note of the contents of this letter. It was written by a prisoner in the prison of Santa Ursula, who has since been transferred to the Carcel Modelo.'

At the mention of Santa Ursula the Minister raised his eyes suddenly, took the letter and began to read:

'. . . For two months we were subjected to all sorts of torture and ill treatment. In order to make us confess we were placed in a cupboard in which we could not stand upright. Whilst I was in it a shot was fired only a few inches away in order to frighten me. We were forced into confined spaces where we could only kneel. Irons were shackled to our feet and we were taken to the crypt of Santa Ursula and left there naked amidst human bones and excrement. We were badly beaten and some of us suffered broken ribs and torn muscles and began to vomit blood. We can prove that all this is true. When we came to this prison (Carcel Modelo) some of us had to spend three or four weeks in the sick-bay. One of us was driven mad in the Santa Ursula prison and is now in a lunatic asylum. We were left for three days without food. Nine days was the shortest time that any of us spent in the cupboard. The hair of a German was pulled out one by one. I swear that all this is the truth. . . .'

It was only one letter amongst many others.

'I'm afraid I suspected as much,' said the Minister. 'I do everything I can to prevent such things, but I am not in full control of the situation everywhere. The war we are going through now has no proper fronts. In every province, in every town, in every house, and even in every family, there is an enemy ready to betray us. If we were to relax our vigilance for one moment we should be lost. We must have an efficient police force to deal with that sort of thing and the methods it employs are not always known to us.'

'But Your Excellency, why imprison men in conditions which are so atrocious that they are equally degrading for the men who guard them. I realize perfectly well that I have no right to interfere in these matters, but if you had to listen as I have to the heart-rending stories which come to us you would be unable to prevent yourself from intervening as I am doing today.'

'I don't blame you. You have obliged me to take notice of something I felt in a confused way. But what do you want me to do?'

'Why not keep all your prisoners in the same conditions as those which exist in the Carcel Modelo? The Spanish Republic has built the most humane prisons in the world and called them "model prisons". Let it be the same everywhere.'

The Minister understood, but as I took leave of him his glance seemed to say: 'Don't interfere too much with all these things.'

However, it was our task as a matter of course to visit the unfortunate, those who had been abandoned by the world. It was no business of ours to pass judgment on the reason for their imprisonment, but merely to pay heed to their cries of distress and to make sure that those responsible heard them too. And in this fashion the latest form of our intervention developed.

We had brought about an exchange of hostages.

We had brought about an exchange of messages.

Perhaps we could now save the lives of those condemned to death?

One evening at about this time another Manolo came expressly to me with a preoccupied and anxious air.

This Manolo was a lawyer who undertook all sorts of cases.

He knew a great many people and he heard about a great number of things, but he also knew the value of discretion. He had never belonged to any political party. Without wasting any time he told me the reason for his visit at such an unusual hour.

'I have come straight here from the Carcel Modelo,' he said. 'The Governor, whom I know very well, gave me this letter. Look at it.'

'Muy señor mio, I am an Italian prisoner of war. I have just been told that I am to be shot at five o'clock tomorrow morning. I am giving this letter to the priest who is coming to hear my confession. My conscience is clear. Save my life if you can . . . Semprebene.'

'An Italian prisoner?' I asked. 'Where does he come from? Is he one of those they talk about so much on the Guadalajara?'

These Italians had been very roughly handled by the International Brigade, which had captured about 200 of them.

'No. This fellow is an Italian airman. He was unlucky. His first mission on arriving in Franco's camp was to drop supplies by parachute to the Civil Guards who are still holding out in the Santa Maria de la Cabeza sanctuary near Alicante. There are 700 men there with their wives and children completely cut off by the republican troops and subjected to a regular siege. Semprebene had to make a forced landing in republican territory and he was taken prisoner. He was hauled before a popular court and condemned to death as a fascist and an aggressor. He is only nineteen.'

I looked at my watch. It was eight o'clock. I had nine hours before the execution. I realized at once that if this Italian were executed it would lead to reprisals on the other side. Reprisals lead to further reprisals. That sort of thing was like a rolling snowball. A situation could develop in which each side would automatically execute all foreigners falling into its hands.

I did not hesitate. At nine o'clock I was asking for an urgent interview with the President of the Council, Largo Caballero. I had to wait half an hour and then I was admitted.

Caballero was standing behind his desk when I came in. He was a short thick-set man with greying hair, and one of the apostles of Spanish socialism. His glance had become hard in years of struggle, but behind it one could sense very real humanity. By his side stood his faithful assistant Llopis.

My reception was not warm. The International Committee of the Red Cross was not in very good odour with the Spanish Republican Government. We were reproached for securing the release of Franco's supporters from republican territory without obtaining a fair return from the other side. It was a just reproach as I had good reason for knowing. But at least I could remind him that I had been classed by the Whites as 'a renegade and a miserable idiot'.

'Buenas tardes,' said the President in greeting. He kept his thumbs in the armholes of his waistcoat and made no attempt to offer me his hand. 'What brings you here so late?'

'I beg your pardon, Your Excellency, for disturbing you at this time of the evening. But let me come at once to what has brought me here. I have just learned that an Italian prisoner of war, an air-man, is to be shot tomorrow morning at five o'clock, and I thought . . . .'

'And that's why you've come here?' interrupted Caballero. 'That's perfectly true. The man's a fascist and he has no right in Spain. He will get no more than he deserves.'

'But Your Excellency, the man is a prisoner of war, and the Spanish Republic was one of the first countries to ratify the Geneva Convention. . . .'

'What! That story again! You know as well as I do that the Geneva Convention doesn't apply to civil wars.'

'Yes, of course I know, but just suppose that it did and that both sides honoured it.'

Largo Caballero laughed sardonically.

'Honoured by the rebels? Those liars! Would you believe their word?'

Without knowing it the President was sprinkling salt in the wound. But how could I make it clear to him? I felt that I was losing ground. Eight hours was all I had. And now my case was weakened by the fact that the Basque women were still in Franco's jails! I was troubled and less sure of myself.

It was the President himself who came to my aid. Perhaps my discomfited silence had affected him more than words. He seemed to understand my distress and suddenly his face grew less tense.

'Well, what do you want exactly? Tell me.'

'You see, when I heard of the death sentence on this man I said to myself: for one who is killed here another will be killed on the other side. Then each side will return the compliment, and so it will go on. How could the hecatomb be prevented once it started? It seems to me that if you agreed not to execute this Semprebene you could put him on an exchange list.'

'On an exchange list? Who should we exchange him for?'

'There are foreign airmen and foreign soldiers on the republican side who are now prisoners in Franco's hands. This Semprebene could be offered in exchange for a Russian or a French airman, and both of them could be sent home straight away.'

Caballero turned to Llopis. It was not very reassuring; Llopis was known as an intransigent. He thought for a while, looked at me, and then turned again to Caballero.

'Give him a fortnight,' he said.

'Very well,' agreed Caballero, 'let's give it a trial. If the rebels haven't given us the name of a man they are prepared to exchange for this Italian within two weeks from now justice must take its course.'

Manolo was waiting for me outside and together we went at once to the Carcel Modelo and explained the position to the Governor who took us to see the Italian in his cell. When we entered Semprebene sprang to his feet.

'Que pasa?'

The sight of my Red Cross armlet lit up his despairing face with a flicker of hope.

'Good news,' I said. 'The President of the Republic has agreed to postpone the execution for two weeks with a view to effecting an exchange. Everything depends on Salamanca now.'

I looked behind me as we went down the prison corridor and I saw his anxious face close to the bars. He was weeping with joy and hope.

Semprebene — always well. With a name like that he ought to pull through.

But if within two weeks. . . .

From that moment the telephone lines between Valencia, Geneva and Salamanca were kept very busy.

We urged the Nationalists to make their decision quickly, but they kept us waiting for a week before they replied. However, when they did reply it was more favourable than I had dared to hope. Not only did they agree to the exchange but they proposed three further exchanges at the same time.

The list they forwarded to me bore three names. One was a Spaniard and the two others were Russians. I went at once to see the Soviet consul in Valencia.

Strigunov was a big, burly man with a mop of unruly hair. He was interested at once in what I had to say.

'And whilst we're about it,' he said, 'what's happened to the crew of the *Komsomol?*'

The *Komsomol* was a Russian cargo-boat which had been sunk by the Nationalists in the early days of the insurrection. In announcing the torpedoing the Burgos wireless had reported that twenty-one members of the crew had been picked up.

'Could your delegates find out whether Franco would be prepared to consider an exchange?'

'We can certainly make such a proposal to Salamanca. Will you support me in my efforts to win over Caballero? We simply must put a stop to these executions, because if a single man is executed by one side or the other it will cause the breakdown of negotiations.'

Strigunov would support me I knew because Soviet interests were involved. Largo Caballero would listen to him because Soviet influence with the Spanish Republican Government was powerful. Franco would probably be persuaded because he could hardly want deliberately to sacrifice the lives of his German and Italian allies. And in adjusting these reciprocal interests the Red Cross would attain its own end: set up a barrier against further violence, save lives and at least postpone senseless slaughter.

Gain time . . . Gain time . . . That was our one aim. Whilst we were busy discussing the lists the men who were rotting in jail, expecting every morning to be taken out and shot, would be given at least a respite for a few days, a few weeks . . . And perhaps in the end we should be able to achieve something definite.

The Nationalists had put forward three names in connection with the exchange of Semprebene. From the other side twenty-one were proposed. In the meantime Salamanca had made further suggestions. No sooner had we examined them than we found ourselves no longer in agreement with Salamanca. But Geneva tried again and again. 'Be patient,' urged our delegates to Franco. 'Be patient,' I urged José Giral, Irujo and President Caballero.

The only means I had of communicating with Salamanca was via Geneva, which transmitted my message and received the reply and forwarded it to me. One can imagine how many mistakes, corrections and misunderstandings such a complicated means of communication involved. When the situation began to look hopelessly involved the delegates in both camps were recalled and flew to Geneva for joint discussions. Conferences, reports, debates and then home again helter-skelter by plane to our 'capitals' wondering on the way whether anything irreparable had happened in our absence. No.

Days passed. Weeks passed. Months passed. And the lists lengthened. First the single name of Semprebene. Then three more. Then twenty-one, and so on: one hundred, three hundred, a thousand, fifteen hundred . . . Until one glorious day there were two thousand names on the lists.

We felt we were holding these two thousand lives by a single thread, all that stood between the sentence which condemned them and the open grave which awaited them.

To think that only a very small miracle was necessary to save them all; put the ones where the others were, and they would be free.

In the hall of the Hôtel Inglès in Valencia I had often seen a very beautiful woman go in and out. Her bearing was proud and a little disdainful. She was a typical representative of the old aristocracy of Seville.

'Muy guapa,' a waiter whispered to me, 'a highly placed hostage.'

I learned that she was the wife of a Spanish nationalist airman. Although she was being held as a hostage she had been spared imprisonment, and she lived in the hotel under close police surveillance. Her charm and her beauty certainly had something to do with the preferential treatment she was receiving.

At the Ministry José Giral spoke to me about her. He had just received through the British Embassy a list of twenty-one names of Spanish Republicans imprisoned in Seville. General Queipo de Llano had generously offered to exchange them all against this one woman. Giral smiled knowingly.

'Queipo would like to tempt us, but I'm not playing. Make a counter-proposal for us. I'm interested in one man. He's not a Spaniard, but he's a friend of the Republic. His name is Koestler.'

'Koestler? I don't know him.'

'He's a Hungarian, a journalist who has been sentenced to death by Franco for sending reports to a British newspaper. I shall be obliged if you will send an urgent telegram off to Geneva in the matter because his life is in danger.'

'I will do so as soon as I get back.'

'And how are the other exchanges going?'

'You know that Salamanca is interested in airmen. Our delegates there are hopeful, but I must ask you to be patient. It seems that long lists of offers and demands are being prepared.'

'And what about the Italian in the Carcel Modelo?'

Giral knew all about the man through me. I often spoke to him about my visits to the prison, and sometimes the Minister learnt surprising things from the mouth of a foreigner. He was flabbergasted when I told him that I had sometimes been in a position to correct the official lists of prisoners held in this or that prison.

'He's not in very good shape, I'm afraid,' I replied. 'You must remember that he's been waiting two months now in the hope of being exchanged but never knowing whether he will be taken out of his cell one day and shot full of holes. I visit him once a week to keep his courage up.'

Wait . . . Be patient . . . I used those words a hundred times a day at least: in prison to comfort a prisoner, in a government office to soothe a member of the government. So much persistence becomes persuasive in the end. One thing we had already achieved: these despairing men, these men who had been condemned and were now awaiting death, could not be forgotten by the authorities who had sentenced them. Our lists made their suffering and their anxieties known everywhere. Like an urgent appeal their names were there on the desk of the President, on the desks of his Ministers. And against their names were those of their opposite numbers, the men whose deaths would pay for theirs, man for man, head for head, life for life.

Koestler against the beautiful woman from Seville?

Yes, Salamanca was agreeable.

Negotiations proceeded for the carrying out of the exchange. Koestler was at La Linea near the Gibraltar frontier, but the Nationalists would not allow him to cross until the woman from Seville was safely on board a British warship. My friend Leech, the British Minister at Valencia, had the honour of accompanying the aristocratic beauty of Seville on board H.M.S. *Hunter*. Gibraltar was informed by wireless and the obscure Hungarian journalist Franco had intended to shoot was released.

Their fates crossed: Arthur Koestler went on to success. A series of books made his name well known in the world. Eight days later the beautiful aristocrat of Seville went into mourning. Her husband had been shot out of the sky in flames on the Madrid front.

The game went on: list for list, individually and in small groups, lives were steadily exchanged for lives.

Six months had passed since my urgent interview with Caballero. Semprebene was still alive. At last his name was on a list agreed to by both sides. With him a number of other Germans and Italians were exchanged.

One fine summer's morning Dr. Marti, the head of the delegation of the International Committee of the Red Cross in Valencia accompanied them in a police car to the quay where a boat from a British warship was waiting to take them off. A crowd of curious spectators collected.

'Quick,' whispered the escort to the departing prisoners. 'And be quiet.'

Quickly they got into the boat. The engine started up and it put out to sea. Marti remained behind alone on the quay watching them go. In the meantime the crowd had grown.

Then suddenly and well within earshot the Italians in the safety of the boat struck up the 'Giovinezza' at the tops of their voices.

'Ah los cochinos!'

The crowd turned on Marti, indignant and menacing. They did not know that on the other side the crew of the *Komsomol* were at that moment crossing the French frontier to freedom.

CHAPTER III

THE DOORS OPEN

THE war continued pitilessly.

1937... 1938....

The Republicans fell back under Nationalist pressure. Spain was left to her fate. The planes above our heads became more and more numerous. Teruel, which had at first seemed a victory, turned into a rout for the Republican Army, and Franco's troops reached the Mediterranean. The Spanish Republican Government left Valencia for Barcelona.

The inequality of forces now made our mission still more difficult. Salamanca became intransigent. However, we continued to do our best. Towards the end of 1938 I was working with the Red Cross Delegation in Barcelona, Calle Lauria, 95. Life was difficult. Hundreds of women and children besieged us for their share of the meagre resources we were able to distribute; chiefly a little condensed milk and chocolate.

Prison ships with hostages on board appeared in the harbour of Barcelona as they had once appeared in the harbour of Bilbao. For a long time we were refused permission to visit them. However, sometimes our requests were granted and we were allowed to bring some aid to the prisoners.

Air warfare was now added to the horrors of famine, the arrests and the despair of a whole people. The capital of Catalonia became a special target for the bombing planes and their bombs fell at hazard on the houses and in the streets.

I remember in particular one morning in September. I saw the planes coming. As usual they emerged from behind the hill of Montjuich and made their way towards the town. I jumped down the stairs two at a time. Below the Spanish Red Cross officials were getting the ambulance ready. It was not long before the call came. Bombs had fallen on a school in the old quarter near the Generalidad.

I jumped into a car with ambulance attendants. When we arrived we found that the roof of the school and the upper storeys had collapsed burying over a hundred children in the ruins. We set to work desperately to open up the debris. At the same time we had to be careful because still living children might be under the rubble.

We managed to extricate only ten complete bodies. All the others had been blown to pieces. It was atrocious. I saw one of the attendants recover a small blond head. Others picked up what might have been the feet of little angels. Not a single child who had been in the school was still alive.

In my mind I kept repeating, 'This blind warfare is horrible!'

For two weeks after that I did not visit the Nationalist airmen in prison. I just could not bring myself to do so.

But then I tried to be reasonable. How were the bombs different from the shells which had fallen on Madrid? Both were part of the war. It was total warfare I hated, but for the men who waged it and the people who suffered it we had still to go on with our task.

January 1939. The front rapidly came nearer and nearer to Barcelona. The prisons were chock full with prisoners the Republican troops had brought back with them as they retreated.

In the city air-raid warnings followed each other in constant succession. All the military and civilian services were paralysed. In the villages along the coast ten, twenty, fifty cars were waiting for supplies of petrol. When the sirens began, mechanics, control officers, drivers and passengers all fled to the countryside. The chaos was indescribable.

Returning to Barcelona one night Marti and I were caught on the Caldetas road by an air-raid warning. All the headlights of our convoy were suddenly extinguished. Above the noise of aero-engines we heard the sound of explosions not far away. Sudden flashes of light in the sky indicated the bursting of anti-aircraft shells. For all we knew the planes were gliding overhead with their engines shut off waiting for our lights to go on again. Or they might return. We waited for about a quarter of an hour in silence, our nerves tensed. Then we went on again hunched up in our seats.

The streets of the town were filthy. The scavengers no longer removed the waste and a disgusting smell arose everywhere. A shortage of water began to make itself felt. Most people stayed in their houses. Here and there mobs had begun to pillage the food stores. From my window I could see men and women scurrying along with sacks filled with plundered foodstuffs. Isolated shots sounded from time to time. *Paco* was the Catalan word used to describe them in imitation of the short sharp sound.

Requests for food came to us from the prisons. All we could send was a little flour and condensed milk. Our food stocks were almost exhausted.

The relatives of the imprisoned men were becoming more and more anxious about their fate. Some of them came to me to beg me to do everything possible to prevent a massacre or new transfers.

On January 19th I visited the British Embassy to try and find out from the British Minister whether he knew anything about the intentions of the Republican Government towards the 5000 prisoners held in the town.

At the French Embassy I was referred to the assistant military attaché, a lieutenant. He was a little man and he received me with an air of importance.

'What are you so disturbed about?' he asked.

'But Monsieur Lieutenant, the Nationalist forces are less than twenty miles away now. They can be here tomorrow, and the government. . .'

'That's not my opinion,' he declared decidedly. 'Barcelona will not fall.'

I was flabbergasted.

'On what do you base that opinion, Monsieur Lieutenant?'

'How shall I explain that? It's just an impression; like heat and cold.'

I did not pursue the subject.

However, the French Ambassador himself, M. Jules Henry, shared my misgivings and he got into touch with Negrin. A reply came on January 23rd to the effect that there was to be a general transfer of prisoners. But the chaos was so great that the order was only partly carried out.

In the morning of January 26th the Governor of the women's prison of Las Cortes rang us up. She was at her wits' end. The relatives of the prisoners had been outside the prison in large numbers for three days trying to stop any transfers. Five soldiers who had been ordered to remove a number of prisoners had had to abandon their task in face of the threatening attitude of the mob. She was unable to get into touch by telephone with the Central Prison Administration. There was no reply.

Marti and I did not hesitate. It was clear that we must go there.

We drove in our car towards the suburbs to the nearest point of the front line. On the Diagonal, the great highway of Barcelona, we passed several lorries full of soldiers. On entering the Los Hermanos Badios Square we were stopped by a Republican control point. A line of cars was drawn up along the pavement guarded by militiamen armed with tommy-guns. All the cars had been requisitioned to provide transport for the Republican rearguard.

'Bajen. Get out,' ordered a militiaman with a revolver in his hand.

I made a sign to the driver to stay at the wheel and I got out to negotiate.

'You can see that this is a Red Cross car,' I said. 'You have no right to requisition it.'

The man hesitated.

'Where are you going to?' he demanded.

Again he hesitated and then he consulted his chief.

'Siga!' said the latter.

I jumped back into the car and we set off quickly.

At the prison of Las Cortes we drove directly into the courtyard. All around the faces of women were pressed against the bars of the cell windows.

'Long live the Red Cross!' they shouted excitedly. 'Long live the Red Cross! Save us!'

I went to the office of the Governor. She was a fair-haired young woman heavily made up. All the keys of the cells were together in a pile on her desk. Her wardresses were also present, looking awkward and dirty. The anxiety on their rather dull faces was hardly less than that which was finding expression in the shouts of the prisoners. They were no doubt asking themselves with good reason whether the roles were now about to be reversed. The release of the prisoners meant imprisonment for them and they now begged me to afford them the protection of the Red Cross.

'I have always carried out my duties objectively,' said the Governor with her painted lips, 'and I have done nothing but my duty.'

And then she added:

'If you think I ought to open the cell doors and release the prisoners I am ready to do so.'

At that moment artillery opened up behind the prison. It was a Republican battery sending over its last shells. It was soon spotted by the Nationalist artillery which returned the fire fiercely.

There was no time to be lost. I had seen a lorry standing in the prison yard and when the prisoners were released I put the old and the sick women into it. But then they wanted to take their miserable things with them. One of them clung on desperately to an old chair. They could not bring themselves to leave the wretched debris of their possessions behind in the cells where they had lived for months, sometimes for years. In the end I had to raise my voice imperatively.

The other prisoners, who were able to walk, went off on their own surrounded by their delighted relatives.

Then we left. The prison stood empty behind us. I felt sorry for the Governor and I took her along with us.

In the meantime another drama was being played out.

Dominating the harbour and the sea stands the ancient castle of Montjuich which was used as a prison. There were about 600 military and political prisoners held there, and all that was left of the guard was an officer and seven men.

Nationalist warships which had anchored broadside on about three miles from the shore had opened fire on the fort in the belief that it was occupied by Republican troops.

From the Calle Lauria the members of our delegation had witnessed the bombardment, and one of our Belgian nurses, Madame

Perdomo, had decided to drive out to Montjuich with our chauffeur and find out what had happened.

When she arrived the bombardment was still going on. The excited officer in command immediately took her to the sick-bay. A shell had entered through the window of one of the cells and exploded inside blowing off one prisoner's head and wounding a number of others. Panic reigned amongst both guards and prisoners.

The shells came over pitilessly one after the other at regular intervals. In agreement with the officer of the guard Madame Perdomo caused a white flag to be hoisted over the castle and the bombardment ceased at once.

The officer handed over the keys of the cells to our nurse and then, fearing to be seized by the prisoners, he fled with his seven men. But the hoisting of the white flag had also been observed in Barcelona, where it was supposed that the guard had mutinied. A detachment of sixty men was sent off at once to suppress the mutiny. On the way the detachment fell in with the officer of the guard and his men, and he was taken back to the castle with a revolver in the small of his back.

Arriving at the castle the men broke down the gate with the butts of their rifles and then cautiously entered, fearing a trap. But all that awaited them in the courtyard was a Red Cross nurse.

Everything seemed quiet inside the fort. The prisoners were still in their cells, but anguished faces appeared at the bars.

'What are you doing here?' demanded the officer in charge of the detachment. 'And what's the meaning of the white flag?'

'Señor Captain,' replied Madame Perdomo, 'I came up here during the bombardment to prevent the massacre of defenceless men in their cells. There were no more Republican troops on the hill and I had the white flag hoisted to stop the bombardment.'

The captain was flabbergasted, but the calm assurance of the woman impressed him.

'We thought there had been a mutiny,' he declared. 'I have been sent up here to shoot everybody. However, there's been enough bloodshed. But my orders are to hoist the Republican flag again. Barcelona has not yet surrendered.'

The white flag was hauled down and the Republican flag hoisted in its place, then the soldiers went off. The fighting was coming closer.

Half an hour later the bombardment opened up again even more heavily than before. There was now no hope of making the Nationalists believe in a surrender so our nurse hurriedly tore off two strips of red cloth and sewed them on to the white flag. A prisoner then climbed up to the ramparts and hoisted it above the Republican flag.

At once the bombardment ceased.

Six hundred men raised their eyes full of hope to where the red cross on the white ground fluttered from the mast.

On January 26th at half past one the first tank rolled down the street and came to a halt before our quarters. The crew consisted of German soldiers. Perched on top of the tank was a smiling woman giving the fascist salute to the crowd. I recognized her as one of the released prisoners from Las Cortes. It was a German Jewess who had been arrested and imprisoned as a Trotskyist.

During the afternoon the balconies of Barcelona began to cover themselves with red and gold monarchist flags, and a great nationalist standard was hoisted on the Tibidabo hill. An endless column of Requetes in red berets, Phalangists and Moors with their patient mules moved slowly down towards the town.

By evening Barcelona was completely occupied.

However, fighting was still going on to the north-west where the Republican Army was being rolled back towards the Pyrenees and the French frontier. The Republican forces had taken thousands of hostages and prisoners with them. What might happen to them at the last moment?

To get over to them there was no longer any question of crossing lines. There was only one way to continue my task: to go round the Pyrenees and enter French territory at Hendaye, cross France and re-enter Spanish Republican territory through Port Vendres.

I went to see Colonel Ugria, the chief of the Nationalist Police, to obtain the necessary papers. Would he recall the 'renegade and miserable idiot' who had been denounced so violently in Salamanca's communiqué?

I found him in the same office where I had always gone to obtain permission to visit the prisons of the Republic, to comfort, save and exchange Nationalist prisoners.

He handed me my *salve conducte* stamped with the five arrows of the Phalange and smiled.

'Amongst the papers left behind by my predecessor I found this one which might interest you.'

On a sheet of paper with the heading of the Republican Police, and which had followed me around everywhere for three years, from Madrid to Valencia and from Valencia to Barcelona, was my name:

'JUNOD, Marcel, delegate of the International Red Cross.'

And below there was one word, underlined twice in red ink: '*Ojo.*'

Or 'Keep an eye on'.

THE SECOND WORLD WAR

CHAPTER I

SEPTEMBER 1939

'LIEUTENANT JUNOD.'

'Here, Colonel.'

'Look, here is my list of patients. I had to take all their names in a hurry before you arrived. The list is a scribble and full of blots. Copy it all out afresh and then this evening go and visit them.

'And just a moment; I had forgotten. You are my medical officer attached to the staff of the First Army Corps. Thus you will attend to officers of field rank. If any of these gentlemen prefers to see you in his own room instead of coming to you, or if you are asked for outside the normal hours, do your best to oblige. But you're used to that sort of thing, aren't you? Didn't you work for the Red Cross?'

'Yes, sir.'

'Here you'll just do your work like anyone else.'

What the devil was this colonel thinking of? As though I were incapable of removing a few ink blots and attending with tact and compassion to the higher officers of the Swiss First Army Corps, who had just been mobilized!

That list was never finished.

At the beginning of September 1939 a letter from the International Committee of the Red Cross recalled me urgently to Geneva. Released from my military duties I was seconded to the Committee.

The Committee was once again meeting in the little Villa Moynier and trying to estimate the crushing task which was to devolve upon it during the course of this second World War, or what might perhaps be called the first totalitarian war.

The invasion of Poland by both Germany and Russia, the entry of Great Britain and France into the war with the moral support of the United States, and the fighting which had been going on for six years between Japan and China and which was soon to spread over the whole Pacific area — all these things suggested that before long the nations of the whole world would be engaged in this gigantic conflict. And we knew that in the past twenty years the means of destruction had made terrifying progress, and that during the desperate struggle itself they would make still further and still more terrible advances. We knew too that the war which had just begun, and whose end no man could foresee, would not spare the non-combatants; that, on the contrary, it would cause them terrible sufferings, inspired and exacerbated by the flood tide of passion whipped up by every ideological war: police inquisitions, internment camps, forced labour, confiscations and collective persecutions.

And what weapons, what means were at the disposal of the strictly humanitarian cause we had been called upon to serve against this sudden explosion of violence which was rapidly spreading over the whole world?

Nothing but the two Conventions which we had already seen in action in Abyssinia and Spain; the one concerned the protection of the wounded and the other the protection of prisoners of war.

Surely it would be a vain hope to rely on the efficacy of arrangements which pre-dated the first World War and sometimes even the Franco-Prussian War of 1870.

It was with sadness and bitterness that I re-read in the little *Memorandum of International Conventions* re-issued by the Swiss Federal Government in 1939, the famous Petersburg Declaration signed on December 11th, 1868, by all the civilized nations of the world:

Considering that the progress of civilization should have the effect of alleviating as much as possible the calamities of war;

'That the only legitimate object which States ought to propose to themselves in war is a weakening of the military forces of the enemy;

'That for this purpose it is sufficient to disable the greatest possible number of men;

'That this object would be exceeded by the employment of

weapons which should uselessly aggravate the sufferings of men who have been put *hors de combat*, or shall render their death inevitable.'

And further on:

'The contracting parties reserve the right to come to a subsequent understanding whenever a definite proposition shall be formulated with regard to improvements which science may bring about in the future in weapons of war, in order to uphold the principles which they have accepted and to conciliate the exigencies of war with the laws of humanity.'

The three Hague Declarations of 1890 and 1907 each open with the words:

'Inspired by the sentiments expressed in the Declaration of St. Petersburg. . . .'

One forbids warring powers 'to launch projectiles and explosives from balloons or in any other similar fashion'. The two others condemn the use of asphyxiating gases or dumdum bullets. It would be too naive to suppose that such prohibitions would be respected by the carriers of flame-throwers or by the crews of modern bombers.

In the same way we should have to consign that admirable 'Regulation concerning Land Warfare' of 1907 to its proper place amongst the historical documents of the past — and amongst our fugitive illusions — although theoretically it was still in force:

'Article 25: The attack or bombardment by whatever means, of towns, villages, dwellings or buildings which are undefended is prohibited. . . .'

'Article 46: In occupied territory, family honour and rights, the lives of persons, and private property, as well as religious convictions and the freedom of religious worship must be respected. . . .'

How much remained of all those noble intentions whose principle was solemnly enunciated in the words: 'the laws of war do not concede to belligerents an unlimited power with reference to the choice of means of injuring the enemy'. How proud civilized mankind had been to formulate such conceptions so far in advance of the old laws of war which had held sway even towards the end of the nine-teenth century!

Since the end of the first World War the representatives of all countries had gathered together on no less than ten occasions in order to adapt these humanitarian restrictions on the waging of war to the growing progress of modern technique, but they had never succeeded in coming to any agreement.

A project for the limitation of air warfare put forward in 1923 at The Hague never got beyond the project stage. The Disarma-ment Conference called together by the League of Nations was unable to come to any agreement.

At Geneva in 1929 the International Committee of the Red Cross proposed two Conventions. The one was a modification of the Convention of 1906 for the amelioration of the lot of the sick and wounded men of armies in the field. Laid before fifty-two States it was ratified in the following years by almost all the governments of the world.

The second proposal was born of the first World War. It referred to the treatment to be accorded to prisoners of war and it was laid before the governments of forty-eight countries. By 1939 it had been ratified by thirty-six governments, but two governments in particular had still not ratified it, the governments of the U.S.S.R. and of Japan.

What was to become of the inhabitants of towns destroyed from the air by concentrated bombing such as we had already seen in Poland? And what, above all, was to happen to the populations of occupied countries, handed over without any protection, without the guarantee of any Convention, to the mercies of the conqueror?

The problem was not a new one. The International Committee of the Red Cross had already tried — perhaps too tentatively — to make the peoples of the world understand the perils to which they might all be abandoned without protection in any new war. In 1934 all the nations of the world had come together in Tokio at an International Conference of Red Cross Societies and had listened to the great project of the Red Cross for the protection of civilians who might be bombed, interned *or deported*. But in the five years which had passed since then not a single government had come forward to ratify the proposal.

What happened during the Spanish civil war ought to have been lesson enough. The blind destruction, the summary executions, the wholesale shootings, the persecution of whole classes, the persecution of religion, the mass arrests of political prisoners, were all a warning of what horrors were to come. I remembered the bodies of the little children in Barcelona. I remembered Bilbao with its destroyed houses and the howling mobs who had tried to sink the prison boats in the harbour and drown the hostages.

And I remembered the miserable mud huts in Abyssinia blown to smithereens by bombs; Dessie reduced to ashes; the wandering skeletons on the Sidamo tracks; the plains of Kworam swamped with mustard gas; and the thousands of victims raising their contaminated and burned arms towards the Emperor: 'Abiet! Abiet!'

All that would now be outdone ten times, a hundred times. We knew all that, and we might have been excused if we had felt overwhelmed by the magnitude of our task.

But not a word of pessimism passed the lips of our President Max Huber when all the delegates of the International Committee of the Red Cross were assembled before him and he explained our task and showed us what we could do and what we should try to do in each of the belligerent countries to which we were being sent.

Our weapons? Two Conventions.

The staff at our disposal? In the little Villa Moynier that day there was only a handful of devoted men, three secretaries and five typists. And at the bank there was a credit of 120,000 Swiss francs.

But more than ever the spirit of the thing was there, and I already knew what it could do and what it could achieve for men who no longer had any rights and who still belonged to the world of their fellow men only by their sufferings and their destitution.

CHAPTER II

'THEY REFUSE TO UNDERSTAND'

ALL was quiet on the Western Front. France and Great Britain felt safe behind the concrete ramparts of the Maginot Line. A few unfortunate sheep were blown up by mines in the Forest of Warndt.

But in the east Poland was overwhelmed with a deluge of fire; held in a rapidly tightening vice; crushed between the Red Army and the gigantic assault of the German tanks, she shed her blood in streams. A long period of martyrdom had opened up for the Polish people.

I had chosen Berlin as my post and for a long time I was the only Red Cross delegate not only in Germany but in all the countries which fell subject to her by right of conquest.

On Saturday morning, September 16th, 1939, I was already installed in the Hotel Adlon, whose roof flew a line of Nazi flags to celebrate a series of victories: Posen, Ostrov, Katovitz, Tarnov, Cracow . . . And the list was extended with each special edition of the triumphant German newspapers.

My first days in Berlin were spent in visiting government offices. Relations with Geneva had to be established. I had to make contact with the German Ministry for Foreign Affairs, the famous Auswärtiges Amt, with the German Red Cross and with the Wehrmacht. I had to find out to what extent we should be able to give assistance, to inspect the camps, to gather information on the situation of the internees without offending the highly susceptible Gestapo.

Throughout the territory of Hitler's Reich there were many hundreds of foreigners who had been arrested and interned at the beginning of the war merely on account of their nationality: the nationals of hostile countries and of countries under their protection.

The first thing was to discover what sort of treatment the German authorities proposed to accord them. After a number of discussions the Germans agreed to accord them the benefits of the Geneva

Convention despite the fact that they were not prisoners of war in the ordinary sense — provided there was reciprocity. That was a matter of very great importance, and it was borne out during the whole course of the war. Almost all these civilian internees survived their internment, and the mortality rate in their camps varied between 1 and 3 per cent according to nationality.

But it was not long before the arrangement led to protests in Berlin. We were informed that reports from Posen and Bromberg in Western Poland, which had just been conquered by the Wehrmacht, showed scores of cases in which German civilians had been murdered by the Poles before their retreat. I was requested to go there and take note of these atrocities on the spot. Geneva agreed that I should do so on condition that no evidence of mine should be published in the press or used in any official document, and that the Germans should agree that during my visit I should be allowed to visit civilian and military Polish prisoners.

Berlin accepted and on September 24th an army car came to pick me up at the Adlon. Two Germans accompanied me, a representative of the Auswärtiges Amt, a convinced young Nazi, and a representative of the Wehrmacht, a regular officer, with monocle and riding whip, who was much less enamoured of the new regime than his companion was.

As we drove down the Unter den Linden and passed the Soviet Embassy, the officer made a gesture with his hand towards the building and observed with an icy smile:

'Unsere neuen Freunde (Our new friends).'

The young diplomat took the ironic observation perfectly seriously and declared importantly:

'The Russians are charming fellows. We Germans always have understood the Slav soul.'

The first stage of our journey was accomplished along one of the famous *Autobahnen*, Hitler's motor-roads. The two ribbons were separated by a third ribbon of grass running between them. The second stage took us over ordinary tarred roads. The country was dismally flat. As we approached what had been the Polish frontier habitations became rarer and rarer. Sometimes we passed an isolated farm with a squat tower and a high wall giving the appearance of a castle: remnants of the former strong points of the Teutonic Knights.

The young man from the Auswärtiges Amt had obviously been instructed to indoctrinate me with a little pro-Nazi propaganda and he went on and on about the marvellous results obtained by the Hitler regime, its wonderful military successes, and the brilliant victory of its tanks over the Polish cavalry. The care with which he followed my least movement whenever the car stopped indicated that he had also been instructed to keep a very watchful eye on me.

We arrived at Posen in the afternoon. It was soon obvious that I was to be received by the German military authorities. All I saw of the Poles was a few pedestrians, and they scurried along keeping close to the walls.

We were escorted at once to the Town Hall where German officers and officials were engaged in taking down statements from relatives of the men who had been killed. After about an hour of this I declared that I had heard enough. I reminded my hosts that I was not present as an official investigator and that I would take no notice of any evidence apart from that which I was in a position to obtain personally. However, I put one question:

'What nationality were the victims?'

'Why, Germans, of course. Volksdeutsche.'

'Excuse me, I mean what was their formal nationality, what passports did they hold, Polish or German?'

'Ach! They were Volksdeutsche. The Treaty of Versailles had made them Polish, but in reality they were absolutely German.'

'Yes, I see, but from the point of view of the Polish Government they were legally Polish citizens. I am afraid that complicates the matter.'

I could not say to the Germans what I instinctively felt. If there were to be any serious investigation into the affair then, above all, the Poles would have to be heard, and the attitude of these Volksdeutsche before the arrival of the Wehrmacht would have to be gone into. I did not continue the discussion.

That evening there was a gala dinner in the former castle of

Wilhelm II. An immense table in the shape of a horseshoe was laid under the impressive vaulted ceiling of a medieval hall. My two bodyguards presented me to the commanding general of the neighbourhood and he invited me to take a seat on his right. Standing motionless behind their chairs seventy officers were waiting for the general and me to take our places. On each plate was a pork cutlet, a little butter, a slice of cheese and a large hunk of bread. To drink there was cocoa and beer.

'Ja, Herr Doktor,' the general observed jovially, 'our meal is frugal. It is our custom that the officers should eat the same as the men. However, observe the beauty of the dinner service.'

He bent towards me and whispered confidentially:

'We had to shake up the Polish caretaker a bit before he consented to produce the linen and porcelain of the Kaiser.'

And he laughed immoderately, instantly putting an end to all conversation.

'Ja . . . Prosit meine Herren. Zum Wohl, Herr Doktor.'

At the end of the meal the general's orderly came along with two small glasses and a bottle of liqueur. The general himself poured it out, a glass for me and a glass for him.

'Zum Wohl, Herr Doktor.'

The officers looked on. When it was over they rose as one man and stood respectfully at attention behind their chairs.

'Ah,' sighed the general. 'It's no joke being stationed here. Curfew at seven o'clock and the streets deserted. But this evening we have a cinema performance. We found some films the Poles had received just before we arrived. If you care to come along you will be my guest.'

I went and was given the honour of a box next to that of the general. The performance began. And what appeared on the screen? A French news reel of the July 14th celebrations in Paris. French troops marched along the Champs-Élysées passing beneath the Arc de Triomphe and before members of the French Government, cheered by masses of people on all sides. The coming war was casting its shadow before. Daladier spoke of the glorious task the French Army would perform, as it had done twenty-five years before, if justice and freedom were attacked anywhere in the world. There was not a word, not a movement in the auditorium. Hitler had decided that there was no anti-French sentiment in Germany.

After the main film, the airy and light-hearted 'Bel Ami', I thought I could at last take leave of my over-attentive hosts, but my two guardian angels were at my side at once to see that I did not wander through the streets of the town without supervision. They accompanied me to the very door of the room which had been reserved for me in an hotel requisitioned by the German authorities.

'If you should require anything,' the diplomat informed me, 'I am occupying the room on your left, and my friend here is in the room on the right. Gute Nacht.'

Even when sleeping I was to be well watched.

When I was alone I felt rather sad. It was not that I was so far away from my own country; it was for Poland. When should I be able to see the Poles instead of this Prussian Army which now lorded it over them?'

'Tomorrow you will be able to see with what savagery the Poles conducted themselves,' declared the Wehrmacht captain.

We went off early in the company of one or two representatives of forensic medicine to visit a cemetery in the suburbs, where I watched the exhumation of three bodies. They were taken to the mortuary and the autopsy was performed in my presence. There was little doubt that the men had died a violent death: fractures of the skull, bullet wounds. The Germans did not neglect a single detail; everything was carefully noted down to be embodied later in a full report.

On leaving the cemetery I bought a newspaper; it was German of course. On the front page the first thing I saw was my name in big print. What was the meaning of that? I turned at once in some excitement to my two companions.

'Look at this,' I said indignantly. 'I had your solemn promise...'

'Impossible!' exclaimed the diplomat, and pretended to be very angry. 'I will telephone to the editorial office in Danzig at once.'

'You can spare yourself the trouble,' I declared brusquely. 'For me this mission is at an end. I refuse to be shown anything else whatever.'

'But really, you can't do that. We've much more interesting things to show you at Bromberg.'

'I don't want to see them. And now if you please, mein Herr, make arrangements for my visit to your prisoner-of-war camps. That will be the last thing I do here.'

My energetic tone convinced the other that I was not prepared to let myself be tricked again. Later on they offered to take me to Brest-Litovsk where the Russians had reported the finding of forty murdered German non-commissioned officers in a Polish prison. The Auswärtiges Amt had the naivety to promise me once again 'the strictest incognito'.

'You will see. This time all precautions will be taken. You will leave on your own by plane with an American reporter.'

Pitiful trickery, tempting stratagems . . . They could not prevent my hearing the real cries of distress.

On September 27th I visited the first prisoner-of-war camp. There were 2500 prisoners. They slept on straw in what had once been stables. Near by were 600 civilian prisoners. The food was sufficient, but the conditions were very poor.

'The arrangements are, of course, only provisional,' said the officer of the Wehrmacht who showed me round. He seemed himself to be unfavourably impressed by the scene.

It was the civilians who had most to complain of. They seemed to have been arrested anywhere, in the street, in their homes, at their place of work. All men between the ages of seventeen and sixty-five had been brought in indiscriminately 'for purposes of identification'. They had not been allowed to take anything with them. The soldiers had at least their uniforms, some of their equipment and sometimes their packs and blankets.

This particular camp was no worse than the others. There were hundreds of them throughout Poland, all as miserable, all just as 'provisional'. Throughout the month of October I visited a number of them along the roads and in the neighbourhood of towns. And everywhere I had to be content just to *see*, to catch a glimpse between the grey uniforms which barred as much as possible of the terrible reality from me. I did succeed on one occasion in speaking alone to a representative of the prisoners, but it was only for four or five minutes, and then my guardian angels surrounded me again, urging me to press on, because of the time, and trying to make me forget by a flow of conciliatory words what I had just learned.

Gradually I learned to divine what the Germans did not show me, to understand the double sense of words, to perceive the distress conveyed in the silence of a prisoner in the presence of his forbidding guard. I needed an infinite fund of patience because I realized the influence a few words whispered into the ear of the commandant after my departure might have . . . an almost imperceptible reserve, a casually suggested improvement. In the hope of that I had to suffer the obsequious attentions of my guides and their ceaseless vigilance. I had to pass over the most eloquent signs of the cruelty that war had brought to the Polish people and pretend not to have noticed them.

On all sides the evidence of fear and intimidation was only too visible. Pedestrians went out of their way at the mere sight of a uniform, children fled when one offered to shake hands with them, and the women with their pale handsome faces framed in black shawls fell silent at our approach.

Why did the Germans surround me with such a wall? There were very few foreign observers in Poland at the time, and no doubt they would have preferred that none at all were there.

What was the explanation? The ruined countryside, the frightful misery in the devastated villages, the wandering families, the lost children, the men kept in stables like cattle? No, it was because the Poles were disappointing them.

'Ach, die Polen!' sighed Governor Frank when I met him in Cracow. 'They refuse to understand. If they would only be reasonable we would give them a nice little Poland of 14 million inhabitants under our protection. But they won't co-operate. They're not even prepared to govern themselves.'

I made no comment. I was anxious to obtain permission to set up an investigation committee to inquire into the fate of the missing. I had already been allowed to arrange for the sending of certain urgent requirements from Switzerland.

My work was more important than trying to convince Governor Frank why the Poles were unwilling 'to understand'.

By the beginning of November the war in Poland was already over. The Germans and the Russians had made contact at Brest-Litovsk. Very little was known about the regime established in the Soviet zone. However, a few message cards did reach us from newly established internment camps organized by the Soviet authorities in White Russia.

'I should like to go to Warsaw,' I declared one day.

'Ach!' exclaimed my guardian angels. 'Unfortunately that's very difficult. All the bridges have been destroyed and the roads have not been repaired yet.'

'But the transport of the Wehrmacht has no difficulty in getting wherever it wants,' I objected.

'Very well,' they agreed reluctantly, 'we'll see if a car can get through.'

The car could get through all right. The bridges had certainly been destroyed, but there were already temporary structures thrown across the rivers at their side. We even passed through some villages which were still intact, but further on the countryside had been razed for miles. Blasted trees, broken walls, the ground torn up by thousands of shells all bore witness to the heroic and desperate resistance put up by the Poles in defence of their capital.

'Stop here,' I said suddenly to the driver.

The car came to a halt. My two guides looked at me in astonishment. We were in the open countryside. There was not a house in sight along the road as far as eye could see. But in a field on the left was a man with a horse ploughing a furrow through the sandy earth pitted with shell craters. He was a Polish prisoner. I had recognized him as such from his cap.

'I want to speak to that man.'

The Pole had left his sabots in one corner of the field and was working bare-footed. When I came near his wretched figure came clumsily to attention behind the plough.

'Sprechen Sie deutsch?' I asked.

'Ja. Wenig.'

'A little.' That would do. I told him that I was from the Red Cross, but he did not seem to understand me. I tried to reassure him, but his eyes were fixed on the two men in German uniform behind me. I was, of course, in civilian clothing.

'Are you married?'

'Ja.'

He twisted his cap nervously in his toil-hardened hands.

'Any children?'

'Ja, zwei.'

He raised two fingers to make the number quite clear.

'Where are they?'

'In Warsaw.'

And then turning to his work again he repeated several times in a broken voice:

'Dead . . . All dead . . . Bombs. Bombs.'

I went back to the car followed by my two guards. An hour later we reached the suburbs of Warsaw. The factories and working-class houses were in ruins. Debris obstructed the street, causing bottle necks and traffic jams, where the drivers abused and cursed at each other until they finally succeeded in getting past. Along the broken crumbling walls queues of people waited silently in front of one or two shops which had been spared destruction.

The air was foul with a horrible smell of decomposition. Fifty thousand bodies were still under the ruins or hastily buried in the public gardens, where the soft earth had allowed the survivors to dig graves. Gangs of men worked ceaselessly to recover the bodies, which were afterwards cremated or buried in common graves.

The side streets had often been so devastated that they were now little more than paths. Out of 18,000 houses no less than 8000 had been completely destroyed. Amidst these terrible ruins wandered crowds of miserable, trembling and hungry people.

The car drove to the Hôtel Europeiski, one of the few which was almost completely intact. It was now the headquarters of the German Staff and once again I found myself completely surrounded by Germans.

My room looked out on to a large square which was dominated by the damaged dome of the Bruhl Palace. A horse had just fallen down in the square below my window. Immediately a crowd of people, some with table knives and some with pocket knives rushed forward. The sight interested me so much that I determined to observe it at close quarters. I left my room without attracting the attention of my custodians. They were not in the hotel foyer and I went out unguarded into the streets of Warsaw.

By the time I got down into the street the crowd had almost disappeared, and all that remained of the horse was a skeleton on which several poor devils who had arrived too late were working in an endeavour to find a little flesh left.

Seeing my obvious astonishment a more dignified pedestrian stopped and addressed me.

'I presume you are a foreigner, sir?'

On hearing who I was he introduced himself.

'Prince Lipkovsky at your service. I also belong to the Red Cross. During the eight days of the siege I worked in a first-aid station which was established in the cellars of that bank there.'

Only the ground floor was left of the building he indicated.

'Yes,' he said, 'the building itself was destroyed in the bombing, as you see, but the basement was intact. From that cellar I made I don't know how many journeys to such hospitals as still remained in order to get bandages and the catgut that our surgeons required. Each journey was dangerous, of course, and one never knew whether one would get back or not. The bombardment went on ceaselessly. When one wave of planes had dropped its bombs the artillery opened up. The wounded were brought into us day and night. We could never get any sleep and we were famished. I really don't know how we managed to stand it.'

I listened silently. It seemed as though this man had been sent there just at this moment to guide me through the town and tell me about its terrifying ordeal. I realized too the urge this Pole had to confide in a foreigner, and particularly in a Swiss, and to make him a witness to the martyrdom of the Polish people.

'The two last days were horrible,' he said. 'No one dared go out any more. There was no water and no electric light. The entrance to our cellar, like the entrances to almost all the other shelters, was obstructed with rubble. The dead had to be left where they had fallen and the stench was frightful. We could do no more for the wounded around us, and many of them were already dying.

We walked together through the streets and brushed against other pedestrians who had experienced the same horrors.

'When finally everything fell silent,' the prince continued, 'we knew that our soldiers no longer had any ammunition with which to hold out.'

He stopped and indicated the ruins of the town with a gesture.

'We had to pay heavily, very heavily. But even that does not matter. We fought and we did not surrender.'

On our way I looked into a park of blasted and uprooted trees, and there in the middle, intact by some strange chance, stood a statue of Chopin.

'We shall never surrender,' said the prince slowly.

We were now far away from the Hôtel Europeiski, and as we walked at hazard through the streets my companion told me from time to time what this or that ruin in this horribly devastated quarter had formerly been. Before a heap of ruins he stopped:

'This was the German Embassy,' he said. 'They did not spare even themselves.'

Sometimes a building looked intact, but it was nothing but a façade drilled full of holes.

'Artillery damage,' said the prince. 'Not so bad as the bombs.'

Then he took me by the arm.

'We won't go any further in this direction,' he said. 'You see the barbed wire at the other end of the street. It surrounds the ghetto and it is guarded day and night. No one is allowed to enter or leave. There are 300,000 Jews there, and heaven knows how they're existing. Perhaps a boat or two brings them food over the Vistula, because one of the limits of the quarter is marked by the river. Their situation is dreadful. Typhus is reported to be raging there to such an extent that there is no longer anywhere the sick can be taken to. The Germans are searching for the Chief Rabbi everywhere, but they won't find him.'

Gradually we returned to the centre of the town. It grew dark and it became difficult for us to pick our way through the debris.

On taking his leave of me the prince observed:

'We are in November now Monsieur. There will be no clearance work before winter sets in. Think of the sufferings of hundreds of thousands of people without homes in the cold and the snow.'

At the Hôtel Europeiski I found my two guardian angels anxiously awaiting my return. No doubt in future their watchfulness would be more vigilant than ever.

The hospitals I visited in the following days were not much better off than the Ghetto infirmaries. Hundreds of typhus cases were brought into them daily. The wards, the corridors, even the staircases were encumbered with the sick and wounded, the amputated and the tubercular. There were no more beds for patients and no more bandages and medicaments. I had some difficulty in finding out the real situation. Even when I spoke to the doctors I could not get rid of the German eavesdroppers — and many people refused to talk at all in the presence of these German uniforms which followed me like shadows.

I was informed that the National Committee of the Polish Red Cross wished to see me. My two guardians raised no objection to taking me there. They accompanied me to the threshold of the room in which I was to meet the members of the committee. When I opened the door the Poles rose, a little shocked to see the two grey-green uniforms behind me.

I had had enough. I turned towards them and demanded energetically that they should leave me alone with the Poles. The Nazi pretended not to understand my objection and adopted a very jovial attitude.

'But why, Monsieur? We can stay here. We shan't interfere with you in the least. You can talk about whatever you please.'

'No, sir. One thing or the other. Either you show sufficient confidence in my integrity and leave me alone as long as I consider it necessary or I shall not take any part in this discussion and then I shall return to Berlin at once.'

He appeared disconcerted at my firmness and he looked inquiringly at his companion. In the end they left me alone with the Poles.

Despite the sadness on their faces and their obvious exhaustion there was very great relief when the doors closed with the Germans on the other side.

'We have been expecting you for some time,' I was told. 'We were sure Geneva would send someone to us. Now we can tell you what has happened here.'

'Alas,' I said, 'as you have just seen, it was not easy to get here at all, and I am fearful for the future. But now that we are together let us see what can be done.'

We then discussed the tasks before us: first of all to obtain news of the Polish refugees in Hungary and Poland, where they had gone with a part of the Polish Army, and then to do what we could for the prisoners of war and the civilian internees. We organized a system of inquiry and messages, which was to work until the end of the war — with varying success, but with good results on the whole. Then we discussed questions of aid and medical supplies. All this was interspersed with heart-rending confidences concerning the harshness of the German regime, the brutalities of the occupying forces, the arbitrary arrests and the alarming reports which were coming in from the Russian zone.

All these Poles had experienced a terrible tragedy within the short space of two months: relatives missing or killed at the front, dear ones killed at home in the bombardment, houses destroyed, the absence of news, famine ... They were still numbed by the suddenness and the magnitude of the catastrophe, and they clung desperately to the new life-line I was establishing between them and the powerful and generous world they had known, which they now no longer knew, but which, they felt, could not have abandoned them altogether. Geneva was their great hope. It represented the spirit of justice which would put an end to the horrors and the bloodshed. A splendid hope that I must not disappoint. But how fragile and illusory!

A few days later 'a grave incident' took place. In communicating it to me my Nazi diplomat — oh how little diplomatic! — grinned with triumph.

'They haven't told you about it?'

'Who should have told me about it?'

'Your good friends of the Polish Red Cross. But perhaps there are some things the Poles don't boast about.'

The German newspapers in Warsaw were making a great to-do about the affair it appeared. A German soldier had found a tin of fresh yellow paint and with it he had painted a partition in one of the stables reserved for the horses of the German Kommandantur. The job was well done, but a few hours later the vet had to be called to attend to the horses, and he found that they had all been poisoned. Their lips were swollen and full of blisters, and before long they all died of gastro-enteritis. On examining the newly painted partition it was discovered that the beautiful yellow paint was in fact mustard gas.

This time I was again expected to serve as a witness to the inhumanity and barbarity of the Poles. I was taken to see Professor Richter, who had been entrusted with the scientific investigation into the affair by the German Governor.

'We have found where the gas came from,' he informed me encouragingly. 'Just imagine, the Poles had an enormous stock of toxic gases in Fort Pilsudski. Incidentally we are going to show it to you.'

In the half-demolished fort there were piles of cases. One or two of them were open. The professor produced a container identical with the one which had held the 'yellow paint'.

He handed it to me and I examined it and then read out:

'Gelb-Kreuz Gaz,' and underneath in smaller lettering: 'I. G. Farben, Berlin.'

I handed it back to the professor and pointed to the marking.

'I have no comment,' I observed.

With that my part in the investigation was at an end.

CHAPTER III

TEN FOR ONE

FOR a month Hitler had been hurling his tanks and planes against France. His parachutists were sowing confusion and fear behind the Allied lines. The big towns of the north fell one after the other to his armies. Gradually Germany devoured more and more of the country. A flood tide of civilians, troops, cars and horse-drawn waggons, everything and anything on wheels, poured back towards the south.

In Berlin I occupied my room in the Hôtel Adlon and fretted under the restraint to which I was subjected. The waiters were every day becoming more and more cock-a-hoop, but occasionally one of these stiff-shirted black-bowed fellows would lean over me with a friendly eye and murmur: 'Poor France. We didn't want that.'

I had been in Berlin for six months working on behalf of the Allied prisoners, of whom there were not many at that time, perhaps 800 all told. I knew almost all of them by name. But now it seemed that the period of the 'phoney war' was over.

Suddenly on June 7th, 1940, I was urgently summoned to the Auswärtiges Amt. The same official who had usually received me so amiably was now cold and distant and declared in an icy voice:

'Monsieur, we have been informed that the French are executing our parachutists even when they are captured wearing German uniform. That is contrary to the Geneva Convention which Germany and France have both signed. The Führer is not prepared to tolerate such things. He will shoot ten French prisoners of war for every German parachutist who is killed.'

I felt my throat tighten. His brusque tone, so different from the way in which he usually addressed me, seemed to indicate that something had already been decided. Was it only a threat? Or had such a cruel order already been issued? I protested indignantly.

'I regard your information as impossible,' I declared. 'I cannot believe that the French would. . .'

'We know,' he interrupted me stiffly, 'and that's enough.'

'At least before you indulge in such harsh reprisals give me a chance to warn the French Government. I will do my utmost to get to Paris as quickly as possible to institute inquiries.'

'You would arrive when the war was over. You would be unable to pass through the lines.'

'I don't need to cross the lines. I can easily get to France through Switzerland. At the same time I would visit German prisoners of war in France and report back to you concerning the result of my inquiries. Have confidence in me.'

He shot me a suspicious look, then he hesitated, and something in his eyes gave me a little hope. He picked up the telephone receiver. The man who soon began to talk to him at the other end of the line was a person of some importance I realized. I listened to the official putting my case. His voice grew calmer.

'Certainly, Herr Minister . . . Most certainly, Herr Minister.'

The official hung up and then turned to me.

'Very well,' he said. 'There is a train that leaves for Nuremberg this evening. Go by that, and whilst you are there inspect a camp for French prisoners of war. You will be able to see how the German Reich treats its prisoners. From there you will go on to Switzerland and then into France.'

'Can you at least give me an assurance that . . .'

'I feel sure that if your report reaches us within twelve days nothing irreparable will have happened by then.'

Twelve days. . . .

I think that from that moment on I did not count the days but the hours.

I arrived in Nuremberg on June 8th, and found German officers waiting for me at the station. We drove at once by car to the prisoner-of-war camp. It was quite near the town and it was not long before I saw the watch towers and the triple row of barbed wire around it.

It was a beautiful June day. The sky was clear and the sun was shining.

Between the typical long, low, barrack-like huts were hundreds of French prisoners with their tunics unbuttoned and their hats on the backs of their heads, pale, tired and listless. They all seemed numbed by their incredibly rapid defeat. Some of them could still display an air of mockery and they looked ironically at the officers who accompanied me.

'Et puis après?' their looks seemed to say.

The representatives of the prisoners were gathered together in one of the huts. Their leader was a French general without either hat or helmet. He had lost all his effects. The top of his head was quite bald, but at the sides his grey hair was over-long and fell down over his ears. Apparently there was no means of getting a haircut here. The Germans looked at him contemptuously. A number of French officers standing with him understood my reaction, and one of them, a handsome strapping fellow with a tired and rather sceptical air, shrugged his shoulders eloquently.

I made a note of their requirements, assured myself that they had enough to eat and were provided with reasonable sleeping quarters, and then I left. 'I must get to Paris as quickly as possible,' was my thought. 'Get there in order to save hundreds of you good fellows, many of you fathers of families, from being shot out of hand.'

They knew nothing of what was passing in my mind, and perhaps they judged me harshly for the briefness of my inspection.

When I was leaving the camp I passed a hut before which a roll-call was taking place. The men were drawn up in two lines and in turn each shouted out his name and the name of the town or place from which he came:

'Moreau — Lyons.'

'Cazoubet — Montaubon.'

'Forestier — Limoges.'

So long has passed since then that I may no longer have the names of the places correctly, but I have certainly not forgotten the names of the men I heard by chance: Moreau, Cazoubet and Forestier.

For days afterwards they sounded in my ear like a litany: Moreau, Cazoubet, Forestier; Moreau, Cazoubet, Forestier. . . .

In the evening I arrived at Ulm station where I noticed an unusual concentration of police. As soon as the train came to a halt it was invaded by members of the Gestapo.

'Your papers.'

I presented my Swiss diplomatic passport.

'Swiss,' exclaimed the man with a sudden light in his eyes. 'Stay where you are and don't move.'

'Why?' I demanded. 'I am going to Switzerland. Kindly allow me to continue my journey.'

'Keep quiet,' he replied. 'I have my orders.'

I was flabbergasted. A dozen and one suppositions arose in my mind. Had Switzerland been attacked? That would mean internment. I thought of all my comrades who were on the other side of the frontier. I thought of my urgent mission, of the German parachutists, of the French prisoners of war whose lives I was trying to save. No, I thought to myself, it can't be. The thing's absurd.

A moment or two later the man returned and made as though to pass by.

'Wait a moment,' I said. 'I have another document I can show you.'

'What sort of a document?'

'A military one,' and I presented a safe-conduct which had been made out for me in Berlin in some connection or the other. It was issued by the O.K.W. or Headquarters of the Wehrmacht. His face changed at once as he read it and he sprang to attention and saluted.

'This train is not going on to Switzerland,' he said in a very different tone, 'but you will be able to get a connection in the morning.'

He collected my baggage and accompanied me to a hotel where he caused them to produce a very good meal in spite of the lateness of the hour. Then he left me with another respectful salute.

In the meantime I was wondering anxiously what could have

happened, but I was not prepared to risk any inquiries from the people around me. After I had eaten, a waiter accompanied me to my room carrying my baggage. His attitude was strange. It was a mixture of suspicion and a certain pity. Once we were in my room and the door was closed behind us he whispered:

'Have you heard the news yet? Germany has declared war on Switzerland and the Wehrmacht has already crossed the plateau in the direction of Lyons.'

I saw him out of the room and remained behind alone, my mind in a whirl. Was that true? The Gestapo man had told me there would be a train to Switzerland in the morning. Was that another little trick? The insoluble contradictions dejected me but I was so tired I quickly fell asleep.

One of the twelve days was already gone.

In the morning I rushed for the papers. The first one to come into my hands was the *Frankfurter Zeitung*, and there in banner headlines was the announcement: 'Italy enters the war on the side of Germany. Mussolini's speech.' There was no mention of Switzerland at all.

Later I learned that Moscow had broadcast an item on the probable invasion of Switzerland. The waiter must have heard it and, seeing the unusual concentration of police and Gestapo, put two and two together. However, I remained vaguely disturbed.

The train took me not towards Switzerland, but towards Austria. The frontier between Constance and Basle was really closed and the train had to make a long detour to find a frontier post open at Sankt Margarethen.

All day long the steady rhythm of the wheels repeated the three names 'Moreau, Cazoubet, Forestier' in my brain like an obsession. All day and all night as well, because it was ten o'clock the next morning before I sprang out of the train at Kreuzlingen.

I crossed Switzerland at once in the hope of catching the express for Paris that evening from Cornavin, but when I arrived I learnt that there were no more trains for France.

At least I was able to go home for a few hours. I slept with my windows wide open to the sky of a beautiful June night. It was not long before I thought I was having a bad dream. I could hear the great drumming of many aeroplane engines in the sky. Suddenly quite awake I ran to the window and looked down into the street and saw that people were coming out of their houses and looking anxiously upwards. It was no dream. Suddenly a red rocket streaked across the sky and burst. Detonations sounded close at hand. The bombing had begun.

So it really was war this time? I went to find out what information I could. No one knew what to make of this sudden act of aggression. There had been no wireless announcement of any sort which might have warned us. 'That's the Germans all over,' someone shouted indignantly.

But the next day we learned that it had been British planes after all. They had mistaken Geneva for Constance, whose position was vaguely analogous, but on the other side.

However, our information service had not failed to notice the concentration of large German forces on our northern frontier, and it seemed that the only reason why the Germans had not attacked had been the rapid collapse of French resistance.

But at the moment no one knew what was actually happening in France. I wanted to leave at once, but there was no authority to issue a visa or even to give me any reliable information. The only definite thing I could discover was that there were no more trains leaving for the north. On June 14th we knew the explanation: the Germans had entered Paris.

Where was the French Government? How could I get to it? The official at the Auswärtiges Amt had agreed to a respite of twelve days, and I realized that my problem was to find the German prisoners and talk to them before the Wehrmacht arrived to liberate them. But in the meantime the precious days were passing and I could not get out of Switzerland.

I had been worried at losing a whole day between Ulm and Kreuzlingen, but I was to lose no less than seven days in Geneva.

Since there were no trains I decided to use my car and take a friend. But where should we make for? The most confused rumours were current. Marshal Pétain was said to have placed himself at the head of a provisional government which was now either at Tours or Bordeaux. Civil war was said to have broken out in the south.

Neither the telephone nor the telegraph was working. And even when we got into France and stopped at local town halls they could give us no real information.

As in Spain, I had painted big red crosses on the mudguards of our car. As soon as we stopped anywhere in France we were immediately surrounded by groups of people who demanded news of us. One thing was clear, in a very short space of time a great number of men had gone to join the first 800 prisoners in Nuremberg and the other Stalags I had visited. Some said that the Germans had taken 2 or 3 million prisoners.

'How can we get into touch with them?' we were asked.

'Write an ordinary post-card to Geneva addressed to the Central Prisoners-of-War Bureau,' I replied. 'But be patient because we don't know anything yet either. Above all, put your own names and addresses clearly on your cards so that we can reply to you as soon as we learn anything.'

But many of these unfortunate people no longer had any fixed address.

We drove on through the night until five o'clock in the morning when we arrived at Séte, right in the south of France. All the hotels, boarding houses and refuges were packed with fugitives.

'Is it true that the French Government has left for North Africa?' I asked.

'No. It's still in Bordeaux.'

So in the morning of June 18th we turned the car towards Bordeaux.

Ten days had passed since I left Berlin.

At Marmande, just over sixty miles from Bordeaux, we met German motor-cyclists chugging along serenely between detachments of French troops. The French were all still armed, but completely indifferent to the Germans. Mixed up with the military was a heterogeneous crowd of civilian refugees. It was an uninterrupted procession of vehicles of all sorts, lorries carrying factory equipment, peasant carts loaded with miscellaneous household goods, mattresses and so on, and children sitting in chairs. The armistice had not yet been signed and the great exodus continued.

On the other side of Marmande we met the first French military control point.

'On ne passe pas.' said the French captain.

'I am on an important official mission,' I explained. 'The lives of hundreds of French prisoners are at stake.'

'On ne passe pas,' he repeated obstinately. 'They are my orders.'

'Listen,' I went on. 'I have just come from Berlin. . . .'

'Useless to talk, Monsieur. If you want to go to Bordeaux take the train.'

'Is there a train to Bordeaux?'

'Certainly there is. There's one that ought to be running into the station now.'

We turned about and hurried to the station. There was, in fact, a train standing at a platform. We seized our cases, left the car in the station yard, took tickets and raced for the train.

'What about the car?' asked my companion.

'It will have to wait till we come back,' I replied. In my heart I had already said goodbye to it, but the great thing now was to get to Bordeaux at all costs.

I will not attempt to add one more to the many descriptions of what Bordeaux looked like on June 18th, 1940. It was something like a dispensation of providence that in that incredible chaos I at once found the man best fitted to understand my mission and to assist me to carry it out without further loss of time: Herr Stucki, the Swiss Ambassador.

'Obviously there's no time to lose,' he declared as soon as I had told him the situation. 'I will take you to Marshal Pétain at once. You probably know that he has just placed himself at the head of the French Government.'

At the Marshal's headquarters I was received by M. Charles Roux. I was filled with terrible apprehension. In face of the catastrophe which had descended on France what would the fate of the men whose lives I had come to save matter? But I also knew that a terrible mechanism was poised waiting to go into action, and if once it was let loose to avenge the supposed murdered parachutists there would be nothing to stop it.

'Ten for one . . .' 'Ten for one . . .' And again I heard the litany of Nuremberg — 'Moreau, Cazoubet, Forestier.'

I spoke with more assurance than I felt.

'In Berlin the French are charged with having executed parachutists, and the Germans are threatening horrible reprisals. Even an official denial at once would be valuable. And then there's the evidence of the German prisoners you have in your hands. May I see them?'

Charles Roux sent me off to the French War Minister, General Colson.

He was installed at the Hôtel de Ville and it was there I went to find him. I had to wait in a vast reception hall. I was alone with my companion, but there were three men there, two of whom I knew quite well; they were standing together talking: Laval, Marquet and an Air Force general. Then Laval left the group to go into the War Minister. Soon afterwards Marquet followed him.

The Air Force general remained behind. A few minutes later two Air Force officers came in, a colonel and a captain, and I was privileged to hear the following conversation:

'Mon général, we have come to you in the name of all our comrades. . . .'

'What do you want?'

'We have come to beseech you not to capitulate. This very morning we have won two striking victories thanks to our Devoitines.'

The general remained silent, and the colonel insisted:

'Mon général, we must leave France.'

'Where to?'

'To North Africa.'

'To North Africa? But you're mad. What for?'

'To fight on, mon général.'

'Do you know what resources we have in North Africa?' the

general asked grimly. 'A hundred thousand men and ammunition for three weeks. And there's not a factory there to turn out even bullets much less shells.'

I saw the colonel grit his teeth and there were tears in his eyes.

'Very good, mon général.'

He saluted smartly and went away with his companion.

Immediately afterwards I was called into the War Minister's office. With him was General Ménard, whom I knew well from the days when I was working on behalf of the Spanish refugees.

'In Berlin,' I began, 'the French are charged. . .'

A few minutes later I had all the necessary papers authorizing me to visit any camp for prisoners of war or for civilian internees in the south of France. An army car was placed at my disposal and we left at once for Toulouse.

'My telegram must go off before tomorrow evening,' I had told General Colson.

In passing through Marmande I was agreeably surprised to notice my car still standing intact where we had left it. We reached Toulouse in the night and the next morning — it was already June 19th — we set off for a château in the neighbourhood where some hundreds of German officers were interned.

The place was lovely. All the German officers were stripped to the waist taking a sun-bath in the grounds. The discipline of these German prisoners was flabbergasting. When I asked to speak to their representatives one after the other of them came up, clicked his heels and gave the Hitler salute.

I did not want to ask straight away the question which was exercising my mind so greatly so I asked simply:

'Have you anything to complain of in your treatment?'

Yes, they had to complain that there were only 100 beds in the château for 300 officers. One or two of them complained of rough treatment at the time they were taken prisoner, but not one of them had heard that any of his comrades had been shot.

'Are there any parachutists amongst you?'

Several parachutists were brought up and introduced to me. I spoke slowly and clearly in order that there should be no mis-understanding whatever:

'Listen,' I began. 'In Berlin the authorities believe that German parachutists have been shot out of hand after being taken prisoner either by French soldiers or French police. Reprisals are being planned: ten French prisoners of war are to be shot for every German parachutist who has been killed in this fashion.'

After a long silence in which they looked at each other a German colonel spoke:

'We know nothing about any such case.'

What a relief! But in order that my investigations should be complete I still had to see the German non-commissioned officers and men who were interned at Vernet in the Département Ariège. That meant hours of driving over congested roads, but at last I arrived at the camp, which I knew well, for I had often visited it on behalf of the Spanish refugees when they had been interned there. It was an old brick works and very ill suited for the new purpose for which it was being used. There were 2500 men interned there in very bad conditions and the food they received was barely sufficient. All the prisoners were well informed about the military situation and they were discussing a mass break-out to go to meet the advanced elements of the German Army, which were not more than perhaps 100 miles away by this time.

In Vernet I gathered the representatives of the prisoners together and I succeeded in convincing them that the best thing to do was to remain calmly where they were and await events. I also made it very clear to the French that it was in their own interests to treat these German prisoners as well as they possibly could because at least a million of their own people were already in German hands. But above all I asked group after group the same dread question that had troubled me ever since I had left Berlin:

'Is it true that German parachutists. . .'

I only wished that the official of the Auswärtiges Amt who had been so sure of his information had been there to hear their replies.

I even went on that dreadful June evening to Argèles to interview German civilian prisoners. There too during the last days of the

Spanish civil war I had seen thousands of hungry men and women in rags flooding down from the Pyrenees. This time the prisoners had come from the north, transferred sometimes even from as far as Belgium in cattle trucks. Hundreds of Germans and Italians now occupied the same miserable huts.

Internment huts in Nuremberg, internment huts in Argèles. They seemed like stark signposts along that path of human misery the world is fated to travel from war to war. Will the only change ever be just a change of occupants?

My work done I hurriedly left that hell behind. Always in my mind was the fate of those other prisoners on the other side.

'And now to the Post Office. Quick. . . .'

It was already the night of June 19th, but my telegram would take only a few hours with official priority to reach Geneva and then go on to Berlin.

Have visited 100 officers and 2500 men prisoners of war and 1000 German and Italian civilian prisoners. Situation of the prisoners precarious in view of situation. Report on parachutists apparently completely erroneous. No prisoner knows anything about executions–Please transmit urgently to Auswärtiges Amt.

The next day without knowing that perhaps their lives depended on that telegram the three French prisoners of war would answer the roll-call as usual:

'Moreau – Lyons.'
'Cazoubet – Montauban.'
'Forestier – Limoges.'

CHAPTER IV

THE LOST HEARTH

THE armistice between Germany and France was signed at Rethondes on June 25th, 1940. A veil of mourning descended over the whole disorganized land. So many people had been driven on to the roads, swept along by the exodus, separated by the war, the fighting and the retreat that nothing was any longer fixed and secure, nothing was any longer reliable, not even an address at which one could be sure to find one's nearest and dearest.

Whole villages and even towns in the east and the north together with their administrative bodies, their schools and their universities had emigrated to the south. A black line cut France in two, from Switzerland to the Loire, from Tours to the Pyrenees. On account of that frontier line, mechanically straight such as one usually sees only through desert areas, a strange new geography sprang up according to which Metz was at Toulouse, Colmar at Périgueux and Strassbourg at Clermont-Ferrand.

The 'Free Zone' was full of lost children and distracted parents. In a desperate attempt to find their nearest relatives people placed their hopes in a miracle; they pinned up pathetic notices here and there in the towns, on the doors of cinemas which had been turned into night shelters. . . .

Other missing men were far away and made no reply: the prisoners of war.

Where were they? How many of them were there? The French General Staff was unable to give any figures, even approximate ones. Whole armies had been captured in the east trapped in the useless cement works of the Maginot Line. Whole regiments had been taken in their garrison towns. They had left their barracks only to march off, disarmed, to the north.

The suddenness of her overwhelming victory took Germany by surprise, too, and she was overwhelmed by this vast mass of prisoners. Where could they be put? Huts and encampments were hastily erected. Another geography arose all over the Third Reich: that of the Stalags and the Oflags.

Even in Berlin the military authorities were unable to give any figures for the number of prisoners. Another influx swept them up towards the forests of Bavaria or the plains of Silesia. They too were lost on the long journey whose end they could not know, until finally they became a mere cipher, a few Roman figures and an initial. But at least it was an address at which they could at last receive news of their loved ones, whose fate worried them more than their own.

What had happened to the brother who had left on one of the last boats for North Africa or England? Where was the wife who had gone off with the children and a few poor household possessions on a lorry between Valence and Montauban? Where was the Jewish friend who had gone into hiding under a false name in some village in the mountains? Where were all those who dared not return to their homes for fear of religious or racial persecution, or would not return because they had taken up the struggle again against the invader?

How could all these people find each other again? Or at least get news of each other, discover that they were still alive?

The exchange of letters between prisoners of war and their families is provided for in the Geneva Convention, but no one foresaw the extraordinary situation which actually developed; this time it was the prisoners who had lost all traces of their families.

As so often, we had to improvise a solution to meet a situation which no jurist had ever foreseen. And the idea was born in action out of those countless pathetic notices pinned up throughout France by anguished families trying to find their lost members. Geneva became the great notice board of stricken Europe, where millions of people sought their friends and relatives.

I submitted the project to the Prisoners-of-War Bureau in Berlin.

The first reaction of the officer in charge, Major Breyer, was a point-blank refusal.

'We are already doing everything the Convention demands. Every prisoner in our hands is allowed to send a post-card to his family. If the families themselves have disappeared or changed their addresses that is no fault of ours.'

'But you know yourself that thousands of those post-cards never reach the hands of those for whom they are intended. The prisoners are eating their hearts out in anxiety and their families are unable to get into touch with them.'

'It's up to the postal authorities to see that the post-cards are delivered to the people to whom they are addressed. It is not our responsibility.'

With an impatient gesture he indicated a well-bound volume on his desk. Every paragraph in it was carefully annotated.

The Geneva Convention!

'But after all, Herr Major, the Geneva Convention was never intended as a sort of Bible. There are no agreements which can be carried out properly if the spirit of the thing is lacking.'

'Well, what is it you want us to do?'

'Permit each of your prisoners to send another post-card, this time to the Central Prisoners-of-War Bureau in Geneva, and we will then do our best to see that they reach the men's families.'

A long report of our conversation and my proposal was then sent off to the Wehrmacht authorities. It came back two days later with the note 'accepted'.

Our people made the same approach to the French, but their administration was in such chaos that no one seemed in a position to make a decision. The old liaison organization which maintained relations between Geneva and the War Ministry was now dispersed in various sub-offices between Lyons and Clermont-Ferrand.

The thing was simple enough, but where was the man to settle it?

When I left for Vichy on October 12th, 1940, I had no idea that before matters could be settled the personal intervention of the Chief of State and his war minister would be necessary.

The famous Hôtel du Parc was still open to the public despite the fact that it had now become the seat of the new French Government. I found myself lost in a crush of chattering visitors all acting as though they were persons of importance. Busy secretaries and dispatch carriers threaded their way through the groups. I was directed into a large hall still furnished with its old lace-decorated chairs and couches. Around the marble tables the survivors of the political shipwreck of the Third Republic were endlessly discussing the fate of France and mapping out the future of Europe.

I was kept waiting for hours. My request for an audience seemed to have been forgotten.

At eight o'clock in the evening a door opened and Marshal Pétain entered. Having finished his dinner he was coming down like all the other guests of the hotel to take his coffee in the hall. I rose and almost immediately an officer of his suite came towards me, a man who remembered having seen me in Bordeaux.

'What mission brings you to us this time?' he asked.

'It's a question of the French prisoners of war again. . . .'

'Wait a moment,' he said and went away. Then he returned.

'The Marshal will receive you himself tomorrow morning at nine o'clock.'

When I arrived at the Hôtel du Parc at the time arranged I was immediately met by a guard who took me to the second floor where the Marshal occupied a suite of three rooms at the end of a corridor. I was shown in at once.

The windows looked out on to the offices of a thermal bath, and the room had been sketchily turned into an office with a few books, one or two leather arm-chairs and a table covered with dossiers. The old Marshal was alone, very upright in his black morning coat. He invited me to sit down and then listened attentively to what I had to say.

'We shall never forget what Switzerland has done for our prisoners,' he said with emotion. 'Tell them that in Geneva, please. But how is it that in this matter of the prisoners and their families you have not got into touch with the French Red Cross?'

'Because there are three separate organizations in France, Monsieur le Maréchal, and they have not established a working agreement with each other even to this day.'

'I shall insist that they amalgamate and form one organization, and that will facilitate their own work and the work of your committee.'

And then suddenly something seemed to strike the Marshal.

'What are you living on?'

'Charity', I replied.

'But hasn't France done anything about it?'

'The matter was discussed in Paris last February, but no decision was ever taken.'

'I will see to it myself.'

The Marshal called his private secretary, Dr. Menetrel.

'Arrange a meeting for Dr. Junod with Weygand this afternoon,' he said. 'The matter is urgent.'

A few hours later General Weygand with three other generals received me in a room of the Hôtel aux Ambassadeurs.

'I have been told that it is a question of our prisoners and their families, Monsieur. What can we do about it?'

'The International Committee of the Red Cross has succeeded in obtaining permission for all French prisoners of war in Germany to write a post-card reporting their capture to Geneva. Those French families who are seeking to get into touch with prisoners need now only write to Geneva. Not long letters, of course, which would be difficult to classify, but brief post-cards along the lines of the cards prisoners themselves are entitled to send. When these cards then come together in the same file the contact between prisoners and their families will be established at once.'

'That is all perfectly clear. You can count upon my full support. I will take steps to see that public opinion is informed and that the necessary cards are made available.'

That was by no means the end of our difficulties. Strange as it may seem, the biggest difficulties arose between Germany and the occupied territories. No postal communication whatever was permitted from northern France to the south or to foreign countries. A Parisian was not allowed to get into touch either with Berlin or Geneva.

The same problem but in an inverse sense arose in Geneva. Twenty sacks of cards and letters from prisoners of war to their families in the occupied zone were already lying in the Central Post Office at Berne.

I succeeded in obtaining the assistance of one of the officials of the German Consul, a man named Maier, to get them transferred from Geneva to Paris. Maier was a South German, young and athletic, and he knew France well. We piled the sacks into his car and mine and set off. Since we were unable to go direct from Switzerland into the occupied zone we had to go by way of Lyons and Vichy. That great detour created the impression that we had come directly from the unoccupied zone and were carrying diplomatic mail.

At the bridge over the Loire at Moulins the black and white striped bars of the new frontier control post barred the way.

'Embassy business,' snapped Maier, and the precious post went through.

In the middle of the bridge Maier's car slowed down and stopped and I drew up beside him. I was quite shocked. Were we to be stopped after all?

'Look over there,' he said. 'Look at the reflection of the trees in the water, and that bank of sand in the distance.'

And then, understanding I think, that the letters with which our two cars were crammed were addressed quite as much to those trees, to that tranquil water and to the magnificent country around as to the lost hearths, he started up again.

'Let's step on it. They're waiting for us in Paris.'

Our sacks were handed over to the Red Cross and I returned alone to Geneva. A month later I met Maier again. He had prolonged his stay in France and had just returned from Marseilles.

'Do you know,' he said, 'I passed the demarcation line again in much the same circumstances as we did together.'

'But you didn't have any more mail?'

'No, but I had an escaped prisoner with me.'

He indicated the number plates of his car, issued in Geneva and bearing the 'CH' of the Swiss Confederation.

'He thought I was a Swiss and so he stopped me on the road between Nevers and Moulins. I saw him dodge out from behind some bushes, emaciated and unshaven, and still wearing his military greatcoat and trousers. As soon as he spoke I knew what it was all about. "Could you give me a lift and drop me a couple of miles or so from the demarcation line?" he asked.

'In the car he told me that he was trying to reach his wife and four children who were in Valence but from whom he had had no news for six months. And they didn't know what had happened to him. I immediately thought of the cards we had carried for the others, Junod, and it seemed worth while to me.'

'And what happened when you got to the demarcation line?'

'I told him to stay in my car, but he didn't want to. "If they catch me you'll get into trouble," he said. I thought up a story to tell them if they asked for his papers, but, in fact, we had no difficulty at all and we passed through easily. When we had got away from the post my prisoner jumped for joy and got hold of my arm and squeezed it. "Ah!" he exclaimed in delight. "Only a Swiss would have done that." When we got to Valence he found his family easily enough and I was introduced to his wife and his children and to all the friends who came up to welcome him and meet his "Swiss saviour".

'I didn't dare enlighten them.'

CHAPTER V

THE GREAT WHITE SHIPS...

F OR months that same letter had been lying on my desk. Each
time I returned to Geneva, after having visited the prison
camps, where the winter had been so hard, it was still there.

British Red Cross Society, London
September 7th, 1940

Dear Sirs: We have the honour to inform you that 36,000 parcels
have gone off today for Geneva. They are intended for British
prisoners of war in Germany. Please be so good as to inform us
without delay. . . .

A note was pinned to the letter on which the arrival of some of
the parcels was noted over a period dating from December 1940
to March 1941. Two thousand seven hundred parcels went from
Lisbon to Marseilles on board a Portuguese sailing vessel, and a
Swedish freighter took another 3000 to Genoa. That was all.

In six months 30,000 parcels had been lost, and all those sent since
by the British Red Cross had suffered the same fate. The prisoners
waited, and the parcels failed to arrive.

There was only one port in Europe still open: Lisbon. It was
there that the parcels sent from the United States, from Australia
and from New Zealand piled up. Even to get them that far
British ships had to run the gauntlet of submarines in the Atlantic.

The means of communication between Lisbon and Switzerland
were still more problematical. Spain had only just emerged from
three years of civil war. The country was disorganized and lacked
rolling stock. Only neutral freighters had a chance of touching in
at French or Italian ports. On board those small vessels there was
no possibility of supervision, and there was a great deal of pilfering.

The prisoners waited, but the parcels failed to arrive.

After having put in at Marseilles a Portuguese freighter took on board some heavy cases which the customs authorities passed after only a casual inspection. When the vessel arrived at Gibraltar three British officers, more dead than alive, crawled out of them. Berlin was furious at the trick and threatened to stop all neutral shipping.

Blockade.

Counter-blockade.

And the prisoners still waited.

'What can we do about it?'

'There's only one solution,' I said.

'And what's that?'

I knew that the plan I was about to propose was very daring, but all the projects of the Red Cross had at first seemed impossibly optimistic and impractical.

'Why not take the whole thing into our own hands, charter ships and let our own flag fly on the high seas? Switzerland owns her own ships. Why shouldn't the Red Cross have its own ships?'

'The German navy wouldn't allow it.'

'The British Admiralty wouldn't like it.'

A journey to Berlin secured the provisional agreement of the German naval authorities — provided the British Admiralty also agreed. Germany had no interest in stopping the supply of food-stuffs to a famished continent.

Obtaining London's agreement began to look more difficult. An exchange of telegrams produced no result.

'Very well,' I said. 'I must go to London myself.'

The pessimists tried to dissuade me.

'The designs of the Admiralty are impenetrable. Their reply has been unfavourable because military considerations are against the whole affair.'

In the International Committee of the Red Cross a timid voice made itself heard.

'Let us go together Herr Doktor.'

The voice belonged to a thin, frail and retiring elderly lady: Mlle Odier. She was always dressed in a dark blue costume which looked as though it were her old nursing uniform. Her voice sounded timid and hesitant but only on account of a serious throat operation. Her health was poor but her eyes sparkled with vitality, and there was, in fact, nothing timid or hesitant about her. The same fire and faith burned in her still. For anything connected with the Red Cross there was no limit to her courage and determination, but her appearance and her voice lent something truly pathetic to all she did.

'I am quite sure that we shall succeed in persuading the Admiralty,' she said confidently.

I don't know even now on what air field we landed by plane from Lisbon. The train which carried us to London travelled at night and there was a strict black-out everywhere, both in the villages and in the towns. The shapes of ruined buildings against the sky became more and more numerous as we rolled into London, and reminded us that a ceaseless air battle had been fought out for months in the skies above it.

Little blue lights seemed to dance a ballet in the London night. I compared the great activity of London, living constantly on the alert, with the heavy silence which reigned over Germany's towns, where at that time British air raids were still infrequent.

As our taxi drove up the Brompton Road I turned to my companion.

'At this hour the Frankfurterstrasse in Berlin is deserted.'

It sounded strange. I was probably the only traveller arriving in London who could say casually:

'The other day in Berlin. . . .'

But now I had to forget all I had seen in Germany. I had no right to say a word. And when I returned to Germany it would be the same with regard to my presence here.

It was seven o'clock when we arrived at the Admiralty.

'What is your business?' we were asked.

'The First Lord has been good enough to give us an appointment,' said Mlle Odier.

But the First Lord begged to be excused and sent us his private secretary, who was a giant of a fellow in naval uniform with fair hair and a slight stoop. In his blue eyes and in the lines of his face one could read a great tiredness, but he addressed us with such a charming smile that he won us over immediately. No doubt we had taken him away from important work, but from his attitude you would have thought that the only thing in the world which interested him was our business. His first words were to express Britain's thanks for our work.

'What you are doing for our prisoners is really splendid.'

Mlle Odier did the talking. It was moving to hear her describe the food situation in Europe and the misery of the occupied countries.

The officer listened attentively, and if he remembered that Europe was a besieged continent he said nothing, but something spoke eloquently. On the wall behind him between the clock and the chimney piece of this comfortable English room a red lamp began to flash, it was the air-raid warning: the Alert.

'Germany is crammed with prisoners,' said Mlle Odier. 'The prisoners which interest you in particular are not very numerous, but think of the others: the French and Belgians, the Dutch and the Poles. They are your allies and their plight is terrible. The winter which has just passed was bad enough, but the next one will be worse.'

The winking lamp replied:

'Every night bombs fall on London.'

Mlle Odier pleaded the cause of the hungry peoples. She quoted alarming figures concerning the infant mortality rate and the stunted growth of children. Poland had been starving for over a year. In a few months' time the martyrdom of Greece would begin.

And the red lamp retorted: 'We are experiencing the hardships of war too.'

I told him about my visits to the prisoner-of-war camps.

'It's not merely a question of food,' I pointed out. 'Clothing is wearing out and we must try to replace it. That means millions of tons to be transported.'

'Yes,' replied the secretary of the First Lord, 'I understand that quite well, but we are blockading Europe and Germany is blockading us. Why don't you use neutral ships?'

I told him of our experiences with the cargo boats plying between Lisbon and Genoa.

'Can't their hulls be painted white with a green stripe like hospital ships?'

'But those markings are reserved for hospital ships,' I objected. 'We want to transport food and clothing. We must think of something entirely new, something not provided for in the Geneva Convention.'

From outside came the sound of a muffled explosion. No one moved. When it was quiet again the British naval officer went on as though nothing had interrupted our conversation.

'Well, what is it exactly you propose?' he asked.

'We want to have our ships sailing on the high seas under the Red Cross flag in exactly the same way as stretcher bearers and ambulances with the red cross can move about freely on the battle field at agreed times. Our ships would be painted white and at night their red crosses would be illuminated. The International Committee of the Red Cross would take full responsibility for their cargoes. Their time-tables and their routes would be communicated in advance to both sides.'

The representative of the First Lord thought for a moment. I imagine he was weighing up all the objections to the proposal. After all, the International Committee of the Red Cross was a private organization. To regard its flag as being on the same footing as a national flag would be something unique in naval history. Could the indispensable 'navicerts' be granted to ships flying such a flag? The movement of our Red Cross ships on the high seas would raise a thousand complicated problems for the great and secret network of warships which patrolled the seas, kept an eye open for the enemy and engaged him at sight.

And then there would be other problems for us to resolve with other ministries and other authorities: the entry of ships bearing food and clothing into the ports of blockaded Europe would mean that a loophole was being opened in the blockade.

We greatly feared that all these obvious difficulties would lead to the rejection of our proposal. The winking red lamp did not allow us to forget that the 'Alert' was still on, and it seemed to say to us reproachfully:

'These men have a heavy task to perform. Is it reasonable to ask them to turn their attention to something which has nothing whatever to do with the immediate war effort?'

'What you are doing is admirable,' the Englishman murmured. And then he got up.

'Wait here a minute if you please.'

We sat there for half an hour. Thirty minutes of silent waiting. We were well aware of how much depended on the answer which must now come. It was the lives of thousands of prisoners. Later on urgent assistance could be brought in the same way to starving populations.

The door opened and we saw at once that the expression on the officer's face was frankly relieved and happy.

'I think you've won,' he said. 'His Lordship has no objection in principle to the carrying out of your plans.'

Several months later there were already a number of sizeable vessels flying the flag of the International Committee of the Red Cross sailing both in the Atlantic and the Mediterranean. They plied between Genoa and Lisbon, where stores of foodstuffs, clothing and medical supplies were unloaded from the United States, South America, Canada and New Zealand.

Our ships sailed openly over seas where all other vessels were extremely anxious to conceal their presence, where submarines lay in wait for their prey, where convoys turned away from the usual sea routes and camouflaged their navigation lights after dark. But at night the immense red crosses of our ships glowed out brightly over the sea.

The new maritime service created in this fashion found a tireless and energetic abettor in the person of Carl J. Burckhardt, a member of the International Committee of the Red Cross at the time. The President of the new organization was a Zürich business man, Herr

Fröhlich. Gradually all the difficulties which stood in the way, material, financial and technical, disappeared, and the scheme worked well.

The biggest difficulty was to secure the simultaneous agreement of London, Washington, Montreal, Berlin and Rome on the exact time at which any of our ships might put to sea. The timetable of sailing and the route to be taken by each ship was carefully arranged beforehand. Each captain knew that once he was at sea the least deviation from the agreed course could prove fatal.

At each port the unloading of the cargoes was closely controlled by a representative of the International Committee of the Red Cross, and the cargo itself was always accompanied by a responsible delegate of the Committee. In this way pilfering, damage in loading and unloading, misuse and so on were kept down to a minimum. We were now far beyond our heartbreaking disappointments with the little Portuguese and Swedish cargo boats.

Two big Belgian ships held up in Lisbon by the war and the blockade and counter-blockade became the *Caritas I* and *Caritas II* respectively. A third Red Cross ship bore the name of the great founder of the Red Cross, *Henri Dunant*. By 1944 they had shipped 400,000 tons of foodstuffs, 33 million parcels and 130,000 tons of medical supplies.

On land we still had to solve the problem of transport into Germany. In Genoa and in Marseilles our delegates engaged in ceaseless disputes with the military authorities over the use of available rolling stock. Everything passed through Switzerland, and in order to exempt that enormous movement of merchandise from customs duties 'free ports' were established at Biel, Vallorbe and Geneva.

'Come and see it,' said Henri Wasmer, the head of the Relief Committee, on one of my many visits to the Villa Moynier. 'I'll show you one of the most important transit depots in the world.'

He took me to the Palais des Expositions, which had been placed entirely at the disposal of the Red Cross. The vast hall of the main exhibition building was piled high with pyramids of cases and parcels. On one side goods trains arriving from France and Italy were unloaded, and on the other trains leaving for Germany were loaded.

'We sort out and distribute the stuff here according to the instructions of our delegation in Berlin,' said Wasmer. 'And the great thing is that in all this vast flow of goods from America to Germany the percentage of loss is negligible. At no time are the parcels out of our sight, and their final distribution is checked by an invoice which is returned to us.'

Five hundred workmen and 300 clerical employees were engaged in the work of the Relief Committee. The telephone bells were ringing constantly.

'Berlin calling. Marti here. Dossel Camp has run out of parcels. Batch number 2781 seems to have been held up somewhere. Will you check up?'

Over there our representative Dr. Roland Marti had covered the walls of his office in the Ballenstederstrasse, where our headquarters in Germany was established, with maps and graphs. Each camp was marked on the map with a little red cross. The least change in its complement was carefully noted. Constant touch with the representatives of the prisoners in the camps and with the O.K.W. allowed us to follow the history of the parcels up to their delivery to the smallest labour detachment.

The lorry carrying the parcels would pull up in some little village in Thuringia or Silesia. The representative of the prisoners would call his men together:

'Swift, Goodwin, Hartley. . . .'

And Swift would take his parcel back to the hut, well packed and bearing the bright label: 'American Red Cross Parcel.'

'Here you are, boys. Here's another one.'

Men like Swift, with parcels opened on their knees, can have had no idea of how much persistent effort, how many difficulties surmounted, how many obstacles overcome, they represented.

And as they unpacked them there appeared a series of smaller packets containing sugar, flour, tea, butter, meat, biscuits and a welcome packet of cigarettes.

Having enjoyed that parcel Swift and his friends could look forward confidently to the receipt of another one. Whether the interval was long or relatively short, there was always the next parcel to be counted on.

In order to carry it to him through a besieged continent, blockaded and impenetrable, we had to open the gateways of the ocean.

CHAPTER VI

UNHAPPY ARCADIA

FROM my bungalow at Kavaklidere I had a fine view over the gardens sprinkled with red roofs which made up the town of Ankara.

On the hill opposite were a few low-built houses and military ramparts which were all that was left of the ancient city of Ankara, to which Kemel Attaturk had given a rebirth twenty years before. His work now lay spread out before me in a valley of roses. The architecture of the town was monotonous, and each garden looked exactly like the other. In the distance beyond stretched a grey and ochreous plain covered with sand and withered grass.

The diplomatic residences were the most beautiful buildings in the town, and I had for my neighbours Russians, French, Americans and Finns. Ankara had gradually become one of the few capitals in the world where the foreign diplomats of all countries were still assembled. Friends and foes could still be met with there in the two main restaurants, in the Ankara Palace, and to an even greater extent at Karpisch's, the famous Russian restaurateur.

In September 1941 war had flared up again in the east and a line of fire cut through the whole of Eastern Europe from the Gulf of Finland to the Black Sea. I had come to Turkey to see if we could establish an office for the exchange of information concerning German and Russian prisoners which would operate more easily than in Geneva. But the negotiations were dragging and there seemed little prospect of their ever coming to anything.

One morning the messenger who puffed and blowed so much when he climbed the hill to bring me the evasive replies I invariably received from Berlin and Moscow, produced a telegram instead. It raised a new problem and gave me quite a different source of anxiety. Our delegate Brunel, who was in Athens, had sent an S.O.S.

'Food situation in Greece extremely grave. Mortality increased sixfold in last two months. Catastrophe inevitable unless outside help arrives quickly.'

Brunel rightly thought that it would be easier and quicker to send foodstuffs through Turkey than by any other route. But had he reckoned with the proverbial slowness of Near Eastern negotiations?

I went at once with his telegram to my friend Raphael Raphael, the Greek Ambassador, whose residence was not far away.

'Read this,' I said simply and handed him the telegram.

'Yes, I know,' he replied sadly. 'For two months now I've been wrestling with the Turks, the British and the Americans in order to get flour, a ship to transport it in and the necessary navigation permits. But the British are reserved and the Turks claim that the Germans are making all the difficulties.'

'Would you like us to take further steps together?'

As though seized with a sudden hope Raphael exclaimed:

'I think you've come just at the right moment. Your intervention might be decisive.'

From that time on we were indefatigable. In conference after conference I brought all my influence as the delegate of the International Red Cross to bear and I called on the assistance of everyone who could hasten or facilitate our success. Rana Tarhan, a prominent Turk, gave me his full support. He was President of the Red Crescent Society, which stood for the same high ideal under the emblem of Islam as did the Red Cross in Christian countries.

The Turks were slow to arrive at a decision. They maintained a very prudent reserve towards all the belligerent countries, whose diplomatists incidentally were competing with all their skill and adroitness to obtain the chromium of Anatolia.

When finally the Turks had guaranteed the purchase of the foodstuffs and decided which ship should transport them we had to obtain the consent of the two adversaries, one of whom occupied the country whilst the other inexorably blockaded it.

Mr. Jordan, the commercial attaché of the British Embassy, was all in favour of relieving the sufferings of women and children, but he insisted that men should not benefit.

'You really must see that His Majesty's Government can never agree to feed factory workers in Greece who are working for the enemy. . . .'

'Yes, of course, I understand that, but think of the refugees in Thrace who have been driven from their homes and are now completely without resources.'

And then the Germans demanded the right to control the cargo. They were afraid that some secret message might be sent through a neutral ship.

My reply to both was that the Red Cross would take full responsibility. A responsible delegate of the International Committee would supervise everything and make quite certain that none of the food parcels came into any other hands than those it was intended for.

It needed a great deal of patience to reconcile all these contradictory demands. Every proposition made by one side immediately aroused the suspicion of the other. We had to meet and overcome the outspoken objections and to divine those which were not expressed. It often happened that I left the German ambassador, von Papen, after a discussion and went straight to the British Embassy to hold further discussions, or crossed the road a dozen times backward and forwards from the Greek Embassy to the Italian Embassy, which almost faced each other, silent and hostile, on opposite sides of the street. And even when the agreement of an Ambassador had been secured we had to wait until his government confirmed it.

At last the great day arrived when agreement was obtained on all sides. The 'navicerts' were signed, the foodstuffs loaded on to a cargo-boat, the *Kurtulus*, and I went off to Istanbul to see it put out to sea.

Amidst the confusion of cargo boats and sailing ships which had been immobilized in port for months by the war I immediately spotted the glistening white hull of the *Kurtulus*, on whose sides the last touches were being given to the brilliant red crescents which took the place of the red cross. Before long its luminous wake disappeared in the blue haze of the Golden Horn.

The telegram I sent to Geneva to report the departure of the

Kurtulus crossed a telegram which Geneva had sent to me instructing me to leave Ankara for Greece. Brunel, it appeared, was over-whelmed with work, and in that famished country, which the invaders were abandoning to its fate, our task was becoming more and more difficult every day.

My friend the Greek Ambassador did not conceal his lively pleasure when he heard that I was to go to Greece.

'Take the whole affair into your own hands,' he advised. 'When you have seen the terrible sufferings of our people with your own eyes you will be still better in a position to defend our cause. The ship which has just left will help us to hold out for a few weeks longer. But after that. . . .'

I had to go to the Germans to ask for permission to enter Greece. Von Papen gave it to me without any difficulty and even proposed that I should go to Athens by plane: the Junkers plane which maintained the service between Ankara and Kifissia would save me two weeks and a very tedious journey by train.

The journey by air via Sofia and Salonika was not without its excitements. Hardly had we crossed the Bulgarian frontier than we ran into a thick fog which covered the whole countryside. It was impossible to find a way out of it or to see where we were going. The plane increased its height, descended again and flew round. A sudden break in the thick mantle of fog showed us a surface of water.

'Impossible to find Sofia in this,' the pilot observed calmly. We shall have to come down on the water. Even without floats we ought to be able to surface all right. The plane will keep afloat for twenty minutes.'

He switched off the petrol and the engine cut out. Down we went in a glide towards the water. Clinging to our seats we awaited the inevitable shock.

Suddenly almost level with us a red light became visible through the fog, and then a green light on a pylon.

'The air field,' we all shouted in unison.

Another second or two and we should have crashed by a million to one chance right on the airfield of Salonika which we had been trying to find for over an hour.

The pilot started up the engine with a roar, the plane gained height and a little later we made a perfect landing. We waited for the fog to disappear completely and then started off on the next stage of our journey, which was accomplished without incident in a radiant Attic sun and under a perfect blue sky.

The Island of Euboea, Mount Hymettus, the Parthenon. . . .

I soon forgot those famous names to devote my thoughts to a people now dying of hunger amidst its classic temples, its colonnades and its eternal marbles.

I took out Brunel's telegram and re-read it: 'Catastrophe inevitable unless outside help. . . .'

And whilst the shadow of the Junkers plane swept over the glistening waters of the Bay of Phalerum I thought I saw the flag of distress flying from the Acropolis.

The small blue and white Greek flag hoisted on one of the corners of the sacred hill was hardly distinguishable. Much higher, flying from a huge mast, was the great red flag with the white circle and the black Hakenkreuz of Hitler's Third Reich. Lower down the tricolour Italian flag hung over the classic façade of the Parthenon.

But only the Greek flag looked at home in the great bare court-yard with its mutilated statues. The invaders had not dared to strike it and since the first day of the invasion the Greeks had refused to remove it. There it flew, torn and tattered in the wind, a symbol of their pride and their distress.

'All these people are suffering terribly,' Brunel told me in the car on the drive to the centre of Athens. 'The Greeks have always been poor. They have never found much to live on in their arid soil. All their food came to them by sea and now the sea is closed and nothing more comes into the country. And nothing is being carried on the one railway line from Salonika, which is still choked with military traffic. Formerly there was at least plenty of oil for cooking purposes, but now the olives, like the vines, are withering because of the lack of chemicals to keep down the parasites.

'Look at those half-starved people and their wretched children who go around begging or looking for something to steal. Somehow they're managing to exist, chiefly on roots. The more fortunate of them may get a little fish, a few grains of maize, a handful of dried raisins.'

In the streets were walking spectres with the light of fever in their eyes. Here and there old men, and sometimes young ones, sat on the pavement leaning back against the wall. Their lips were moving as though in prayer, but no sound came. They stretched out their hands for alms and then let them fall back weakly. They would sit in the same place for days. And then one morning one or the other of them would cease to move at all. Pedestrians passed backwards and forwards before them without paying them the least attention. Each one asking himself when his own turn would come. Hearts grow hard in their own misery.

'Refugees from Thrace,' said Brunel. 'After the Bulgarian occupation about a million of them arrived, and that exodus very greatly worsened the situation. Thrace always provided about one-third of all the Greek wheat harvest, which, in any case, was enough to feed only about half the population of Athens, which has greatly increased since the war. The refugees can't go out into the surrounding countryside to get hold of a few vegetables because the surroundings of Athens consist entirely of pine forests, sand and rock.'

It did not take me long to find out that there was no exaggeration in the sinister picture which had been presented to me. Every morning when I left my rooms in Herodotus Street to go to the offices of the Red Cross Delegation I came across two or three corpses on the way. They were the unknown casualties of everyday life in Athens. No one would come forward to identify them. No one would claim their bodies for burial. Their bodies had, in fact, been dragged to the spot, far away from their own hovels, by their families, who wanted to keep their food cards for a few precious days.

And yet the cards themselves were becoming almost useless, because there was so very little left to distribute. The time came when for a whole month the only thing obtainable with them was about half a pound of salt and a little soap.

The situation was the same in the country and at the coastal ports. There were no more cattle and no milk for the children. No nets and no hooks, no petrol and no fishing boats. Many houses had been destroyed, and nothing was being reconditioned or rebuilt because of a shortage of materials and labour.

There was no more seed corn, no more fertilizers, no more medicaments. In the malarial districts of Macedonia and Thessaly there were no longer any chemicals to spray on the ponds and prevent the emergence of the dreaded anopheles mosquito. Malaria was spreading and there was no quinine. The workers engaged in draining the marshes had themselves been decimated by the scourge.

Brunel had not exaggerated: 'Catastrophe inevitable unless outside help. . . .'

The cargo of the *Kurtulus* allowed us to distribute half a million basins of soup over a period of two months.

In Athens the scene was one of distress and depression. Everywhere in the populous quarters of the town there were long queues of silent people waiting for the distribution of the soup. Huge boilers, holding either 80 or 160 quarts, had been set up in improvised kitchens. On presenting their food cards these people received a plate of hot soup each, to keep them going. The Athens hospitals were provided with condensed milk, bandages and medical necessities. Special centres were opened for the children.

'The mortality rate has dropped by 60 per cent,' the municipality of Athens announced after five weeks.

But over and above the tangible misery, easy to observe, which both the German occupants and the British Ministry of Economic Warfare allowed us to combat, there was another great volume of distress which we could not forget: that of the prisoners of war.

They could not come to us for help; we had to go to them. Far away in the camps of Tatoi, Thebes, Salonika and Larissa, their mouths were stopped, and their appeals came to us only through the intermediary of courageous individuals who broke through the wall of terror and suspicion erected around the camps by the

Gestapo and the Questura, just as in the days of the Spanish civil war we had learnt about the happenings in Santa Ursula.

And how many Greeks there were who had been arrested by the authorities of the three occupying powers, Germany, Italy and Bulgaria! Hostages seized indiscriminately after some action of the Greek resistance, peasants who had resisted the requisitioning, pedestrians who had been caught on the streets after curfew. The Averoff prison in Athens was full of partisans, workers and intellectuals. There were even a number of foreign prisoners, British in particular, former prisoners of war who had escaped and joined the Resistance movement only to be recaptured by the occupation forces.

Brunel's assistant Gredinger, a Swiss business man who had been in charge of the Nestlé works in Athens for many years, now devoted almost all his time to assisting them. His fluent knowledge of Greek permitted him to open many doors which would have remained closed to us.

He was guided to prisons and prison camps, whose existence was sometimes unknown to us, by a Greek Red Cross nurse, Madame Zafari, who carried out a thankless task with never-flagging enthusiasm. She was the wife of a banker in Athens and therefore a member of the Greek *haute bourgeoisie*, but in connection with her work to help the prisoners locked away in secret prisons she would say gratefully: 'The communists are my best friends.' Tirelessly, using every possible means of transport, German or Italian lorries, motor buses and peasant carts, she would scour the remotest provinces to collect reports of her oppressed compatriots.

Gradually an atmosphere developed around the work of our delegation which reminded me strongly of that which had existed four years before in Spain. There was no civil war in Greece, but the arbitrary and repressive measures of the occupying powers were no less cruel: unexplained internments, deportations, torture. For us the same problem arose each time: find the whereabouts of the missing person.

In this task we had no official standing whatever. Only the initiative of a delegate plus good luck and, above all, persistence, could break down the resistance of a police official, the governor of a prison or the commandant of a concentration camp.

'You have no idea what tricks I have to get up to before I can gain access to the camps,' Gredinger said to me one day. 'I arrive unexpectedly with tins of corned beef, bundles of old clothes and some Red Cross parcels. I leave a tin on the desk of each of the officials whose job it is to prevent my getting in, but there's enough left for a distribution once I manage to get inside.'

'Oh, indeed, I have a very good idea, my dear fellow,' I replied. 'I've done that sort of thing too often myself.'

A few days later Gredinger approached me with a confidential air.

'Tell me, Doctor,' he said. 'Have you ever heard of a certain Captain Savage?'

'Do you mean Captain Alistair Savage of the Second Queen's Royal Regiment? In that case, I most certainly have. His name is in people's mouths from London to Calcutta. The British Red Cross has inquired about him in Geneva and all the delegates in the Middle East have been questioned.'

'That's the man. Six months ago I came across traces of him and then lost them again. He was taken prisoner in Crete after the fantastic fighting in which every creek and every rock was bitterly disputed. He was wounded in the head and the shoulder, and looked after at the Kotinia hospital here; then he escaped. Naturally he joined the Resistance movement and the Italians recaptured him and put him in the Averoff Prison. There they tried to make him talk. You know what that means. But he's a tough fellow and they couldn't get him to open his mouth. He held out under the torture without saying a word.'

'How did you find that out?'

Gredinger smiled disarmingly.

'I have been able to let him have a Red Cross parcel from time to time, thanks to the good offices of a caribinier, a nice fellow who's rather partial to a packet of cigarettes.'

'And you say that Savage has now disappeared again?'

'That's it, Doctor. One fine day he was taken out of prison and sent off to an unknown destination. That is to say he's being held incommunicado in some camp or prison. For weeks I've been trying to find out where he's held and now I think I know.'

'Where?'

Gredinger made a significant grimace.

'Larissa camp.'

'Right, let's go there together tomorrow.'

'Exactly. Madame Zafari will go with us and I think we shall get inside without much difficulty. I'm glad you're going to come along because I've got a letter from his mother and I'd rather like you to give it to him.'

Larissa is about 125 miles from Athens. A lorry went ahead of us carrying foodstuffs and clothing for the prisoners.

After Levadia the road climbs high into the mountains through a rocky country with patches of pines and plane trees. From the Pournakari Pass there is a view over the Bay of Lamia and the Atalante Canal. The wooded coastline of Euboia and the tranquil sea stretched out before us would have made us forget all about the war for a while but for the fact that from time to time along the road emaciated women and children stretched out imploring hands to us for help as we passed.

Leaving the famous Pass of Thermopylae on our right we descended into the plain of Spercheios. At the other end were the terraced houses of Lamia with its thermal wells and its baths to remind the beholder of the distant times of Turkish occupation. But suddenly a sharp command reminded us of a very different invader.

'Halt! Papers.'

The stop was very short and then we drove on over the bare hills of Othrys, up and down over the last foothills of the range, coming out into the vast golden plain of Thessaly, and reaching Larissa in the afternoon.

The town was half destroyed. Suffering a double blow, many of its houses were destroyed in the earthquake of March 1st, 1941, and the next day it was made the target of hostile bombers.

The camp was two or three miles from the town, cut off from the dusty barren countryside by a double row of barbed wire.

'There are only civil internees here,' the officer in charge of the guard sought to assure us. 'Ordinary criminals. The Red Cross Convention authorizes you to visit only prisoners of war.'

Gredinger pretended to be very perplexed at this information.

'Do you really mean, Monsieur, that we have made this long journey for nothing, and that we must now go back without having unloaded our lorry?'

No, the officer didn't really mean that and he took counsel with the Italian doctor who was with him. In the end we were allowed in to distribute our consignment. First we had to see the prisoners, of course, before we could apportion the things justly.

So there we were, allowed to visit a camp which was protected by no kind of Convention, and into which no stranger was supposed to penetrate. A thousand prisoners were cut off from the world in this camp, but at least we were able to see them, make a note of their names and take details of the most alarming cases in order to be able to raise them later with the occupation authorities.

An Italian doctor led us to the camp hospital. About thirty malarial and tubercular patients were in such a state that it was obvious that their lives could be saved only by speedy transfer to a proper hospital or sanatorium. When I pointed this out the Italian doctor flung up his arms.

'But who's going to pay for it?' he asked.

In the last room we visited we found a mother and her daughter. They were the only two female prisoners in Larissa. They were Egyptians who had been arrested in Volo. Why? No one seemed to know. No one had bothered about their fate because there was no Egyptian Consulate in Greece.

Sixty men were held in close quarters in a near-by hut. Their only crime was that they happened to have been born in Crete. They had been waiting for three months for permission to return home.

On a third hut was a big notice, 'Quarantine'. The men in it were kept at about ten paces from us by guards with fixed bayonets.

'Don't go near them,' an Italian advised. 'They've all got the itch.'

And according to the same man we were not allowed to go near a hut marked 'Convicted' in which there were 200 to 300 men condemned for various offences: political espionage and ordinary criminal offences. They were an extraordinary mixture of thieves, anarchists and black-market operators. Their conditions were extremely bad and they were all dirty and in rags. The weather was already cold and there was no glass in the windows of the hut.

In the next hut were 'intellectuals'. No sooner had we entered than we were surrounded with a jostling crowd of them. There were lawyers, doctors, journalists and heaven knows what other professions represented. They were all in a parlous condition, emaciated, unshaven, their hair untrimmed, and dressed in rags. Most of them were suspected of being in touch with the enemy. They all spoke at once in great excitement. Each man attempted to explain his own case and to convince us of his complete innocence. Many of them begged for clothing and blankets. All of them were without news of their families.

In this immense confusion I noticed a group of men at the far end of the hut who had not come forward. They remained seated on their beds. From their calm bearing and from their physical type I realized at once that they must be English, but I was surprised to see them dressed in civilian clothing, shorts and torn shirts. I went up to them and they explained that they were all recaptured prisoners of war. As they had obtained civilian clothing after their escape they were now treated as *franc-tireurs*. They had all been condemned by Italian courts to sentences ranging between four and forty years imprisonment.

I took up their case with the Italians and succeeded in obtaining permission for them to wear British uniforms which the British Red Cross Society had sent to our delegate in Greece via Geneva. Their obvious pleasure at the idea of new uniforms was a deep satisfaction to us. I took advantage of the general good spirits to whisper to one of them:

'Have you any news of Captain Savage?'

'Yes, he was here about a fortnight ago.'

He nudged me.

'Look! In that hole.'

Through the window of the hut I saw a hole in the ground just large enough for a man to turn round in.

'We can hear him groaning every time they take him back after a new beating,' the Englishman whispered. 'He's being driven mad. And now he's caught malaria. He ought to be in hospital.'

I then went straight up to the Italian officer who was accompanying us.

'Where is Captain Savage?' I asked point blank.

His embarrassed air at this direct question showed me clearly that there was something disagreeable in connection with Savage's fate. Taken by surprise by the question he declared that Savage was in hospital.

'I want to see him,' I said firmly. 'I have a letter for him from his mother which has already been censored by the Questura.'

The Italian found it impossible to refuse and he agreed to take me to see Savage when the visit to the camp was over.

Our inspection was almost concluded when I noticed another hut to which we had not been taken.

'What's in there?' I asked.

The officer looked casual.

'Only communists,' he replied.

I went inside and I was immediately struck by the cleanliness and order which prevailed. The contrast with the dirt and confusion which reigned in all the other huts was striking. There were more men in this hut, but they remained drawn up in a line and quite silent. They all looked at us, but their faces remained expressionless. As no one made any attempt to speak or come forward I raised my voice.

'Is there anyone here who speaks French or English?'

Two men then came forward and I questioned one of them in French.

'Have you any complaints or any requests to make?'

The man turned towards his comrades, thought for a moment and then said slowly:

'No, we have no complaints to make, but we have one request. We want to be treated like everyone else here. Every time anything goes wrong in the camp we get the blame. And that is quite unjust. The officer will tell you that we always obey orders, and ours is the only hut in the camp with any discipline. We should be much obliged to you if you could persuade them to stop punishing us for anonymous offences.'

All this was said very calmly and the silence which reigned in the hut was impressive. I looked at the Italian officer and he shrugged his shoulders impatiently.

It is always a difficult matter to intervene in disciplinary matters. Our authorization covers inspection and relief, no more. But I could at least assure them that as far as our task was concerned they would not be treated unjustly.

'We have brought food and clothing with us,' I said, 'and I will see to it in person that you and your comrades receive a fair share.'

When the distribution was at an end we left the camp for Larissa to visit the hospital there. It was an old and rather dilapidated building guarded by sentries. After long negotiations with the officer in charge of the guard a carabinier led us to the room shared by Captain Savage with another prisoner.

He was sitting on his bed when we entered. He was terribly thin and his face was pale and drawn; his lips were dry and cracked and his eyes had sunk back into their sockets. When we came in he looked at us with indifference.

When I told him who I was he showed no interest whatever. I pointed to my Red Cross armlet and to a paper with his name on it, but nothing seemed to affect him, except that when he read the card and saw the name of his regiment, the 2nd Queen's Royal Regiment, I thought I detected a flicker of life in his eyes. Had he made a despairing effort to communicate his distress to me? Or did he want to make me understand that I should not question him? The Italian who had accompanied me was still at my side. I had to be cautious.

Even when I gave him the letter from his mother there was no reaction. I showed him the writing so that he might recognize it and I put it into his hand but he let it drop on to the bed without making any attempt to read it.

'Would you like to write a few words to your mother so that she will know at least that you are alive?' I asked.

There was not the slightest sign of understanding in his fixed look. If the man were simulating madness in order to escape the questioning of his persecutors then his self-control was incredible. For half an hour I remained with him at the foot of his bed without being able to secure the message which he was either unable or unwilling to give.

I turned to the Italian.

'Will you please call the chief doctor.'

My Italian colleague was not long in coming. I introduced myself. When he looked at Savage his face bore a worried look. I took him to one side.

'This man is very ill,' I said. 'Traces of oedema, probable uraemia and he seems mentally unhinged. He shouldn't be here at all. He must be taken to a hospital where he can receive the treatment his case requires.'

The Italian made a gesture of helplessness.

'I quite agree with you,' he said, 'but it doesn't depend on me. You must raise the question in Athens.'

The day after my return, I went to see the Italian Minister, Ghigi, with whom I had one or two matters to discuss; the affair of Captain Savage was one which was particularly close to my heart and I was now well equipped to plead his cause.

'Savage!' exclaimed the Italian Minister, 'but he can no longer be considered as a prisoner of war. You don't realize that he has been sentenced to a thirty-year term as a *franc-tireur.*'

'Yes I do,' I replied, 'but the treatment now being accorded to him and the state I found him in when I visited the hospital of Larissa suggests that he won't live to serve his thirty-year sentence. It would be most regrettable if anything of that sort were to happen to a British officer.'

'What do you want me to do?'

'The only way to cure him now would be to put him into the

care of his own people, British medical men who have been captured and are now in your hands. The best thing to do would be to send him to Italy.'

Ghigi looked thoughtful. Could he decide the matter on his own? He would probably have to discuss the affair at great length with the Questura.

We began to talk of other matters, but I was thinking all the time of the man who was being burnt up by fever in his bed in that remote hospital in Larissa. Perhaps it was that which inspired the sudden gesture with which I ended our interview.

We smoked whilst we talked and I had noticed the envious eye the Italian Minister cast on my Dunhill lighter. Suddenly the idea came to offer it to him.

After a very little diplomatic hesitation he accepted the gift joyfully. When I left him I said:

'Whenever you use it, Monsieur, please think of Captain Savage.'

A few weeks later I heard that Savage had been brought back to Athens to the prison hospital of Averoff and that he was gradually recovering.

He had been saved from Larissa, where I am quite sure he would have died, but that was not the end of his tribulations. He was transferred to Italy, as I had requested, and taken to the Carcere Giudiziare in Bari, and from there to the Instituto Penale in Aquila where at long last he was with his compatriots.

One day Geneva received a reassuring message from him for his mother: 'Send fifty pounds through the International Red Cross. Quite well but need new clothing. Don't forget a leather waistcoat and some breakfast food.'

From then on the delegates of the International Committee of the Red Cross followed his movements and we were in touch with him when he was finally liberated from the German camp, Oflag 79.

I don't think Captain Savage of the 2nd Queen's Royal Regiment realizes that he owes his life in all probability to a Dunhill lighter. What, exactly, did that short flicker in his eyes in Larissa hospital mean?

Athens still suffered terribly, but she lived on. During the terrible winter of 1941 we were able to distribute 800,000 bowls of soup. In addition we had 450 feeding centres for 100,000 children over seven, and 130 nursery centres for 74,000 infants.

The *Kurtulus* had already made five voyages between Istanbul and Piraeus, and it made its sixth in January 1942.

One morning Brunel came into my office greatly upset. The *Kurtulus* had suffered shipwreck in the Dardanelles and gone down with its precious cargo.

An S.O.S. went off to Ankara at once and the Turkish Red Crescent Society fitted out a new ship, the *Dumlupinar*. We managed to keep up the soup kitchens in February and March, but for weeks there was no bread.

The means at our disposal for keeping up the work were very limited. We never had more than enough to last us two or at the utmost three weeks. A cargo of 5000 tons kept us going for no more than ten days. And even then there was only about half a pound a day for 12,000 or 15,000 hungry mouths. And can a man be rightly regarded as nourished when all he has from one day's end to the other is a bowl of vegetable soup?

Happily the International Committee in Geneva had gone elsewhere to get us further supplies and the Swedish Red Cross sent us the 5000-ton ship *Hallaren* loaded with flour. Switzerland sent us tins of condensed milk. Italy sent us some corned beef and Germany sent us a few wagonloads of potatoes.

Then another Swedish ship, the *Sturebog*, was placed at our disposal in the Mediterranean to bring us British wheat stored in Egypt.

It was high time. We had got through the spring of 1942, but the preceding winter had sadly depleted our resources whilst the coming summer promised only a very poor harvest. On the black market — which existed in Athens as it existed everywhere — the prices of the sparse quantities of foodstuffs obtained by trafficking with the occupying forces went up to fantastic heights. A loaf of bread cost several hundred drachmas and a little oil or sugar several thousand.

Suddenly the news spread round Athens like wildfire: the *Sturebog* is berthing. Bread is coming!

It was true. The flour arrived and we had bread for three weeks.

The joy at the news brought people flocking to Piraeus. The police had all they could do to clear the quays of the milling crowds and to drive off the numerous boats which harassed the *Sturebog*, their occupants offering to do the most fantastic deals: a Tanagra statuette for a tin of corned beef, for example.

The winches began to creak and rattle over the holds, and the crowds fell silent. All that could be heard was the rattle of chains as the grapples were lowered into the hold. Followed by thousands of eager eyes they rose again swinging sacks of flour in the air against the blue sky.

I had gone down to Piraeus with Gredinger to meet the young Swiss who represented the International Committee on board. He was a big fellow in a green shirt and shorts, wearing a Red Cross armlet. I spotted him leaning against the deck-house watching with obvious emotion the scene which unrolled before his eyes for the first time.

'Hallo, Heider!'

'Dr. Junod? Bonjour.'

He invited me with a sweeping gesture to come on board and I made my way towards the gangway where the German sentry recalled me to reality.

'Pass, please.'

Gredinger had thought of everything and he produced our papers and a little later we were in the Captain's cabin with Heider. The Captain was a real sea-faring man, delighted to welcome us, but not so pleased at the presence of a German official who had attached himself to us.

Heider was anxious to land, but that was strictly forbidden. That was understandable enough. The *Sturebog* was to leave when its cargo was discharged, within a few hours, and the Germans were not willing for more people to see the position in Greece than was absolutely necessary.

Gredinger was anxious to know when we could expect the next cargo.

'We shall be back again in a month,' declared Heider with youthful enthusiasm, and the Swedish Captain nodded his head gravely above his cigar to confirm it.

But as we were going down the gangway afterwards I shouted back:

'Take good care at sea. Your red cross should protect you, but you never know what disagreeable adventures might happen. Keep your eyes open.'

What presentiment was it that made me shout that warning? For three weeks we impatiently awaited news that the *Sturebog* had arrived back safely in Alexandria. Geneva inquired vainly after her whereabouts in London, Rome, Berlin and Ankara. The *Sturebog* was lost at sea and we began to think we should never learn anything about her fate.

Then one morning on the coast of Palestine two Bedouins going along the shore found a body half buried in the sand. They retrieved it and then discovered that the man was alive. A few vestiges of pyjamas were still on the emaciated body. The man was little more than a skeleton but he was breathing faintly. They stopped a British lorry on the coastal road and the unfortunate man was taken to hospital in Haifa.

He was the sole survivor of the *Sturebog*, a Portuguese sailor. Gradually he recovered and after a week he was able to tell his tale.

The day after the departure of the *Sturebog* from Piraeus two Italian planes flew overhead. They flew round in circles and had plenty of time to observe the huge red crosses painted on the ship's white side. Nevertheless they dropped a bomb which cut the *Sturebog* in half.

'The ship went down in a few minutes,' said the Portuguese. 'Fortunately a life-raft on the deck released itself automatically, and nineteen of us — those who were sleeping on deck — managed to crawl on to it. All the others in the cabins, including the young Swiss Red Cross man who was with us, had not time even to realize what had happened.

'The Captain and I were the only ones who even had pyjamas on. All the others had just tumbled naked out of their hammocks. They were naked under the broiling sun, and hadn't a stitch to cover themselves. Faint with heat they plunged into the sea and remained in the water for hours, but when they crawled out again their state was worse than ever because their burnt bodies could no longer stand any sun at all.

'We knew that the wind would carry us to land. With careful rationing we had enough to eat and drink, but we could do nothing to protect ourselves against the cursed sun. Those who had bathed in the sea had blisters all over their bodies and the salt ate into their wounds. On the third day they were burnt to the bone and began to die one by one.

'At the end of the first week there were only nine of us left alive on the raft. At the end of the second week there were only three.'

'How long were you on that raft altogether?'

'Nineteen days. The Captain died last. The day before I caught a glimpse of land, a thin line on the horizon. When the raft drifted near enough I plunged into the water and swam ashore.'

With the sinking of the *Sturebog* our last hope of getting any flour was gone. Once again our stocks were depleted and our stores empty. We had to find some new means of assistance, some different system of getting food.

Geneva busied itself with our plight and repeated its *démarches* in London and Washington. Stockholm willingly agreed to supply ships, but in order to be able to sail them outside Scandinavian waters it was necessary to obtain German permission to waive the condition that half the Swedish mercantile marine should always remain within the Skaggerak. Made uneasy by the growing volume of goods which managed to break through the blockade, the Ministry of Economic Warfare hesitated for a long time before giving its agreement, and our President Carl Burckhardt had to go to London in person to try to arrange matters. A commission was organized to meet in Stockholm. It all took time, and in the meantime nothing tangible happened to allay our anxiety.

More than ever before Brunel's first warning was coming true: 'Catastrophe inevitable unless outside help. . . .'

How could we make those men whose task it was to wage ruthless warfare sympathize with our anxieties? How could we make them realize the magnitude and the urgency of the tragedy which was developing before our eyes? How could we make them *see* those men and women who were weaker than children, those children whose arms and legs were nothing but skin and bone!

I was about to leave for Geneva, and was strapping up my cases when a young woman was announced. It was Amelita Lycouresos, a Greek nurse who was in charge of the distribution of milk for the infants.

On my table she placed two green files. There were no reports inside but a hundred photos, each complete with exact details. The camera had been at work in the children's homes, in the distribution centres and in the hospitals, and the result was a series of pathetic pictures of small stunted and deformed bodies of children it was difficult to believe were still alive.

'Here you are, Doctor,' she said. 'Here's the best proof you can possibly have. Take them with you to Switzerland. Tell the people there that every day in Athens and everywhere else in Greece, one can find thousands and thousands of children in a similar plight. Unless they do something for us before next winter sets in there won't be anyone left alive in my country.'

At the mixed commission assembled in Geneva of members of the International Committee of the Red Cross and of the National Red Cross Societies horrified faces bent over the photos I had brought with me. The diplomats were shown them too.

Soon afterwards the Swedish Minister informed us that the steps taken by the Swedish Government and the Swedish Red Cross Society were about to bear fruit.

'Leave for Berlin and Stockholm,' said Carl Burckhardt.

At Berlin after a short conference with the representatives of the German Navy and of the Swedish Legation it was agreed that nine Swedish vessels with a total capacity of 50,000 tons should be permitted to leave Swedish waters.

In Stockholm the British and United States Ministers were present in person at a conference at the Swedish Ministry for Foreign Affairs.

The need for systematic relief for Greece had at last been recognized and the volume was generously fixed at 15,000 tons of wheat monthly, which would permit us to distribute about half a pound of bread to 2½ million Greeks per day, and in addition about 200,000 pounds of dried milk would suffice to save the lives of 100,000 new-born babies.

Those who held the keys of the blockade did not hesitate now to show themselves generous. They had seen the photos of the children of Athens.

In the interior of Arcadia there is a little village named Issari which clings to the side of the mountain which overshadows Megalopolis. Deprived of bread and oil its inhabitants had managed to keep alive for a year eating roots, leaves and acorns.

At the beginning of autumn the village schoolteacher wrote to us:

For three weeks now, or even longer, the people in my village keep asking the same question: 'Do you know if the flour has arrived?' and I have to answer 'I don't know'. Anxiety is now at its height and it is reflected in the pale and drawn faces all around. And then at last we heard that a lorry had arrived at Megalopolis. Immediately all eyes lit up and people even seemed to walk more freely. A young man climbed up into the belfry of the church and set the bell ringing. The half-starving village crier, dressed in rags and with bare feet, ran through the streets of the village shouting: 'Tomorrow, Wednesday, everyone should assemble before the church of St. Nicholas for the distribution of food.'

Deep emotion spread through the village and the women crossed themselves and prayed ardently for those venerated people who were working to save thousands of human beings from a most dreadful death. Many people passed the night which marked the end of the famine in prayer.

At last the day came. All the inhabitants flocked towards the church of St. Nicholas. Men, women and children emerged from their holes and one might have thought an army of skeletons was on the march. Soon the square in front of the church was full to overflowing with a fantastic crowd of scarecrows who could hardly stand on their feet. Many of them dragged themselves as far as they could and then sank down on the grass from where they could see the bend in the road round which the saving lorry must come. But the certainty of being saved in the nick of time restored a little animation to their exhausted bodies. They all felt a need to talk, to tell each other how they had managed to survive, by what miracle they were still in the land of the living.

A number of children managed to climb trees and rocks in order to be the first to see the little cloud of dust which would herald the coming of the precious lorry.

At about ten o'clock a great sigh told us that they had seen something. Men and women went down on their knees, their hands crossed over their breasts, and from their lips rose the hymn of Christ arisen. And in the silence that followed the end of the hymn a child's voice sobbed out:

'There they are! There they are!'

CHAPTER VII

FORTRESS AND PRISON

T HE 'Swiss Air' plane left Zürich early in the morning in the direction of Stuttgart and Berlin. It was my fourth or fifth journey into Germany since the beginning of the war. With me I carried the Swiss diplomatic mail, which our Political Department had requested me to take to our Legation in Berlin.

Almost all the passengers were Germans: diplomats or business men returning from various missions. One or two of them were accompanied by their wives.

At Stuttgart we touched down for a customs examination. We gave up our passports and our baggage was trundled away to the customs hall for examination. My two personal cases were placed on the bench with all the rest and grim-faced men in grey-green uniforms proceeded to make a careful examination of their contents. Then the passengers began to make their way back to the plane whose propellors were already turning. I remained behind alone in the hall. No one had made any attempt to examine my cases.

With some misgivings I approached one of the customs officials.

'What are you waiting for? I shall miss the plane if you don't hurry.'

The thought obviously did not disturb him.

'Bedaure,' he said, 'but your passport is in the hands of the Gestapo.'

And with an obsequious gesture he invited me to wait in the bar.

I was nonplussed by the strange happening. A hundred and one thoughts raced through my brain. Must I fear an arrest? Vainly I tried to think of some explanation which would fit the facts. Had I committed any imprudence on my former visits? If I had the Germans would blame the International Committee I represented. No, I thought, that's impossible. My conscience is perfectly clear.

'Herr Ober, ein Helles,' I ordered.

The barman served me with a deliciously refreshing German

pale ale, and for a moment I forgot the unpleasantness of my situation. Although the true horrors of Germany's concentration camps
were not very widely known at that time, towards the end of 1941,
the prospect of a stay in Dachau was uninviting enough.

The plane had left at nine o'clock according to schedule, leaving
me behind, and it was midday before 'the gentlemen' for whom I
had apparently been waiting put in an appearance. It was easy
enough to recognize them for what they were from their heavy
gait, their small green hats crammed on to closely shaven heads, and
the disagreeable looks on their faces.

'Herr Doktor Junod?' one inquired formally, though he pronounced it 'Youknowd'.

'Yes,' I replied. 'That's right.'

'Come with us, if you please.'

I knew that any objection would be useless, but I protested
nevertheless.

'For what reason are you interrupting my journey?' I demanded.

'You will learn soon enough. You have been placed in the hands
of the Gestapo and we have been instructed to take you there.'

I got into a car with them and it drove off in the direction of
Stuttgart where it finally pulled up before a big building of grey
stone. One of the detectives took my cases but I did not let go of
the sealed bag which contained the Swiss diplomatic mail.

On the fourth floor I was taken into a comfortably furnished
room with a sofa and a leather arm-chair, but with barred windows.
Soft music came from a loud speaker on the corner of a large desk.
A broad-shouldered official bade me a courteous 'Guten Morgen.'

'Sit down, please. Make yourself comfortable.'

He could hardly have been more friendly.

'But please make no attempt to go away or to use a telephone.
You may not communicate with anyone outside this building at
any time.'

'Will you at least inform the German Red Cross, the O.K.W.
of the Wehrmacht and the Auswärtiges Amt of what has happened
to me?'

'Certainly, I will give the necessary instructions.'

'And what do you propose to do with me, may I ask?'

'I am waiting for instructions from Berlin.'

I gave up trying to understand. Gradually I began to feel in-different to the whole proceedings. Fortunately I had with me a book I was reading, a book on tiger hunting in Bengal, and the fascinating adventures which it described helped me to forget the adventure I was now in process of living, the barred windows I had noticed on my entry, and the presence of the official who treated me with such politeness.

By the middle of the afternoon I had finished my book so I stretched myself out at full length on the sofa and before long I was fast asleep. It is a gift I enjoy of being able to sleep anywhere at any time when I have nothing better to do.

I was wakened by a gentle shaking of the shoulder. It was seven o'clock.

'Wake up,' said a voice. 'You are being taken to dinner.'

I sprang to my feet in sleepy bewilderment, and the sight of the detective reminded me of my situation. Immediately I thought of the messages I had asked him to pass on for me.

'Have you received any reply from the Auswärtiges Amt?' I asked.

'I'm afraid not,' he replied with a smile of the deepest regret.

I learned later that he had taken care to inform no one of my arrest apart from his own superiors.

A detective escorted me to a little café in the neighbourhood where I had an indifferent meal. When we returned everyone was in a great hurry to get me to the station, because apparently it was the Gestapo in Berlin who wished to interrogate me.

A special second-class compartment had been reserved for me and my two guards in the train which left for Berlin at eight o'clock. They took it in turns to watch me closely but they obstinately refused to follow up any conversation in which I tried to engage them. Perhaps they had been told that I was a dangerous spy or some redoubtable criminal.

Throughout the night I tried to find some explanation for this changed attitude of the German authorities towards me. I had always carefully upheld the objectivity doubly imposed upon me by my mission and my nationality, even when sometimes things I had witnessed had made me indignant. I certainly had very definite views on the Hitler regime but I had never expressed them publicly and as far as I could remember I had never committed even the slightest indiscretion in my work as delegate of the International Committee of the Red Cross either in Germany or elsewhere.

Thinking over in my mind all the incidents in which I had been concerned and all the cases in which it had been my duty to intervene I could not repress some misgiving, even anxiety. The knowledge that my conscience was clear did not prevent my fearing the worst. I was very much in a position to know that innocence is not a safeguard for a man once he falls into the hands of certain police forces. It is very easy to let a man disappear. An accident followed by official apologies and polite expressions of regret, and the matter is finished.

My only hope was to warn someone from our delegation in time. But how could I do that? The German official had repeated to me on several occasions: 'On no pretext whatever may you get into touch with anyone outside.' The blinds of the windows giving on to the corridor had been carefully drawn. However, I worked out a plan whilst the dawn began to show through the carriage windows, and I prayed to heaven that I should be able to carry it into execution.

The train arrived at Anhalter Bahnhof in Berlin at 8 o'clock in the morning. At least my guards had spared me the humiliation of handcuffs, and this last vestige of consideration encouraged me to suggest to them that we should get some breakfast at the station buffet. But all there was to have was cold beer, which I drank with disgust. All the time my eyes searched the great hall, which was crammed with soldiers and shaven-headed civilians, for the sight of an acquaintance. I was prepared to give a message for our Red Cross Delegation or for the Swiss Legation to anyone who looked worthy of confidence, but it was likely that the business of my companions was clearly visible to anyone who cared to glance at them, and no one else made any attempt to sit at our table.

When we had finished our beer one of the detectives rose and telling his companion to keep a close eye on me he informed me that he was now going to telephone to his superiors for instructions as to where I was to be taken. I reacted immediately to that and assumed an indignant air. I thumped on the table.

'What do you mean, where I'm to be taken? Naturally to the Hôtel Eden where a room has been reserved for me. Tell your superiors that before meeting them I want to take a bath and have a shave. You can accompany me. After that you can do what you like.'

The people in the neighbourhood were already looking at us curiously, and the detective put on a very friendly air and informed me that he would do everything he could to oblige me.

I had remembered opportunely that the head of our Delegation in Berlin, my friend Dr. Roland Marti, who had been with me in Spain, was living at the Hôtel Eden. He must have been astonished to find that I had not arrived with the Zürich plane the evening before. If he had then telephoned to Geneva to inquire about my absence they would have told him that I had left on the plane as arranged. Even if I could not get into direct contact with him my presence at the hotel would certainly be reported to him.

Half an hour later the detective informed me to my great relief that there was no objection to my proposal. The police car set off through the streets of Berlin.

On arriving at the Hôtel Eden one of the detectives went off and the other accompanied me to the reception desk. The reception clerk recognized me at once and came forward to ask me whether I had had a good journey.

'Quite well all things considered,' I replied and I gave my guardian an ironic look. 'Did Dr. Marti reserve a room for me?'

'Yes sir, Room No. 573. His room is No. 553.'

So we were quite close together on the same floor, the fifth as it transpired.

On getting out of the lift I let the detective go ahead of me to Room No. 573. It so happened that Dr. Marti's room was between the lift and my room. My heart beat harder. The detective was a few paces ahead. Before he could turn round to prevent me I suddenly opened Marti's door. By great good fortune he was in his room.

'Hallo, Roland!'

'Welcome, Marcel.'

Marti was typing near the window of the room. I went up to him, but already the detective had hurried back and now he took me by the arm. Marti was astonished at the gesture of restraint.

'You're not alone, Marcel?'

'As you see,' I replied. 'This gentleman is from the Gestapo. Let the Auswärtiges Amt know at once that I am under arrest.'

That was all I could say, but it was enough. The angry detective had dragged me unceremoniously out into the corridor and bundled me into my own room and closed the door. I was undisturbed. I had succeeded in doing what I wanted to do, and now I knew that steps would be taken on my behalf.

A hot bath was very comforting after all the excitements of the past twenty-four hours, and afterwards rolls and butter and coffee restored me entirely.

My detective was joined by two others, and they watched me dress. They all jumped to their feet when the door opened and Dr. Marti came in accompanied by an official of the Auswärtiges Amt who had come along at once in reply to his phone call. The young diplomat, whom I knew quite well, apologized to me for what had happened and promptly took the leader of the detectives outside into the corridor to discuss the matter with him. I just had time to tell Marti what had occurred when the two came in again talking animately, and a name which continually recurred in their conversation was 'Prinz Albrechtstrasse'. It was clear that the detective intended to take me to the headquarters of the Gestapo, which were in the Prinz Albrechtstrasse and that the representative of the Foreign Office was objecting. In the end, however, the latter gave way before the all-powerful representative of Himmler. At least he was allowed to come with me, but the same favour was not accorded to Marti.

We went off to the Prinz Albrechtstrasse and I took good care
not to leave the diplomatic mail behind. I had not let it out of my
sight for a moment since the whole affair began. Once we were
inside the doors an army of officials in uniform and mufti took
charge of us. Gates opened electrically to let us pass and we went
along innumerable corridors lined with green filing cabinets stacked
up to the ceiling. We were kept waiting for a short while in an ante-
room, and, not knowing what might happen to me, I thought it
best to entrust the Swiss diplomatic mail to the representative of the
Auswärtiges Amt. Then I was ushered alone into the office of Ober-
kriminal-Kommissar Fischer.

Fischer rose when I came in and shook hands with me.

'Guten Morgen, Herr Doktor.'

He had pale blue eyes and the keen, cold look of a Nazi policeman.
I was probably pale with the excitement and upset, but I was very
calm and determined to remain so.

Fischer invited me to sit down in a chair on the other side of his
desk. On my left stood one of the detectives I had seen in the Hôtel
Eden, whilst a young typist sat silently behind her machine to take
down my interrogation.

It was certainly only as a matter of form that Fischer inquired
about my past activities, for by his side was a voluminous dossier
which bore my name and which no doubt contained all possible
details concerning my life. In particular that dossier must have
grown very considerably in connection with my activities in Spain,
and, in fact, he referred to it indirectly later. His first question
somewhat perplexed me.

'Herr Doktor, tell me, do you know any French officers in
Geneva?'

'Yes certainly,' I replied, 'quite a number.'

'I wonder if you could give me the names?'

The form was conciliatory, but the tone was rather more peremptory. I mentioned a number of names, but obviously the name
Fischer had in mind was not amongst them, and he maintained his
inquisitorial attitude. He offered me a cigarette and I lit his as
well as my own.

'Try and remember someone else, a French officer whom you perhaps met amongst the Reds in Spain.'

Immediately I realized who it was he meant. It must obviously be Colonel Bach, who had been entrusted by the League of Nations with supervising the withdrawal of the International Brigade from Spain. But what on earth could Bach have to do with the present affair? I now recalled having met him again in Geneva at the beginning of the war. I sensed that Fischer was trying to follow my thoughts and I felt a vague apprehension, because we had always spoken our minds very freely to Colonel Bach. However, I could not remember anything compromising which had passed between us.

It was my turn to offer Fischer a cigarette. The movement helped me to regain my composure. My hands did not tremble as I offered him my case. The fact would not have escaped his keen eye.

'So, you now remember Colonel Bach,' he said.

He spoke as though he had read my thoughts. It was useless to deny it, and in any case I hate telling lies.

'Yes,' I replied. 'I remember having dined with him one day in Geneva.'

Fischer was unable to suppress a movement of satisfaction. Immediately he took a letter out of the dossier, and read it to me. It was written in French and the text was approximately as follows:

Mon Général: Recently I met one of my friends who had just returned from Germany. He is quite a well-known person internationally. He believes that the Germans have considerable stores of poison gas, quite sufficient to poison the whole of Paris. . . .

Fischer looked straight at me.

'That letter is signed by Colonel Bach,' he said. 'Can you remember anything now? A conversation perhaps?'

I recalled that on that evening the subject of poison gas had been touched upon, but we had not been alone and other people had taken part in the discussion who had seemed much better informed than I was. However, I had no desire to bring anyone else into the matter and in particular I wished to avoid providing Fischer with the slightest argument which might be used later against Colonel Bach.

'If the possibility was mentioned it was only by way of comment on statements which were appearing at the time in all current military and technical works. Nothing that I saw in Germany in connection with my mission could have given me any confirmation of something the whole world feared even before you entered the war.'

I deliberately made no mention of the mustard-gas containers I had been shown in the cellars of Fort Pilsudski.

'In any case why do you attach such importance to that letter?' I asked.

'It is addressed to General Gamelin, the Commander-in-Chief of the French Army.'

'But what has it got to do with me?'

'Just this, Herr Doktor: there is a second letter. . . .'

Fischer played his cards effectively. He consulted the dossier again and read me another letter, carefully emphasizing each word:

Mon Général: The friend about whom I wrote in my first letter is Dr. Marcel Junod, the delegate of the International Committee of the Red Cross in Germany. I beg you to destroy this letter as soon as you have read it.

Not without pride Fischer went on:

'We found those two letters together with all the papers of the French General Staff in a staff train we captured on the Loire.'

This statement was followed by a long silence which I finally broke.

'Herr Kommissar,' I began as calmly as I could, 'the task of a delegate of the International Red Cross is a difficult one. He sees a good many things, travels from one country to the other and crosses frontiers when no citizen of the belligerent countries may do so. He is aware of what is going on in both camps, and his investigations and his connections with the military authorities provide him with a good deal of material, not directly related with his mission, which the other side would give a great deal to know about. Since the beginning of the war I have been in Germany on four different occasions, including many weeks in Berlin, Hamburg and Munich. I have also been to Warsaw, Oslo, Athens, Paris and Bordeaux, and to Geneva, Stockholm, Lisbon and London. And now to tell you the truth I think it no mean tribute to my discretion that the utmost you can find to reproach me with in all that long time is the echo of an after-dinner chat which took place two years ago and whose subject matter might have been taken from any Allied newspaper of the time.'

I felt very certain of myself now and I spoke with firmness and confidence. Fischer himself seemed to realize that his accusation had turned to my advantage in his hand, but he was not prepared to give up as easily as that.

'I can't believe you,' he said. 'We know Colonel Bach very well, and if he transmitted this information to the French General Staff it was because he was following his profession.'

'I've no doubt he was,' I agreed. 'Just as you follow yours.'

I looked straight at Fischer and said deliberately:

'I see what you believe: you think that I am an agent of the Deuxième Bureau.'

The vestige of a protest gave me the opportunity of adding:

'If you think that then your whole Gestapo isn't much good at its job, for it certainly isn't true.'

Fischer seemed convinced and the smile returned to his face. We began to talk in a much less strained tone, and in the end he abandoned all suspicion, but at the same time he pointed out the dangers of conversations after my return to Switzerland from missions in Germany. I willingly accepted his point of view and I decided that the affair should be a lesson to me.

The future showed that the lesson was not lost on others as well as on myself. At no time when I crossed the frontier on my subsequent missions to Germany, or at any time when I was in Germany or the occupied countries, was I ever bothered in the least with the disturbing attentions of the Gestapo.

On returning to the Hôtel Eden Marti met me with a broad smile.

'So they've let you go?'

'As you see, my dear chap. Let it be a lesson to us to keep a watchful eye on all our conversations, even the most harmless. Our words sometimes make extraordinary detours before they finally turn up again on a policeman's desk.'

Marti's three assistants at our delegation in Berlin, Rubli, Descœudres and Schirmer had nothing to say. I turned to them:

'Well, let's get to work now.'

The measure of our work was that of a besieged, occupied and conquered Europe, a Europe in chains, where millions of people were now living in concentration and internment camps, behind new frontiers born of the fortunes of war, in impassable zones surrounded by barbed wire whose limits varied with the extent of the field of battle itself and turned the whole continent into a fortress — or a prison.

Germany had attained the peak point of her conquests: in the north her forces were at Oslo, in the south at El Alamein, in the west at Biarritz and in the east at Stalingrad. Within that vast quadrangle the people of twenty countries chafed at the German yoke. Since October 10th the Wehrmacht had been immobilized before Moscow. American supplies reached the Russians via Teheran and Vladivostock. British tanks were being unloaded at Murmansk and from under the jackboot of the conqueror there rose the great hope of the Resistance.

At the same time the sufferings of the peoples increased. Norway, France, Belgium, Holland and Yugoslavia had just experienced a hard winter. Poland had become a province of the Reich at the mercies of its Governor.

'Polen existiert nicht mehr — Poland no longer exists,' replied Colonel Dibovsky of the German Army Medical Corps when I asked for the repatriation of the Polish wounded.

Almost all the wealth of the country had been destroyed during the war either by enemy bombardment or by the population to prevent its falling into German hands. What was left had been systematically pillaged. Greece was not the only country facing starvation.

Hunger also depressed millions of prisoners. The number of prisoners in German hands was so immense that the O.K.W. found it extremely difficult to arrange camps for them all: 1,200,000 Frenchmen, 400,000 Poles, 120,000 Belgians, 70,000 British, 80,000 Yugoslavs were distributed over twenty-three Wehrmacht districts and in 80,000 labour detachments. The immense procession of starveling Russian prisoners — 3 or 4 millions, according to the Germans — trailed through Ukrainia and White Russia; only about 800,000 ever reached Germany.

The deportations were beginning everywhere too. Buchenwald and Dachau were no longer big enough. The Germans had to open Belsen, Mauthausen and others we were still unaware of.

Such was the fantastic total of human suffering. Many human beings had sunk to the lowest stages of misery and destitution. The task of the International Red Cross Committee was to assist and protect them to the full extent of its powers.

Perhaps it is as well to point out that neither its resources nor its possibilities depended on its own good will.

The International Committee had no resources in its own right. It was able to give only what it first received. And it could give only to those with whom it was permitted to get into touch.

During the first two years of the war the extent of its funds and the size of its stocks in kind, foodstuffs and clothing, steadily increased. The 400,000 tons of freight carried by Red Cross ships accounted for a good part of the 35 million Swiss francs which were placed at the disposal of the International Committee. Half of it was contributed by the belligerent countries and the other half was obtained by means of collections in towns and villages all over Switzerland.

The little Villa Moynier had seen its organization grow to such an extent that two big hotels in Geneva and the whole Palais Electoral were hardly sufficient to contain it. Voluntary workers in Zürich, Lausanne, Berne and Basle who assisted with the distribution of the prisoners-of-war correspondence raised the total number of people working on behalf of the International Committee of the Red Cross in Switzerland to 3500.

In military terminology, which is very properly applicable to the permanent place they held in the ceaseless battle, often dangerous and sometimes fatal, on behalf of all the victims of war, they were the base services.

But there were also combatants holding advanced posts in the front line.

Thanks to persistent and scarcely believable efforts the International Committee succeeded in obtaining permission for five or six delegates to visit the German prison camps. The seventh was at Athens, supported by a Swiss-Swedish commission. At Belgrade the Germans tolerated the presence of a representative of the Committee in the guise of a correspondent. It was the same in Paris, but no permanent delegate was ever admitted to any of the other occupied countries.

In all there were eight or nine of us, eight or nine Swiss, and our field of operations was the whole of stricken Europe. And how insecure was our right merely to be there!

No doubt those who expected us always to intervene successfully and to an extent proportionate to the horrors unleashed by the war and to the suffering which had come over the world, those who expected us to make the voice of justice, or simply human charity, heard everywhere, and believed that we were in a position to do so, will now be astonished to learn how absurdly few our numbers were.

The Geneva Convention concerning the treatment of prisoners of war mentions the International Committee of the Red Cross in one phrase only, and a very negative and guarded phrase it is:

'The preceding dispositions shall not represent an obstacle to the humanitarian efforts which the International Committee of the Red Cross may make to protect prisoners of war *with the agreement of the belligerents concerned.*'

The agreement of the Germans to let us aid the Allied prisoners was obtained in part because London and Washington permitted our delegates to give similar aid to the Axis prisoners.

The limits of our operations were strictly laid down by the Convention from which our authority derived, namely to aid the prisoners of war, and it applied to them only.

But even that did not mean that we had the right to aid all prisoners of war, but only those who came from countries whose governments had ratified the Geneva Convention.

And it did not mean that we had the right to visit all the camps where prisoners of war were interned, but only the camps in countries whose governments had ratified the Convention.

The Government of the U.S.S.R. had not ratified the Convention, and because the camps for German prisoners of war in Russia were not open to our inspection the German Government used its right to refuse to allow us access to the camps in which it held its Russian prisoners.

When I consider the limits which were thus so rigorously imposed on our activities I always remember the words of Sidney Brown when I first met him in the library of the Villa Moynier on the eve of our departure for Abyssinia in 1935:

'There are the official Red Cross texts, of course, but, above all, there's the spirit of the thing.'

It was that spirit, the spirit of combat, which we kept alive in us and which so often persuaded us to attempt the impossible, to extend the limits imposed on our action against the efforts of those who just as constantly tried to restrict them still further.

'Let's get to work now.' For Marti, Rubli, Descœudres, Schirmer and myself that meant one thing: 'What can we do to go still further, to reach the greatest possible number of those helpless fellow creatures behind barbed wire and cut off from the world.'

In that little room in the Hôtel Eden which was our only office in Berlin at the time — the big house in the Ballenstederstrasse came later — the five of us were assembled, poring over an immense map of Germany and the occupied areas. Little red crosses marked the spot where the Oflags and Stalags we were entitled to visit were situated. But there were other camps which were always in our minds: the camps where the Russians were held, certain Polish camps which had been withdrawn from our list on the pretext that they were now voluntary labour camps, and, above all, those cursed places surrounded in mystery and secrecy where we knew that human beings were suffering anguish of mind and body: the concentration camps.

'There are 30 million index cards here,' Major Bourwieg informed me proudly as he introduced me into the vast corridors of the former school which was now the Registry Department of the Wehrmacht.

At the same time the department also kept a register of all the prisoners it held in its various camps.

Herr Major Bourwieg was the chief technician of the Prisoners-of-War Bureau. Tall, well-made and soldierly, he was proud of two things: his three sons who were serving their country on the eastern front, and his index cards.

He showed me the letter 'A'. It occupied a floor to itself. Ladders which slid noiselessly along rails allowed easy access to the upper files, and the system was so efficient that it took no more than a few seconds to find all the details concerning a prisoner of war even if he was tucked away somewhere in the remotest of labour camps.

Two years later I met Major Bourwieg again. His hair had gone grey and his back was no longer so straight. On his desk were photos of two handsome young men in uniform. He showed them to me with tears in his eyes, still proud, and told me they had died for their country. Three years later nothing remained of his precious index cards but ashes in the wind.

In the adjoining office Major Breyer was the director of prison camps. He was a chubby little man with lively shrewd eyes. He had an air of good humour which cloaked a fund of typically German energy.

One day he confided to me with an air of profound perplexity a problem which it appeared was troubling his conscience.

'Ach, diese Engländer!' he exclaimed. 'Really, they're getting more and more undisciplined. Just think, Herr Doktor, a report has just come in from Doessel that they refused to eat perfectly good apples. Instead of that they gave them to the pigs and all the pigs died. Our vet discovered that they had stuck razor blades into the apples before giving them to the pigs. Quite a nasty business. What's to be done about it I ask myself.'

'Hm!' I said cautiously. 'That sounds odd. Are you sure of the facts?'

I clearly remembered the report of our delegate who had visited the camp two or three months before. According to him the British prisoners had cause for complaint. There was not enough room for them all for one thing. . . .

'Oh yes,' the Herr Major assured me, 'we know all that. But the trick with the apples. You must understand that we really can't allow that sort of thing to go unpunished. However, I'll pay a visit there myself and make my inquiries on the spot.'

'Would you allow me to accompany you?'

'I was just going to suggest it.'

The next day we got out of the Berlin train at Kassel and were received at the station by officers of the Wehrmacht. Introductions: gloved hands sprang to the peaks of caps and heels clicked. The uniforms were clean but already looking worn. Everyone was extremely amiable. My reputation as the oldest Red Cross delegate in Germany, and perhaps the recollection of the Luftwaffe officers who were 'exchanged' in Spain, gave me a certain prestige and earned me the respect of these men.

Some of the officers had been prisoners of war themselves in the 1914-18 conflict. They remembered that the delegates of the International Red Cross had visited them in their prison camps although the Geneva Convention concerning the treatment of prisoners of war did not exist then. One of them told me with some emotion how he had been received in Riga by the Red Cross after he had made his way on foot for over 300 miles across Russia.

We passed through a pleasant countryside of wooded hills and arrived at Doessel just as day broke and the sky lightened. A keen wind was blowing and I turned up the collar of my coat and hugged my wallet full of papers close to my body. And another involuntary shudder went through me when I saw the metal towers manned by steel-helmeted sentries, which dominated the camp. At the least sign of disorder machine-guns could sweep any part of the camp and its surroundings and mow down those whose longing for liberty might tempt them to make a dash for freedom. I experienced again that feeling of indignation and revulsion which troubles me whenever I see an animal in a trap.

In the meantime the German officers were effusive.

'How would you like to make your inspection, Herr Doktor?'

I was already with the prisoners in spirit. Human beings like myself, but behind barbed wire. I failed to notice what was said to me.

'Bitte, Herr Doktor,' insisted Major Breyer, and repeated the question.

I returned to my official function.

'I am at your disposal.'

At that moment we were joined by a fair-haired little man who gave me a flabby hand. He introduced himself as the *Abwehroffizier*, which meant that he was the representative of the S.S. and the Gestapo in the camp. It was his duty to see and know everything. A word from him was a condemnation from which there was no appeal. His reports went direct to the Gestapo.

We entered the camp between two one-storeyed brick buildings which housed the guard. It turned out in our honour and presented arms.

Before us were long lines of the typical wooden huts I had come to know so well. Twenty-nine of them served as living quarters, two were for meals and one for meetings. Behind three huts reserved for the post and for Red Cross parcels were the boot-repairing and clothing workshops. The camp held 2400 British, Canadian, South African, Australian and New Zealand officers.

In the middle of the camp was a large and muddy playing field strewn with slag. Footballs, cricket bats, golf clubs and boxing gloves indicated clearly that the Y.M.C.A. had passed that way.

When I entered the hut in which the representatives of the prisoners were waiting for me I was greeted with a loud and cheerful chorus:

'Good morning, sir.'

All the officers rose, but the smiles froze on their faces when they spotted the *Abwehroffizier* immediately behind me. I turned to him with a look which told him plainly that I wished to be left alone. He pretended not to understand. I looked at my watch and asked him to come back for me in an hour. He stiffened.

'Ganz unmöglich,' he declared. 'Quite impossible. I must be present at the discussion.'

'No,' I declared coldly, 'that won't do at all. Do you think that our delegate in Great Britain would agree to the presence of a British officer whilst he talked to German prisoners of war?'

At that he hesitated. The British officers were following the clash with eager interest. In the end the German ostentatiously consulted his watch.

'Nun gut,' he said, saluted and turned on his heel.

As soon as he was outside the British officers surrounded me. Their senior officer, General Somerset, introduced himself.

'It's the first time anyone has put that inquisitive mouse outside,' he declared with a smile.

I sat down with them at the table and they offered me English cigarettes. They were already unobtainable in Switzerland. Then for an hour they spoke to me freely.

On the wall the Geneva Convention, printed in English, made an impressive picture. A gramophone and piles of records, and neat lines of books on shelves indicated that I was in one of the most 'comfortable' camps in Germany. Mutual aid had done a great deal to keep the captive in touch with home and relieve the rigours of his enforced exile.

Only once during the course of our talk did an officer risk an embarrassing question:

'What's the news?'

My deliberately evasive reply was understood.

Amongst other matters I asked about the wretched apples and the question produced a burst of laughter.

'A stupid affair,' said General Somerset. 'About a month ago the kitchen authorities distributed apples which were really quite rotten. My officers didn't refuse them but simply flung them into

the waste bins with the rest of the camp refuse. Razor blades were
flung there too, like everything else. That's all there was to it.
Why do they suppose we had anything against the unfortunate pigs?'

There was a sudden knock at the door and the *Abwehroffizier*
entered without waiting for an invitation.

'Excuse me, Herr Doktor, but the hour is up.'

I looked at my watch.

'Just,' I replied.

The prisoners' representatives rose and put on their coats.
General Somerset looked very smart in his khaki greatcoat. He
picked up a giraffe's tail which had once served him as a fly-swatter
in India and probably now reminded him of the more spacious
days he had spent in the Punjab. Together with the *Abwehroffizier*
we now proceeded to make the rounds.

For two hours we went from hut to hut, and General Somerset
provided a running fire of commentary on everything which he
considered worthy of criticism. The presence of the German did
not seem to disturb him in the least.

The huts were certainly overcrowded but each officer had two
blankets and sheets. There was no proper place for them to put
their personal belongings, and there were not enough cupboards.
Kettles were simmering on small fires made of brick for the inevitable cups of tea. The officers complained of the German censorship
which refused to let them have certain books. However, there was
a library of 4000 volumes.

Somerset overlooked no detail. From time to time he brandished
his giraffe's tail at imaginary flies, but there were other forms of
insect life which were not imaginary, and he informed me that the
day before he had disposed of his hundredth flea. Small fry for a
big-game hunter.

In a cemented hall provided with washing basins and four baths
we came across some fine big fellows completely naked, laughing
and towelling themselves down. The steam suggested that the
water was really hot.

'Twenty-three showers for 3000 men isn't anything like enough,'
observed the implacable Somerset at my elbow.

The final hut we visited was kept for the storage and distribution of parcels sent by the British Red Cross. Each man received one a week, which provided them with a supplement of something like ten pounds of food, including meat, cheese, sugar, biscuits and jam, to eke out the camp rations.

'We've got 18,000 parcels in reserve,' Somerset informed me with satisfaction.

'What about clothing?' I asked.

'There's some difficulty there because the Camp Commandant thinks he can distribute it as he pleases, and we don't agree. After all the things are ours.'

After a short discussion an agreement was reached that in future these huts should have two keys, one in the possession of the responsible German official and one for General Somerset.

At the end of my tour of inspection I was compelled to refuse the invitation of the British officers to have lunch with them. It was impossible for me to refuse the prior invitation of the Camp Commandant.

Half an hour later after a very frugal meal with the Commandant and his officers I regretted still more that I had been unable to share the meal of the British officers with their spam, marmalade and cups of Nescafé I had seen in course of preparation in the huts.

On leaving the camp at about two o'clock in the afternoon I came by accident on a sight which made me suddenly forget the reassuring impressions I had received in the Oflag for British officers. A long column of shambling men in a pitiful condition passed me on the road. They looked more like helots dragging invisible irons than prisoners of war. Some of them were wearing old and torn greenish coloured greatcoats which reached to their ankles. On their feet, sometimes bare and sometimes wrapped in rags, they wore wooden clogs. The vestiges of uniform they wore were reminiscent of the Polish Army, but the caps of stuff with little bosses on the top and chin straps which now hung over their ears were unknown to me. I turned to Major Breyer inquiringly.

'Russians,' he said, and as he spoke the one word his face grew hard, almost hateful.

Slowly the column made its way forward to the Russian camp, which was separated from the Oflag only by a double line of barbed wire. A Feldwebel shouted brief commands from time to time which were repeated by interpreters. His hoarse shouts sounded like insults.

Determinedly I turned to Major Breyer.

'May I visit their camp.'

His face showed a series of sudden emotions: first astonishment at such a request, then suspicion of the feeling of pity which must have dictated it, and finally anger at the fact that apparently I had forgotten the columns of German prisoners dragging their way across Russia to Siberia.

'You know quite well that the Russians have not signed the Geneva Convention,' he objected.

'Yes, of course,' I replied, trying to adopt an air of indifference, 'but it would interest me all the same to see the Russians at close quarters.'

He hesitated.

'I understand,' he replied, 'but our instructions on the point are very strict. Incidentally, you probably know them: as long as delegates of the International Committee of the Red Cross are not allowed to visit our men in Russia we cannot let them visit Russian prisoners here.'

'Yes,' I said. 'I understand all that, but this would be an unofficial visit, of course. Without a report and without photos.'

Breyer was obviously perplexed. Our train did not go for another couple of hours. Could he very well refuse to employ the spare time in a visit to the Russian camp?

'All right,' he said finally. 'You shall go in if you like.'

He spoke in a low voice to one of the officers who immediately went over to the sentries.

At the entrance to the camp, on the left, the prisoners went in indian file past a wooden hut which turned out to be the kitchen. There were two large, steaming cauldrons. Each prisoner presented a receptacle of some sort, a basin, an old tin can, or a chipped dish. The man distributing the food was working mechanically and without interest, slopping a ladle of the stuff into each receptacle, sometimes so carelessly that some of it was spilled on to the ground. If a man made a timid attempt to receive his due he was immediately roughly bundled on.

'Pass along. Next man.'

I went closer. The soup was watery and in it floated a few carrots and potatoes and occasionally a piece of stringy meat.

Some of the famished men did not wait until they reached their huts before eating their soup, but reeling along they raised their pannikins to their mouths and drank it off at once. They burned their lips but their hunger was not stayed. Here and there a man tripped up in his oversize clogs and fell into the mud. Comrades helped some to rise, but others remained lying where they had fallen.

To clear a path for us the *Feldwebel* did not hesitate to use his whip. My heart beat faster, but I did not want these Germans to read on my face what I was feeling, and I did my best to remain impassive.

Some of the Russians cast furtive glances at me, and quickly looked away. I tried to make out the expression on those emaciated faces. They seemed indifferent to the whip which lashed their backs. What was going on in the minds of these men from Eastern Europe? Was it revolt or fatalism? In any case they seemed very near the end to me. They seemed to have but one desire: to stretch themselves out and sleep, sleep. . . .

It was impossible for me not to compare the conditions under which they were existing with those of the neighbouring camp. 'We have only twenty-three showers for 3000 men,' General Somerset had complained. Here there was nothing but a few taps in the open. No letters, no parcels and not even cigarettes. Not the least echo from their far-off homes.

In the huts I found that the men slept on the bare boards. Each man had two blankets, but no mattresses or even straw. And the stove was cold.

In the sick-bay one or two patients were stretched out on mattresses. Their eyes were blank and death was already near. One of them was unconscious.

'By the evening he'll be as naked as he came into the world,' said the *Feldwebel*. 'They're hardly dead when their comrades come and strip them of everything. When they've finished they come to me and say: "Kamerad kaput".'

And he added confidentially:

'Sometimes they don't even wait till they are dead. They're just beasts, you know.'

I said nothing. I could not have spoken.

In the train which took me back to Berlin I was unable to efface the terrible picture of these ill-treated men from my mind.

From the Oflag of the British officers to the prison camp of the Russians was only a few steps, but between those two extremes lay the fate of all the prisoners of war according to the severity or the privileges of their camps. But here the contrast was heart-rending because it was present at the same time, in the same place and under the rule of the same victor.

And yet the word 'prisoner' had to do for two kinds of treatment so dissimilar.

Affixed to the walls of the huts in the Oflag for British officers was the text of the Geneva Convention, known to all and respected by the prison-camp authorities. In the huts where the Russians were kept the walls were bare.

On the one hand the prisoner was respected and his affairs were discussed calmly and objectively, and on the other the whip lash descended on his back.

In the fatigue of that night in the train the pictures I had seen that day crowded back into my mind. On the one hand healthy trained bodies, the steaming water gushing over them from the showers, and on the other the emaciated faces raised to drink the thin soup from battered pannikins. On the one hand the steaming tea made on improvised stoves, and on the other the cold stove and the damp and cold penetrating through the ill-fitting planks of the huts.

I returned to the Supreme Command of the Wehrmacht. This time I was not concerned with rotten apples and razor blades, and it was more than a dispute on the application of this or that article of the Geneva Convention. I was out to save a band of slaves from an inhuman fate.

It was with Breyer's chief, General Reinicke, that I had to do this time. It was my second interview with the supreme head of all German prisoner-of-war camps after General Keitel and the Führer himself.

'General,' I said, 'I have just returned from Doessel. Matters in the British camp are now in order I think.'

Reinicke nodded approvingly.

'But I want to speak to you now about something else: the neighbouring camp.'

'Ach, die Russen!'

'Yes, the Russians. Their situation is almost indescribably bad.'

General Reinicke was a professional soldier and I could speak to him fairly frankly. He was perfectly aware of what was going on.

'I know, Doctor,' he replied, 'but you mustn't forget two things: first of all we have to find room for between 5 and 6 million prisoners of war, of whom between 3 and 4 millions are Russians. On the other hand there are thousands of families in this country who can get no news at all of their fathers and sons who have disappeared in the east. Gradually their anxiety gives way to hatred. No, until you can persuade the Russians to apply the provisions of the Geneva Convention to our men we cannot apply its provisions to their men.'

It was a problem I came up against repeatedly: the tit for tat. I did my best to evade it.

'I know all that, General. In fact I conducted part of the negotiations on the point with the Russian diplomats in Ankara. It seemed at first that the Russians were willing to apply part of the provisions of the Geneva Convention, but unfortunately for the past eight months we have been unable to get a word out of them on the subject and we don't know why. However, the International Committee of the Red Cross in Geneva can't be satisfied with leaving matters like that. We are anxious to obtain permission from the Government of the Reich to look after its Russian prisoners as we look after all the others even if reciprocity can't be obtained, and I consider it my duty to raise this question with you now.'

Reinicke thought over what I had said. Around him stood his officers in silence. Some of them seemed encouraging, whilst the cold attitude of others was a clear rebuke to my audacity.

It was quite a time before Reinicke spoke.

'Personally I should not oppose it,' he said slowly, 'and I don't think General Keitel would either, but we regard it as a matter of such importance that only the Führer himself can decide it. I will see to it that you receive his reply in due course.'

The reply never came, and we heard nothing from the Russians either.

The propaganda machines of all the belligerent countries took up the affair and whilst their broadcasting stations abused each other through the ether the bodies of the Russian prisoners piled up on top of each other in mass graves.

Parallel to the tragedy of the Russian prisoners a drama was unfolding in Germany such as the world had never witnessed before. Thousands of civilians of all races and all religions were dying in the concentration camps.

From a distance in passing we had seen the belching smoke stacks of the Mauthausen crematoria but we had not realized that thousands of human beings were being reduced to ashes there. Our suspicions were aroused, however, and we knew that something or other was going on. The memoranda sent out from Geneva to the belligerents remained unanswered.

Because the fifty-two nations assembled in Tokio in 1934 had shown no particular eagerness to sign a convention for the protection of the civilian victims of war these camps remained hermetically closed to us until a vanquished Germany was no longer able to guard their terrible secrets.

Nevertheless, it proved possible to send the first Red Cross parcels with foodstuffs into these camps of death as early as the year 1943, and during the last few months of the war, under bombardment from the air and amidst the convulsions of coming defeat, the white cars of the International Committee of the Red Cross travelled along the roads of Germany to the camps, and parties of Swiss volunteers, assisted by Canadian, French and American prisoners of war, hurried to save the victims from the gas chambers and the crematoria. It is an extraordinary story which will one day be told by those who lived through it.

In the meantime I was preparing to leave on my final mission, one which was to take me to the furthermost ends of the earth; to a part to which Europe, all intent on the approaching victory, gave little thought: the Far East.

JAPAN

CHAPTER I

EN ROUTE TOWARDS THE EAST

THE Persians have a saying: 'In June the heat is so great that even the flies die off. In July it's the mosquitos. And in August ... it's the Americans.'

But the Americans remained unimpressed by oriental proverbs and in a desert not far from Teheran they established a huge camp covering some 15,000 acres, whose organization and standards of comfort soon aroused the unbounded admiration of the subjects of the Shah.

From the near-by mountains they diverted a stream, and its fresh water was used to supply a vast swimming pool laid out with blue tiles. Set out amidst the dunes the huts with their large awnings formed shady avenues. Hot and cold water showers worked perfectly day and night. The doors and the windows of the huts were protected against the incursions of all forms of insect life by a three-fold barrier of fine wire mesh. In every mess an air-conditioning plant kept the atmosphere cool and pleasant, and when the heat of the day was at its height refrigerators permitted the happy occupants to enjoy fruit-juice drinks or Bourbon ices.

This Amirabad Camp was laid out for the Persian Gulf zone at a time when the armies of von Paulus and von Schwedler were driving forward across the sun-parched steppes towards the Caucasus and the Volga. It was one of the three key points through which the western allies poured war material into Soviet Russia. British tanks went via Murmansk; American planes via Vladivostock; and the handy little Jeeps, lorries and all other forms of military transport via Teheran. Within the space of three years no less than 150,000 vehicles of all kinds passed through Persia and Baku on their way into the interior.

I arrived at the camp as a guest on June 20th, 1945, and for the second time since the beginning of the war I found myself at the gates of Russia.

All my attempts to cross that frontier in October 1941 when I had gone to Ankara to open up negotiations on the subject of the prisoners of war held by Germany and Russia had been in vain.

Should I be able to succeed this time?

I had applied for permission to pass through Soviet territory in order to go to Japan. I was to go to Tokio to replace the head of our delegation there, Dr. Paravicini, who had died the year before. Together with me was another delegate of the Red Cross, Margherita Straehler. She had been born in Yokohama and she spoke Japanese fluently and, in addition, she was well versed in all Red Cross questions as they affected the Far East because for four years she had been the head of the Geneva Red Cross service for American prisoners of war in Japan.

When it was first decided that we should go to Japan, eight months before, we had intended to go the easier way via New York, San-Francisco and Vladivostock, but the Japanese had vetoed the proposal.

'It is impossible for us to allow you to enter our country after you have passed through enemy territory,' explained the Japanese Minister in Berne. 'It is a question of dignity for my government.'

And then he suggested a route which would not offend his government's dignity, namely: Cairo, Teheran, Moscow, Siberia and Manchukuo. Russia was, of course, the only member of the grand alliance which still maintained diplomatic relations with Tokio. We therefore took steps to obtain Soviet visas and then waited throughout the winter for a reply from the Kremlin. It arrived on May 28th, 1945, and specified that Soviet visas should be issued by the Soviet Consulate in Teheran.

Everyone in the Amirabad Camp was anxious to assist us. Margherita Straehler lodged with the Red Cross nurses and I was made welcome in one of the officers' huts. Everyone knew that we were on our way to the Far East in order to do our best for 'the boys' who were prisoners of war there.

An American officer of French origin who had lived in Moscow for seventeen years offered to come with us to the Soviet Consulate to act as interpreter. I took with me a satchel full of Red Cross documents, because I feared that all these papers in a foreign language might cause difficulties and I wanted to have them checked before I attempted to take them through Soviet territory.

We were received by a representative of the Consul, a short thick-set man with a friendly face. He rattled off a conversation with our interpreter of which I understood nothing. However, he seemed to be well informed about our mission. The American officer translated: our visas would be ready in two days. But when we were outside he asked me with a sceptical smile:

'Do you really think you'll get through?'

'Why not?' I asked in some surprise, 'hasn't the Consul just told you so?'

'Yes,' he replied, 'but what I meant was: do you really expect to get into Manchuria before the Russians do?'

So the American reckoned with a possibility which I had been trying to put out of my mind ever since I had left Geneva. Even there we had heard rumours of an impending declaration of war by Soviet Russia on Japan, but 'well-informed circles' had launched the rumour so often that in the end we no longer believed it. However, here in Teheran there were a number of reasons for being better informed, and my American friend, who was in close contact with all the negotiations between the Russians and the Americans, would know what he was talking about.

I could only hope that we should arrive in time to cross the frontier into Manchuria before the Russian tanks did. And the race would be won only when the Russian passport officials handed us our passports at the frontier station in Siberia.

Two days later, as promised, the Soviet transit visas were stamped into our passports and I hurried to the Soviet travel agency 'Intourist' to book seats on the plane for Moscow. The 'Intourist' occupied modest offices on the first floor of a house in one of the busiest streets in Teheran. Air connections with Russia had been re-established only comparatively recently and there were very many would-be travellers who were anxious to spare themselves the ten- or twelve-day journey to Moscow by train.

The official, who had just been about to make himself a glass of tea at a steaming samovar, came over to hear what we wanted. As soon as we mentioned our names I had the impression that he knew all about us and that in principle no obstacles were to be placed in our way.

'You will be informed of the departure of the plane in which your seats are booked two or three days in advance,' he explained, 'but if you like you can drop in again in three or four days.'

That didn't sound too encouraging and I communicated my doubts to an American captain, who smiled and replied:

'I shouldn't be in too much of a hurry if I were you. We've got people in the camp who've been waiting for a couple of weeks, and they are business people of some importance for the Russians.'

A further surprise awaited me at the Soviet Consulate when I was informed that there was no one there with sufficient authority to facilitate the passage of my papers through the Soviet customs.

'If you don't want to go through the customs with them why not entrust them to the American diplomatic bag from Teheran to Moscow?' the Soviet official inquired. 'Once you're in Moscow all you need do is to entrust them to the Japanese diplomatic bag and pick them up again in Tokio.'

One or two visits to 'Intourist' produced no result. On one occasion I witnessed an American business man staging a violent scene and declaring that he would return to the United States without bothering to go at all unless he was given a seat in the plane within forty-eight hours. The Soviet official remained unmoved and replied simply:

'We are short of planes; that's all.'

However, the American did get his place within forty-eight hours and we were warned to be ready to leave on July 4th.

Early in the morning we left the camp and made our way to the air field. Two Russians, four Englishmen employed at the British Embassy in Moscow and two American meteorologists were with us. The plane was a C.47 and its bucket seats were covered with

Persian rugs. The baggage was piled up between the passengers and strongly fastened with cord.

We started at five o'clock. The plane gained height rapidly and made for the north to cross the steep walls of Mount Elbruz. On the other side woods and fields stretched away in a gentle slope towards the Caspian Sea. We flew along the coast of Azerbaijan, which has so often been described as the Côte d'Azur of Persia, until in the distance we could see a strange forest of steel derricks close together and surrounding a tawny coloured town — Baku.

We landed amidst oil derricks. By a path edged with flower beds which led to the air field buildings was a statue of Stalin leaning forward and smiling as though in welcome.

For two reasons I was more than a little moved to find myself in Russia at last: first of all at having an opportunity to see, if only superficially, a great country, and secondly at having successfully overcome all the difficulties which up to now had prevented delegates of the International Committee of the Red Cross from entering Russian territory.

When we came to the customs I expected a very strict control. One by one the British and American passengers unlocked their baggage and made their customs declarations, and then it was our turn. But at the sight of our passports the customs officials chalked up our baggage without even examining it.

Then we continued our journey and after a flight of about three hours across the Caspian Sea and the desert-like delta of the Volga Stalingrad came into view. From the air an accumulation of tanks, lorries and wrecked aeroplanes formed an immense smudge of rust before its outskirts.

On the far side were wooded hills, green meadows and fields on which the harvest was ripening. After a further three hours flying at a fairly low altitude the appearance of increasingly built-up areas announced that we were approaching the capital. In the distance the towers and domes of the Kremlin became visible.

At the air field we were met by two attachés from the British Embassy and by Mr. Shirk, the representative of the American Red Cross in Moscow.

'Are you free this evening?' was his first question after the preliminaries of greeting were over. 'Today is the Fourth of July and our Embassy is giving a big reception to celebrate Independence Day and we should like you to be present.'

At the Hôtel National, where most foreigners put up whilst in Moscow, we had a few hours to recover from the fatigue of our journey and prepare ourselves for the reception. From the windows of our hotel we could see the high walls of the Kremlin and the great arch which led into the Red Square in the centre of which the Lenin Mausoleum caught the rays of the dying sun as it set in a blaze of purple.

The Independence Day reception was a sumptuous affair to which all the leading Soviet personalities in Moscow at the time had been invited. Mr. Harriman, the American Ambassador, chatted to Mr. Molotov, whilst Russian and American generals gave each other innumerable toasts.

Mr. Shirk introduced me to Dr. Serge Kolesnikov, the President of the joint alliance of the Red Cross and Red Crescent in the Soviet Union, who spoke at some length on the spirit of sacrifice which he regarded as the basis for the principles of the Red Cross. For him, however, it meant primarily the care of the wounded, the training of nurses and hospital work. Did he know that we were on our way to Japan to do our best for the prisoners of war by virtue of similar principles? If he did he gave no indication of it.

The next day we began to take steps to continue our journey as soon as possible. By plane it would take only two or three days to cross Siberia, but the air lines on the other side of Moscow were not yet available for foreigners and we had to make up our minds to use the slow and dusty carriages of the Trans-Siberian Railway. And even then we were disappointed to hear that we should not be able to obtain places on the train for about a week.

Once again I began to fear that we might find ourselves in the wake of the Red Army. Foreign diplomats whom I questioned anxiously were unwilling to make any prophecies, but the Swedish Minister Soederblom pacified me to some extent.

'Don't worry,' he said consolingly. 'You will have plenty of time to get across.'

I recovered my satchel of papers from the United States Embassy. All I had to do now was to take it to the Japanese Embassy, and I set off to do so without any very clear idea of the way. Before long I realized that I was lost, and there was nothing for it but to approach a policeman.

'Iaponskoie Possolstvo,' I said in my very best Russian, 'The Japanese Embassy.'

Realizing that my knowledge of Russian was more or less limited to those two words the man did his utmost to explain, chiefly by gestures, the way I had to go. Thanks to his kindness in putting me on the right track I arrived safely at the Japanese Embassy where I was received very cordially by the Japanese Ambassador himself, M. Sato. He was fully informed about our journey and promised to cable his government to announce our coming arrival. I handed him over my satchel of documents which he promised to put with the Japanese diplomatic bag.

'I will ask for reservations for you on the plane which leaves fairly regularly from Hsinking for Tokio.'

At no time did he even suggest that we might not arrive in Hsinking owing to the outbreak of hostilities between his country and Russia, and in consequence I resigned myself to suffering my enforced stay in the Soviet capital with less impatience.

We passed the time in wandering freely around Moscow. The streets were always crowded. Everywhere the determined war effort of the Russian people was visible, but at the same time it was clear that the struggle was an exhausting one. The clothing of the inhabitants was well worn and the shops were almost empty. The only really happy faces I saw were those of the children. Observing so many women doing the work of men, and so many young women driving heavy lorries which are usually driven only by men, our thoughts turned to the hecatomb of corpses which the war on the Eastern Front had caused.

On Sunday Mr. Roberts, one of our friends at the British Embassy, proposed to take us out into the country. Very few cars passed us in either direction on the broad tarred highway which runs through country almost as flat as a pancake towards Smolensk. In half an hour we had travelled about twenty-five miles and we came to a stop near barbed wire entanglements and half-collapsed trenches.

'This is the furthest point of the German penetration,' explained Roberts. 'It was on October 10th, 1941.'

In the height of summer in this vast plain devoid of all obstacles and without any natural line of defence it was difficult to see what could have held up the impetuous drive of the Wehrmacht but for those two relentless and powerful allies of the Russian people, the snow and the cold, which came to paralyse all movement.

On July 11th at last we made our way to the railway station, accompanied by our friends of the American Red Cross who had shown us so much kindness during our stay in Moscow. The train seemed endlessly long and it was already packed. Travellers climbed through the windows to settle down somehow inside the carriages, and there were even daring ones between the carriages, standing on the footboards and lying on the roofs.

There was only one sleeping car and there we found the two singles which had been reserved for us. It was an old carriage whose worn lace and dilapidated furnishings dated from before the revolution. On our sleeping places two greyish sheets covered thin and greasy mattresses. My first precaution was to sprinkle everything with D.D.T. whilst two porters stowed away our 800 pound odd of baggage in the compartments under the roof.

The locomotive whistled like a ship's siren. It was the signal for our departure, and after one or two jolts the train began to move slowly.

The Trans-Siberian goes slower than an omnibus at home. It takes nine days to cover the 3000 odd miles between Moscow and the Manchurian frontier, and, counting stops, its average speed is about eighteen miles an hour. A strange convention helped to give us a very relative notion of time: all the railway clocks from Moscow to Vladivostock are synchronized without respect to the progression of the sun. Thus our watches told us that it was midnight when at the end of that seemingly interminable journey we saw the sun rising above the roofs of Tchita.

All along the route we could amuse ourselves by buying what we needed. In the smallest station peasants came to offer us their produce: fruit, vegetables, butter, sour milk, wild strawberries and so on. To offer for sale, that is, and the prices they demanded were exorbitant. For one egg they wanted a dollar. No one purchased without first haggling over these fantastic prices. In the middle of it all the train would move off again, and the bargaining would start afresh at the next station.

There was a restaurant car attached to the train but we had already been warned in Moscow that its prices were prohibitive. A Japanese who had made the same journey in the other direction had spent more than a hundred dollars a day. As we had no time to undertake the long and wearisome negotiations with the Soviet Ministry for Foreign Affairs which might have produced the necessary coupons, we thought it wiser and easier to provide ourselves with a supply of provisions for the long journey. My faithful Primus, brought with me from Geneva, enabled us to prepare some very tasty meals.

As we had to camp for nearly ten days in two very narrow compartments encumbered in addition with bags, cases and trunks we sought to instal ourselves as comfortably as possible. The conductor of the sleeping car obligingly came to our aid. He was quite as old as the ancient lace, and his grey beard gave him such an astonishing resemblance to the last of the Tsars that we immediately dubbed him Nicholas.

Margherita's window was closed and its broken pane was held together roughly by a sort of metal clamp which prevented the pieces from falling out. Nicholas begged her not to attempt to open it. She suffered greatly from the terrible heat, but at least she was spared the black specks and smut belched forth by the engine. I was in the contrary dilemma. After half an hour's strenuous effort I managed to lower the window of my compartment, but when I wanted to close it again I found it quite impossible. When we finally left the train I was almost as black as a sweep, but in return I had enjoyed cool nights.

A Soviet general poked his nose into my compartment, sniffed the appetizing odour of frying bacon, and was obviously delighted at my invitation to share it with us. Two other generals, the secretary of one of them, one or two high Soviet officials, one of whom was on his way to the United States, and a famous woman violinist were the privileged passengers of our sleeper.

At nights we passed through big towns whose names I do not even know, and sometimes we were held up for long periods in sidings. Locomotive whistles sounded and were answered lugubriously in the distance. It was like the sirens of ships lost in a fog. Even in the Newfoundland Roads I have never heard such a sinister concert.

I went to sleep very late, almost at dawn, but at nine o'clock in the morning I was awakened by a knocking on the door. It was Margherita, who wanted her breakfast. The sun shone through the widely spaced boles of a forest of pines and birch trees. At midday we arrived in the first big town I was able to identify. It was Kirov, at the junction of the main line to Leningrad.

Pictures of Lenin, Stalin and Molotov with gigantic inscriptions celebrating the architects of victory hung above the motley crowd which filled the platforms. Many travellers immediately jumped from our train and made their way to a shed where a queue had formed. Something or the other was being distributed.

'Kipiatok,' explained Nicholas.

Margherita's Russian had made astonishing progress, and she translated: 'Hot water.'

I joined the queue with all the rest. *Kipiatok* is a magic word in Russia and it is heard even more frequently than the word *vodka*. At every station queues of travellers immediately form with remarkable discipline and patience before the cauldrons of boiling water which is distributed to them for their samovars.

When we continued our journey we passed many German trucks loaded with material. Lathes, presses and machine-tools were rusting in the open air. No doubt they had become useless for anything except scrap.

Two days after we had left Moscow we arrived at last in the Urals. Beyond the smokestacks of the great industrial town of Molotov we passed through hilly country with pasture land which reminded me somewhat of the Swiss Jura. In the mountainous district the cold became noticeable and it took us a whole day before, beyond Sverdlovsk, we ran again into the suffocating aridity of the Siberian steppes.

By this time we had lost all our accustomed notions of time, space and speed. The villages, laid out in circles, hardly interrupted the monotony of great fields where sheaves of barley and other grains were lying on earth which was almost as black as peat. Herds of cattle grazed peacefully in the undergrowth watched by old women and children.

A general feeling of lassitude created a community amongst the travellers and we found ourselves holding strange conversations. The General's secretary asked Margherita where we came from.

'Geneva,' she replied.

'Geneva? Where's that?' the young woman wanted to know.

'Geneva is the capital of Switzerland.'

'And where's Switzerland?'

It was rather difficult to answer that one.

'Well, it's not so very far from Paris,' Margherita replied, thinking the girl might have heard of the capital of France.

'Oh, I see,' she said vaguely.

Her general showed us a book that he and his colleagues were eagerly studying. It appeared to be an important treatise on military tactics and it was full of notes and photographs. I felt that he was very proud to be able to show me that such a precise and invaluable manual existed for Soviet generals.

Incidentally they were very charming and good-natured chaps and on one occasion they brought players of the guitar and tambourine into the carriage to sing and dance with them and crack a bottle of wine.

As day after day passed I noted our approach towards that point on the map at which it would be quite certain at last that our journey had not been in vain. It was somewhere very far to the east and my map did not even mention the name of the frontier post.

Occasionally we passed important convoys of war material and the sight of all those guns, tanks and planes made me wonder whether they were perhaps intended for something more than mere summer manœuvres.

Troop movements, which we could sometimes divine in the night, retarded our already very slow progress. Before Novosibirsk we had to wait six hours before being allowed to cross the great bridge over the Ob, because beyond the Urals the line is a single one and we had to give way to trains coming in the opposite direction.

After five days and five nights travelling we arrived in Kraznoyarsk on the Yenissei, by which time we had done about two-thirds of our journey.

At that hopelessly slow rate of progress we hardly noticed any change in the landscape. However, the plain was becoming narrower and forests of pines with their red trunks covered the last foothills of the Sayan Mountains, from which delightful streams ran down into the plain. Very often the train stopped in open country, as though to recover its breath, and then many travellers would get out and stretch themselves in the grass or pick bunches of wild flowers in the fields. The locomotive would have to whistle several times before they were all safely back in their carriages again. No one seemed in the slightest hurry, though we were already twelve hours behind our time-table.

A whole week had passed by the time we reached Irkutsk, where we found the railway station full of troops. Two hours later we saw another concentration of troops at a small dirty station which seemed to have been erected pointlessly in the middle of the landscape, but beyond it heavy oil tankers spread plumes of smoke over the green and blue surface of Lake Baikal.

All the afternoon we rolled along its sunlit banks between rocks and pine trees and when we finally left it behind we could see the high mountains which marked the frontiers of Mongolia.

Tchita was quite near now. That is to say it was only a day's journey away, one day and two nights, but they seemed almost longer to us than the rest of the journey put together.

Further inexplicable stops delayed us still more, and the morning of July 19th found us halted near another lake, and if my impatience had not by this time become so great I should have been better able to enjoy its wonderful beauty. The sails of fishing boats stood out against the rose and mauve mist which covered its calm waters. In the distance I could hear the sound of soldiers singing in chorus. Great white birds arose from the reeds at the edge of the lake as the morning light increased.

Margherita stood by my side. She too was thinking anxiously of the time we had lost and of the connection we were supposed to catch at Tchita to take us into Manchuria. Would it wait if the Trans-Siberian were late?

'How many hours are we late?' she asked Nicholas.

Nicholas opened and closed his hand five times.

'Twenty-five hours, Mamutchka.'

The locomotive whistled and the train jolted into movement again. A few miles to cover still, and there was Tchita at last with the inevitable giant picture of Stalin and a crowd of shouting, gesticulating people, through which we saw a tall fellow in a leather jacket elbowing his way towards us. He spoke English and introduced himself with a broad smile:

'Niemkov of the Ministry for Foreign Affairs.'

I hurried to get out our luggage. We might have no more than a few minutes to get from one train into the other.

'What about our connection?' I asked Niemkov anxiously.

'Don't worry about that,' he replied. 'It went yesterday.'

'And when does the next one go?' I asked with a sinking heart. He made a gesture of thoroughly oriental fatalism.

'In a week.'

I began to fear that we should never cross the frontier into Manchuria.

On taking leave of us at the station the Soviet general had shaken my hand warmly and stressed the words:

'We'll be seeing each other again soon.'

Did he mean that he would be seeing me in Hsinking? Obviously it would be useless to ask Niemkov and we had to settle down in Tchita to a week of utter boredom, hearing strange noises in the streets and fearing at any moment to learn that the Red Army was on the march.

If the frontier were suddenly closed our defeat would have been caused by something truly absurd. We had crossed a quarter of the globe; we had been on our way for a month; and we had begun to make our first preparations for the journey about a year before — and we should then be obliged to retrace our steps because we had arrived at Tchita one day late.

There was very little in this garrison town to distract us and prevent our minds from brooding over our unrest and anxiety. If you replace the exuberance of the first American trappers by the oriental placidity of these Mongolians then an outlying town in the Wild West in the pioneering days must have looked something like Tchita. Its long straight streets, sandy and dusty, were as full of ruts and potholes as a river bed.

There was only one hotel. At one time it was no doubt a luxury place patronized by rich merchants and others on their way to China, but all its former glory had faded and only vestiges of its sumptuous hangings were still left clinging to its cracked walls. We inspected five or six incredibly dirty rooms before we found two which were not quite so sordid as their fellows. There was only one tap on each floor in what looked like a lumber room and a notice warned us that to drink the water, or even to use it to clean our teeth, was dangerous.

There was no restaurant. We finished off the rest of our provisions in our miserable rooms, whose doors we were strongly recommended to keep carefully locked at night.

There was only one open-air attraction in the town and that was the so-called Park of Rest and Culture where giant portraits of the Heroes of the Soviet Union rose amidst the trees. Men and women sat quietly on the benches listening to music from a dance floor where couples moved around. The couples were often of the same sex, sometimes two women, sometimes a couple of soldiers waltzing around in each other's arms. One tune seemed particularly popular and there was a burst of applause to secure it again. The voice of Tino Rossi sounded — a little cracked and hoarse because the record had been played so often — melting endlessly under the trees of Tchita:

> Il pleut sur la route,
> Dans la nuit j'écoute . . .

If you happened to ask who Tino Rossi was you were told that he was an American. In that summer of 1945 everything foreign basked for the Russians in the reflected glory of their great ally. On the posters celebrating the fraternity of the allied arms Russian and American flags were much in evidence, whilst those of Great Britain and China had a humble place in the background.

Even Niemkov once said to me with a happy indifference to fine distinctions:

'Yes, of course, you Americans. . . .'

And the soldier who clapped me amiably on the shoulder inquired with evident approval:

'Amerikansky?'

This vogue for Americanism was the only thing which recalled the distant world from which we felt ourselves so terribly isolated. What battles were taking place in the Pacific? What decisions had been come to at the Potsdam conference which had begun whilst we were still in Teheran? We asked for news in vain. There were no newspapers in Tchita, and the only ones Margherita could discover were those which had been brought with us from Moscow on the Trans-Siberian.

When I went outside the town to climb the hills and the undergrowth hid the grey and yellow town from view I found it difficult to believe that I was in the heart of Asia, at the extreme limit of the great Russian plain as huge as a continent, and that I had covered vast stretches of it. The Gobi Desert was at hand, away there beyond the blue mountains which reared up in the south. Towards the north it would take days and days of travelling before one could reach the icy banks of the Lena and the Arctic coasts.

When I turned towards this immensity, when I repeated in an

undertone to myself the ancient names, and listened to their mysterious echo, it was because my thoughts impelled me, thoughts which were closely connected with my mission.

I had crossed this limitless land to go still further and lend a hand to forgotten men. But there were still others and I was unwilling to create the impression that perhaps I had forgotten them.

There were tens of thousands of German prisoners in the Soviet Union. And there were many other men deprived of their liberty who were not prisoners of war. Nowhere throughout my journey had I seen the watch-towers or barbed wire of a prison camp, but throughout those nine days, though I had not dared to say so, I had been constantly on the look out for such signs.

Since passing the Urals I had seen nothing, and I could still see nothing, but fields and forests and little towns each as peaceable as the other. But since the novels of Dostoevsky became known in the Western world our imagination has associated very different things with the name Siberia.

'Tomorrow you will be in Otpor.'

Otpor was the frontier station of the Soviet Union. Two or three miles further on was a little Manchurian village and the first Japanese military post.

Were we going to get through after all?

I was reassured when I saw a Russian loaded with baggage climb into our compartment. It was the diplomatic post for Tokio.

When the train left Tchita it was packed, but gradually the number of passengers got fewer and fewer, and during the past twenty-four hours we had seen more and more signs along the route that war was imminent: troop concentrations, arms depots, convoys of war materials.

The country became completely deserted. As far as eye could see there was nothing but the waving grass of the steppes.

Here and there perhaps were a few houses and a shed or two. For hours the train stood still waiting at platforms which scorched in the sun. The heat was oppressive and heavy as though before a storm.

The train now consisted of only two carriages and in them were just four passengers apart from ourselves: two Japanese diplomats, one of whom had just come from Berlin and the other from Paris, the diplomatic courier and the Soviet Consul at Manchuli.

At Otpor a Soviet official handed us back our passports.

The locomotive whistle sounded. The train began to move towards a little wooden bridge and slowly we crossed the frontier into Manchuria. . . .

CHAPTER II

MEN BEHIND BARBED WIRE

IN September 1941, 60,000 Japanese disembarked in Indo-China. Three months later simultaneous attacks on Hong-Kong and Pearl Harbour started the war in the Pacific.

When the last drop of water had been exhausted in the reservoirs destroyed by the Japanese bombardment the British garrison of Hong-Kong capitulated. That was on December 19th, 1941.

Ten days later coming down from Siam and Indo-China the Japanese advanced along the narrow tongue of land which separates the Gulf of Siam from the Indian Ocean for 600 miles, and reached the extreme limit of the Malay Peninsula.

Three weeks of heroic resistance on the part of the British Third Army could not prevent what Winston Churchill was subsequently to describe as 'the biggest disaster in British military history'. On February 15th, 1942, General Percival, Governor of Singapore, was compelled to sign an unconditional surrender and he was taken prisoner together with 70,000 men.

On February 20th the Japanese landed at Timor at the lower end of the Dutch East Indies and directly threatened Australia. The Dutch forces were gradually encircled in their islands. Sumatra was taken by parachute troops and the naval base at Surabaya was blockaded and bombarded daily. On March 9th Tokio announced the fall of Java and the capture of 90,000 prisoners, including General Starkenborgh, Governor of the Dutch East Indies.

On May 6th the desperate resistance put up for five months by the heroes of Corregidor came to an end. General Wainwright signed the surrender of the Philippine Islands, and 50,000 prisoners marched off into exile along the terrible Bataan route. Many thousands of them perished on the way under the scorching rays of the eastern sun.

That exile was the remotest and the most merciless that any men were called upon to suffer throughout the war. Captured thousands of miles from their own country they were marched off still further to the ends of northern Asia. Crammed aboard Japanese vessels they even suffered bombardment by their own planes. Many of them never reached the camps where the survivors were to remain completely cut off from the Western world behind the fortified coasts of Formosa, in the snowy forests of Hokkaido and the mountainous districts of Manchuria.

Out of 300,000 prisoners captured by the Japanese in the first months of the war in the Pacific 100,000 were already dead when the day of liberation dawned. The 200,000 survivors staggered emaciated and exhausted from unknown villages and prison camps scattered over the island or in the interior of the Asiatic mainland from the rocky shores of the Banda Sea to the Burma jungle.

An almost unsurmountable barrier surrounded them. It was not only the physical prison which held them, or the enormous distances which separated them from their homes and their families and from those who were fighting to liberate them, but their complete isolation amongst a race whose language and customs were completely foreign to them. And in addition there was the wall of silence which their Japanese guards deliberately erected around them.

A letter took a year to reach the place of their imprisonment — and then the Japanese would often leave the post sacks lying unopened for some time.

On rare occasions outsiders were able to penetrate their careful isolation. Three Swiss citizens who had lived in Tokio for many years accepted the thankless task of representing the International Committee of the Red Cross in Japan. On three occasions in as many years they were allowed to pay a short visit to the prisoner-of-war camps in Korea. Twice they were allowed to go to Formosa. But it was not until November 1943, after a year of complete silence, that they were allowed to go to Manchuria, and even then they were permitted to visit only one camp, that in Mukden. They never succeeded in getting permission to visit any of the camps in Burma.

How many other prison camps were there in the burnt and parched mountainous lands in which British, Dutch and American

253

prisoners from Malaya, Borneo, Java and the Philippines slowly rotted, cut off from the world they had known?

Where were the airmen who had made forced landings in Japan or who had baled out? Where were the crews of the ships captured in the southern seas?

Where was General Percival, the defender of Singapore? Where was General Starkenborgh, the Governor of the Dutch East Indies? Where was General Wainwright, the hero of Corregidor?

Only the Japanese knew.

When I arrived at Hsinking on August 1st, 1945, I was determined to do everything I could to find out where these three men were being held and to get into touch with them if possible. Whilst I was in Moscow I had already informed the Japanese Ambassador Sato of my intention and he had promised to cable to Tokio to enlist support for my project, but I did not know whether the Japanese Prisoners-of-War Department, which had kept so many secrets, would be prepared to divulge this one.

As soon as we arrived in Manchuria Margherita and I were, so to speak, 'taken in charge' by a group of Japanese who treated us with great deference as honoured guests but who never let us out of their sight for an instant and who carefully observed all our movements and listened to all we had to say. Amongst them were members of the Manchurian Red Cross Society, but they were all Japanese, smiling, silent — and vigilant.

From the time we arrived at the little hotel in Manchuli where we were to stay until the day we left for Tokio our whole time was carefully mapped out for us hour by hour and devoted almost exclusively to courtesy visits to the local notabilities and to official receptions.

We had already travelled about a thousand miles across the fertile plains of Manchuria with its hills and pasture lands, its fields of maize, barley and soya beans cultivated by Chinese coolies enslaved to the Japanese colonists who had swarmed over the country fourteen years before in the wake of the Japanese army. The Japanese occupation had set its stamp deeply on the countryside and everywhere there was evidence of order, perseverance, methodical effort and discipline. It was visible too in the organization of the 'Yamata' hotels, which were run in exactly the same fashion in all towns, and in the punctuality and comfort of the Manchurian railway service.

'Manchukuo is our most beautiful province,' the old Japanese who had been attached to us as interpreter informed us on every possible occasion. What English he spoke he had learned at an American missionary school.

We spent three days in Harbin, and the noise and tumult of its Chinese streets almost numbed our senses. We were taken for a motor-boat trip on the river Sungari and in the distance we caught a glimpse of Buddhist temples, pagodas and other monuments. A nostalgic memory of Holy Russia of the Tsars was brought to mind by the cupolas of copper above the orthodox churches built by the 35,000 Russians who had fled to Harbin from the Bolshevist Revolution.

In the train which carried us on to the Manchurian capital I was unable to resist pointing out to our guides that our mission would be very inadequately fulfilled if it were confined — as had so far been the case — to a few brief visits to hospitals, even if accompanied by numerous exchanges of politeness and salutations.

'At Hsinking our honourable guests will have an opportunity of expressing their desires,' was the polite but non-committal reply.

The opportunity arrived at an official dinner — the sixth since our arrival in Manchuria — which found us at the table of M. Kaminura, the Japanese Ambassador to the court of the puppet emperor Pu Yi.

The Ambassador's wife was Japanese, but the European elegance of her evening dress of black silk trimmed with white lace, the gentle wave in her jet-black hair and the irreproachable English she spoke suggested a long stay in London.

'Yes, we were there in 1940,' she said, 'just when the terrible bombing began which lasted through the winter. Then when our country entered the war we were repatriated with other diplomats.

And now the whole of Japan is experiencing the fate of London.'

And she added with a touch of nervousness, turning to Margherita:

'You wouldn't recognize Tokio, Madame. It has been razed to the ground. We lost everything, our house, our belongings. It was terrible.'

She did not yet know that in a few days another war, very short, but terribly bloody, would begin for them here.

The Japanese Ambassador was in uniform, as was one of his councillors, M. Miyasaki, whose wife's slender body was clothed in a lovely sky-blue kimono.

At a table decorated with flowers I made the acquaintance of the Japanese national dish 'Sukiyaki' which was served with the very fine wine produced from the Manchurian wild grape.

When the meal was over I asked the Ambassador for a private interview and he led me to his office.

'I should like to discuss my mission with you, Your Excellency,' I began.

'But aren't you going to Tokio?' he asked. 'Once you are there you will be able . . .'

'Yes, I am, Your Excellency, but my work should begin here. The Japanese Government has agreed that I should take advantage of my journey through Manchuria to see the prisoners and find out their needs. Now in this programme which has been given to me. . . .'

M. Kaminura looked attentively at the programme.

'Hasn't it been arranged that when you arrive in Mukden you will have two hours to visit a prisoner-of-war camp there with 1600 prisoners?' he asked.

With deliberate emphasis I asked:

'Does Your Excellency think that General Percival, Governor Starkenborgh and General Wainwright will be amongst them?'

At the sound of those names Kaminura raised his head. Behind his horn-rimmed glasses his slit eyes grew even narrower. He thought for a moment.

'No, I don't think so,' he replied.

'It was two years ago that these officers were last seen — by one of our delegates in Formosa. Since then the International Committee of the Red Cross has reason to believe they have been transferred to Manchuria. I consider it essential that I should be permitted to visit the camp where they are being held.'

Kaminura seemed extremely embarrassed by my bluntness.

'Why certainly . . . Yes, that's true . . . I'm sure Tokio will not hesitate to give you permission. . . .'

But with that he broke off the interview and led me back to the dining-room where Madame Kaminura had caused her guests to be served with iced fruits and champagne.

During the three days in Hsinking I did everything I could to persuade the Japanese authorities to let me see the prisoners. And for that I had to take advantage of the very little time left to me between a great number of courtesy visits, which, it appeared, all proceeded according to the same inflexible ritual. In this way we visited the emperor Pu Yi's Minister for Foreign Affairs, his Vice-Minister Shimomura, General Hata, Japanese Chief of Staff in Manchuria, and General Miura, the President of the Manchurian Red Cross Society.

When we left one palace it was only to enter into some administrative building or the other. Everywhere the ceremony was the same: tea, small cakes, grave bowings. If we had not already gone through a certain amount of training in Japanese courtesy ceremonials we might have thought that the prime aim of the receptions in Hsinking was to provide the various notabilities with some distraction in their idleness.

The imperial town was as young as the emperor whose seat it was. Formerly Changchun, the city had been created a dozen years before by the Japanese and its very name means 'New Capital'. Its modern buildings form long avenues lined with trees all of the same age and all too young to dispense with support.

All the notabilities who received us uttered the same speeches of greeting with the same measured gestures in exactly the same surroundings.

Chinese faces. Japanese faces.

And they all maintained the same embarrassed silence masked by smiles of excessive affability when we mentioned the prisoners of war whose fate was our chief concern.

We left Hsinking for Mukden on August 5th in a train which was packed with Japanese troops. However, there was a compartment reserved for us in a first-class carriage, and although we were the only occupants no one made any attempt to occupy the other seats although numerous Japanese officers were standing in the corridor or sitting packed together in the other compartments. We were watched curiously all the time, but as soon as we raised our heads all eyes turned away.

M. Miyasaki was also on the train.

'Would you be good enough to invite some of these other people who are standing to share our compartment?' I asked.

He smiled gently.

'Please allow me to do nothing of the sort,' he replied. 'You are eminent and honoured guests and if you proposed that ordinary traveller should sit beside you you would lose face.'

Impossible to argue with that outlook. The train sped on. From time to time a conductor passed through the corridors ordering the blinds to be drawn. Through the side of our blind I could see a bridge guarded by soldiers and some barrack-like buildings. Since our arrival in Manchuria I had seen many soldiers and military convoys making for the north. All indications suggested that a Soviet attack was expected and that strong Japanese forces were being sent to repulse an invasion of Manchuria.

Suddenly in our coach an officer began to shout a few words in Japanese. To me they were only incomprehensible syllables:

'Ki ko ka ku . . . Ki ko ka ku. . . .'

All those who were sitting immediately rose from their seats and we instinctively followed their example.

'It is our prayer for the dead and for victory,' explained Miyasaki when everyone had sat down again.

A few moments later someone else began to shout the same invocation and once again everyone rose.

After five hours in the train we arrived at Mukden, the most important industrial centre of Manchuria and the most thickly populated of its towns. A million and a half Chinese and 200,000 Japanese live there in squat houses built of wood and earth. One or two rare modern buildings raise their concrete façades amidst a forest of factory chimneys which belch grey smoke over the plain.

I immediately sent my card to Colonel Matsuda, the commander of all the prisoner-of-war camps in Manchuria.

That evening we were invited to dinner with the Chinese Governor Mr. Yi, whose fine features and gentle expression contrasted strangely with the arrogant airs of the Vice-Governor, a Japanese, who sat next to him.

Mr. Yi informed me that he had abandoned the study of medicine a dozen years before to collaborate with the Japanese occupying forces. When I asked him which he really preferred, his old profession or his present position as Governor, he whispered amidst all those Japanese ears eagerly strained not to miss a word of our conversation:

'It's a question I have not yet resolved.'

Late at night we returned to our hotel in a cab under an extraordinarily brilliant starlit sky. The Chinese driver let his horse pick its own way through the dark streets where pot-holes threatened to upset us on a score of occasions.

At the Yamata I found the visiting card which Colonel Matsuda had left in exchange for my own. He had also left a message telling me that arrangements had been made for us to visit a prisoner-of-war camp on the outskirts of Mukden at nine o'clock the next morning.

Colonel Matsuda was a short man with broad shoulders. He had a big jaw and large teeth and above a turned up nose was a large pair of horn-rimmed glasses under a low brow and a small completely bald skull.

Accompanied by two other officers, each of whom ceremoniously carried a sheathed sabre as he did, he advanced solemnly up the hall of the hotel Yamata. The three Japanese bowed profoundly three times as they approached us thereby erecting at once that barrier of rigid and formal politeness which distanced them so effectively.

We were driven out to the camp. As we emerged from the suburbs, which were separated from the factories only by the width of the road, we came to a large white wall, barbed wire and a watch-tower. The year before the factory had been bombed by the Americans and forty prisoners had been killed.

'Such camps should not be within two miles of the nearest military objective,' I observed to Colonel Matsuda. 'That is laid down in the Geneva Convention. . . .'

But Colonel Matsuda had his reply ready.

'You must not forget, sir, that Japan has not ratified the convention concerning prisoners of war.'

That was perfectly true. However, we had hoped that Japanese recognition of the Convention would be implicit when the International Committee of the Red Cross received a telegram from the Japanese Government in February 1942 with the text:

'We agree to operate the Geneva Convention under conditions of reciprocity and *mutatis mutandis*.'

We were soon to see the Japanese interpretation of that Latin formula.

Colonel Matsuda first took us into the officers' mess, where he sank down into an armchair, invited all those present to do the same, and then made himself comfortable, both hands resting on the hilt of his sabre. About a score of Japanese officers who were present followed the invitation of their colonel and imitated his gestures exactly. Matsuda introduced them to us one by one with obvious signs of complacency. The authority and power of a Japanese official is measured by the number of assistants he has.

Were we in an officers' mess or in a conference hall? Margherita and I had taken our places in two chairs offered to us. The opposite wall was covered with maps and tables, diagrams and statistics.

Colonel Matsuda then proceeded to deliver a lecture for all the world as though he were a professor talking to his students. Sitting on the edges of their chairs and leaning forward in rapt attention the officers interrupted him from time to time with exclamations of wonder and admiration as he delivered himself of a speech they must have heard a hundred times already. It appeared to be a detailed recital of the history of the camp from its foundation, the successive uses to which it had been put, and the continual improvements being made to it.

'When the prisoners arrived from the tropics,' he recalled in a tone which suggested that he was much moved, 'they were in a pitiful state. Dressed only in shirts and shorts they had not stood the icy winter of Manchuria very well. Many of them died of pneumonia and recurrent malaria despite the excellent attention which was showered on them.'

At the end of each sentence, as though lost in admiration at the cogency of his demonstration, he paused for a moment. Raising his right hand in a broad gesture and stamping on the ground with one foot he tapped himself on the neck two or three times, accompanying the strange gesture with a sharp and audible inspiration of breath and ending with a sonorous exclamation:

'Na!'

And all his officers responded immediately with an obedient chorus of 'Na!'

Margherita and I looked at each other in consternation. We were both thinking that the time limit for our visit was two hours and that one of them had already been wasted by this vain babbling. When were we going to be taken to see the prisoners? I interrupted the colonel's flow to express our desire to him.

'Certainly,' he replied. 'Just a moment though. There are still some very important things I have to tell you.'

And he continued his paean of praise for the magnanimity of Japan towards her prisoners.

Young girls dressed in 'war-time kimonos', a blue blouse and baggy trousers, with their black hair braided down their backs, came in with small cups of grey tea and cakes which they handed round, offering cigarettes at the same time. Another half-hour passed and I dared to interrupt the colonel again.

'I am growing more and more impatient to be shown a camp so

well organized and so comfortable and where the prisoners are so well treated,' I said.

This time Matsuda found it impossible to do any more stalling, and so with a great clinking of sabres the party rose and a procession was set in motion.

The first thing we saw was a big yard around which were sheds made of concrete.

The yard was empty and there was nothing in the sheds. Where were the prisoners?

'They're at work,' Matsuda replied with a great display of nonchalance.

'Well, will you please take us to where they are working?'

'Oh, that's quite impossible. It's too far.'

'Perhaps we can at least see their representatives?'

'Na. Na. An unforeseen hindrance.'

Not for the first time in my career as a delegate of the International Committee of the Red Cross I felt anger rising hot in my breast. But I had to keep calm. An unpleasant incident on this very first 'visit' might create difficulties better avoided. And incidentally the colonel was taking us towards a building which appeared occupied.

'And here is our magnificent hospital,' he announced with one foot on its first step.

At the top of the steps stood four men in shirts and shorts at attention. They were the first prisoners of war I had seen in Manchuria.

As our procession mounted the steps after him the four men bowed low, their arms kept tightly to their sides, until their heads were almost on a level with their knees.

In a low voice, and making an effort not to show the indignation which was boiling up in me, I said:

'That's not the manner in which soldiers of an occidental army salute.'

'No, it's the Japanese manner,' replied Colonel Matsuda with his eternal and impenetrable smile.

We were taken along a corridor with sick-rooms on either side. Standing by the wall near each door were three or four sick prisoners all of whom bowed low as we approached. Those prisoners who were unable to rise were seated tailor-fashion on their beds, their arms crossed on their chests, and they too bowed as low as their bandages, wounds or mutilations would permit. When the last Japanese officer had passed they resumed the upright position, their eyes raised fixedly to the ceiling. Never once did their eyes meet ours.

The palms of my hands were wet and Margherita was as white as a sheet. This was indescribably horrible. Matsuda tried to lead us on but I stopped before a group of four prisoners, three British and an American.

'Is there a doctor amongst you?' I asked, trying to keep my voice firm and not betray the emotion I felt.

No one answered, and the Japanese behind me kept silent.

I stood directly in front of a big fellow who towered above me. I could see only his chin and his stretched neck as he looked up at the ceiling. Not a muscle stirred and I repeated my question. There was still no reply and I turned grimly to Matsuda.

'Why doesn't he reply?' I asked. 'Isn't he allowed to?'

The Japanese were stupefied at my audacity, but Matsuda was evidently unwilling to risk an unpleasant incident and he indicated one of the men standing against the wall with the others.

'This Australian is a doctor,' he said.

I went towards my Australian colleague with outstretched hand. I had to overcome a lump in my throat to get out the banal words:

'How do you do?'

The man lowered his eyes, but not to me. It was at Matsuda he looked. It was the colonel's permission he sought. After several seconds which seemed incredibly long his hand slowly rose to mine. I took it and shook it warmly, trying to convey to him all the emotion and sympathy I felt and hoping he would afterwards communicate them to his comrades.

I told him as briefly as possible who I was and why I had come and I tried to get into conversation with him. He replied slowly and in monosyllables and each time before he spoke I could see that he silently sought the approval of Matsuda over my head.

'Will you accompany me on a tour of the wards?' I asked finally.

This time Matsuda intervened.

'No,' he said. 'A Japanese doctor will accompany you.'

I felt it was impossible to insist any further and I let go the man's trembling hand which stiffened back to the attention against his side whilst his eyes rose again to the ceiling.

On leaving the hospital we came across a pile of American Red Cross parcels in the corner of a hut. The journey they had made to get here was an odyssey in itself. From San Francisco they had crossed the Pacific in a Russian ship. At Vladivostock they had been unloaded and sent to the nearest Korean port to be loaded again on to the Japanese ship *Avamaru* which had then distributed its load along the coasts of Japan and China. From Fusan one batch — those we had just seen — had gone by train to Mukden. Others had gone to Singapore, to Shanghai, to Malaya and Borneo. Some of them had even reached the furthermost camps in the Burma jungle.

'Why haven't those parcels been distributed to the prisoners?' I asked.

'I am saving them up for later,' answered Matsuda. 'It's a precautionary measure, because the *Avamaru* won't be bringing us any more; she was torpedoed and sunk by an American submarine. The prisoners will be much better pleased to get their parcels at Christmas than now.'

What was the real physical and moral state of the prisoners in this camp under the vigilant solicitude of Colonel Matsuda? What sort of work were they required to do? Probably the work usually performed by Chinese coolies. I knew none of these things.

Our visit to the Mukden camp ended with an inspection of the cemetery which was a few miles away out in the country. There was a hill on which a large white wooden cross dominated a few hundred smaller ones set out in lines. On my way towards them I picked a posy of wild flowers from the field. The Japanese officers did the same. Pitiless towards the living, they had a religious respect for the dead.

Passing slowly along the lines of crosses I read the names of 200 British, Dutch and American soldiers. A bitter sadness descended on me. I knew that behind me 1600 exiled prisoners in the mountains of Manchuria lost a little more hope every passing day of ever being able to return to their homes. I had been able to see only a few slaves with bowed backs whose lips had remained as silent as these tombs.

'You asked to see General Wainwright?'

It was Matsuda, and the question was put to me on the way back to the hotel Yamata in a calm and detached tone. I looked at him in astonishment, seeking to discover the trap behind his words. He smiled broadly, showing his large teeth, and seemed perfectly content to tell me now that after numerous telegrams had been exchanged between Mukden, Hsinking and Tokio permission to see General Wainwright, which I had asked for so urgently, had been granted.

'We will stay this evening at Sze Ping Hai, and tomorrow we can take the train from there to the camp in Seihan where he is interned.'

'And what about General Percival and Governor Starkenborgh?'

'You will also be able to see them. The Seihan camp is the place of detention for fifteen superior officers whom we regard as important prisoners of war.'

I was greatly tempted to ask Matsuda whether my visit to Seihan would in any way resemble my visit to the Mukden camp, and whether he would show me General Wainwright's room, Governor Starkenborgh's room, General Percival's room and then tell me that unfortunately 'by an unforeseen hindrance' their occupants were somewhere far away from the camp, but I thought it better to resist the temptation.

After what I had just experienced I feared it might be much the same, but I determined to take even that slim chance of seeing and talking to these men. Even if they were not able to speak freely with me as they were entitled to do according to the provisions of the Geneva Convention they would know at least from my presence that they had not been forgotten, that we had discovered their prison and that it had ceased to be inaccessible.

In the train which took us towards the north that evening in the company of Japanese officers I made no allusion whatever to the visit we had made that day or to the visit we were to make to-morrow.

We arrived in Sze Ping Hai in pouring rain and drove through its disorderly Chinese streets with black, white and red signs swinging above our heads. We left the next morning and travelled for three hours along a valley towards the north-east. At the end of the valley smoke-stacks and slag heaps indicated the presence of an important mining centre: Seihan.

We passed through the town by car. Its buildings were grimy with coal dust. Passing the entrance to a mine we came to a halt before a long low building set back in quite pleasant grounds. Formerly, I was told, European mining engineers had lived there.

When our car passed through the gates to the hoarse shouts of sentries we observed Japanese soldiers hurriedly driving one or two men, who had been walking under the trees, back before them into the building. A book left on a bench and a couple of tennis rackets on the grass near an improvised tennis court seemed to suggest that the glowing accounts given me by Colonel Matsuda on the conditions in which the prisoners were held was perhaps rather nearer the truth this time.

'They are allowed a great deal of freedom,' he had said, 'sports, including tennis, and even angling, lectures and so on.'

However, it was clearly impossible to hope to get into touch with them without first having listened to a long lecture on the history of the camp, its geographic situation, and the excellent conditions created here, as everywhere else, for the unfortunate soldiers whom the just fortunes of war had deprived of the honour of fighting on.

This unavoidable lecture, delivered in the Japanese officers' mess with exactly the same ceremonial as at Mukden, lasted an hour and a half. I was boiling with impatience, but I did my best to remain impassive. Later on, in the camp, I proposed to tell Matsuda of my wish to speak to each of the prisoners.

Did he guess my intention? As soon as we had arisen to proceed to the camp proper he caused his secretary to translate the following to us:

'You are authorized to visit the camp provided that you give me your word of honour that you will make no gesture of sympathy whatever to the prisoners and that you will not say a word, even "Good morning".'

Stressing each word he added:

'On your attitude today will depend the whole future of the International Red Cross Delegation in Japan.'

That was clearly because I had shown the temerity to shake hands with the Australian doctor in the hospital at Mukden and to utter a few words of encouragement. The Japanese idea of how a Red Cross delegate should act was now quite clear to me: a silent visitor to silent prisoners.

However, I had to think carefully before protesting. I had been warned that it was not merely a question of my own mission but of the work of our whole delegation in Tokio. An exchange of glances with Margherita assured me that I had properly understood the sense of the warning. I summed up all the risks and turned to Matsuda:

'You have said that there are fifteen superior officers detained here. I will agree not to say a word to fourteen of them, but you must allow me to tell at least one of them that I represent the International Committee of the Red Cross.'

It was Matsuda's turn to think.

'Is that all you want to say to him?' he asked.

'No. I must be able to ask him about his health, to tell him that his family received his last message, and to ask him whether he has any request to make.'

Matsuda sucked in the air violently and tapped himself on the neck as was his strange habit. Obviously, my insistence had put him in a difficult quandary. I knew that his instructions from Tokio were on the one hand to prevent any contact whatever between me and these 'important prisoners' and yet on the other hand to treat me as an 'honoured guest'. They were difficult to combine. Dare he cause me to 'lose face' before his officers? He hesitated, and I knew that I had won.

'Which of the prisoners do you desire to talk to?'

'General Wainwright.'

'Very good. But you will give me your word of honour that you will say nothing whatever to the others?'

'I will.'

It was a strange bargain closed 6000 miles from Geneva in a little park which reminded me to some extent of the grounds of the Villa Moynier but which was situated in the heart of the Manchu country.

We walked towards the grey house, which was less like a prison than a miner's block in the Borinage. A long corridor went from end to end of it with doors on either side, seven on the left and eight on the right.

In surroundings which were so like the familiar surroundings we knew at home I had difficulty in realizing that I was about to come face to face with the hero of Corregidor, the defender of Singapore, the Governor of the Dutch East Indies and twelve other soldiers of high rank whose armies were still fighting everywhere in the Pacific.

And suddenly a disturbing sight presented itself.

There they stood upright and motionless in the middle of the room. I should not have been able to distinguish their faces even if I had not involuntarily turned my head away because they bowed low, their arms close to their bodies, as soon as the sabre of Matsuda rapped on the floor.

It seemed to me that the last man in the row refused to submit to the humiliation and remained upright.

'General Wainwright.'

My emotion was so great that I could hardly utter the words I had to speak. He maintained an icy reserve towards the Japanese around me. Nothing, it seemed, had broken his spirit. His voice was still vibrant as he replied to the pitiful and absurdly abrupt questions which were all I was allowed to ask him.

'How are you?'

'Not bad. My right hip is giving me rather less trouble now.'

'I am happy to tell you that your family is well and that they received your last message safely.'

'Thank you.'

His face lit up at my last question.

'Have you any request to make?'

'Certainly. Can I make it now?'

'No,' put in Matsuda at once. 'It will have to be made in writing to Tokio.'

The ghost of a sceptical smile passed over General Wainwright's lips.

The door was closed behind us. The interview was at an end. It had not lasted two minutes.

I left the house almost hustled out by the Japanese, who seemed to fear that I would shout the 'goodbye' that struggled for expression. I had been able to see them and let them see me; that was all. But at least they now knew that we were aware of their place of detention.

Only prisoners who had been cut off from their world for three years and had seen nothing around them but yellow faces could appreciate the full significance of that pitiful result: two months journey from Europe to China, via Egypt, Persia, Moscow and Siberia, for two minutes restricted conversation with one prisoner of war in Manchuria.

We had gone only a few steps in the grounds when I heard coming from the other end of the house the noise of a violent altercation and then shouts. Suddenly a thin, nervous-looking man broke through the barrier of Japanese sentries and ran towards me. He was very pale but determined. Out of breath he reached us and addressed me:

'Excuse me,' he said. 'I am General Percival. I protest against the fact that you have been authorized to talk to General Wainwright although I am the senior officer here. There is a lot I should like to tell you. Things take place here that you ought to know.'

But already he was surrounded by Japanese guards who sought to take him away. What could I do? I had given my word to Matsuda that I would speak only to General Wainwright and that I would not say a word or make a sign to another prisoner. I had not even the right to explain to General Percival that I was bound by my word not even to give him my hand. I could feel Matsuda's eyes fixed on me and I could still hear his warning in my ears: 'On your attitude today will depend the whole future of the International Red Cross Delegation in Japan.'

I turned to the interpreter and said to him loudly in English so that General Percival should understand:

'This is an impossible situation. Please ask Colonel Matsuda to give me permission to make the necessary explanations to General Percival. When I asked permission to speak to General Wainwright I did not know that General Percival was the senior officer in the camp and he is perfectly entitled to feel astonished that I did not speak to him. The nature of the visit I have been compelled to make here today must truly astonish him.'

The interpreter translated what I said. The Japanese put their heads together and General Percival did not take his eyes off my face.

Colonel Matsuda gave way again:

'One minute only then,' he said grudgingly.

Eagerly I turned to General Percival and explained rapidly who I was, from whence I had come, and the conditions which had been imposed on my visit.

'When will you come again?' he asked.

'As soon as I possibly can,' I replied.

'All right,' he said shortly, concealing his disappointment, 'but promise me that you will come again.'

'I will do all I can.'

The Japanese escorted me away whilst the guards took General Percival back to the house. I still heard his voice as he went: 'Promise me to come back. Promise me to come back.'

I had no need to go back.

On that very day, August 6th, 1945, over a thousand miles from the camp, the first atomic bomb had exploded in the air over Hiroshima.

Three weeks later on mounting the steps of the New Grand Hotel in Yokohama I saw two high officers coming towards me in new uniforms with many decorations on their chests.

'Pleased to see you again, Monsieur Junod,' said General Wainwright smiling. 'MacArthur has allowed us to return your visit.'

And General Percival added:

'This time we shall be able to talk in peace.'

CHAPTER III

OMORI CAMP

W E were to leave Hsinking for Tokio on August 9th, 1945, in a Japanese plane bound for Tokio. We had crossed the frontier into Manchuria twelve days before and for six weeks we had had no idea of how the war in the Pacific was going. The Japanese in Mukden were as badly informed as the Russians in Tchita, and no one listened to the American wireless though for the past three days it had been broadcasting the dreadful news of Hiroshima.

We had begun to think that our fears of not being able to get across the Manchurian frontier in time had been vain. Despite all the troop movements we had seen on both sides of the frontier the Russians had not moved.

On August 8th we went to bed rather late in the Hotel Yamata in Hsinking after having packed our bags ready to leave the next day. At about one o'clock I was awakened by the sound of bells and by tumult in the corridors. I opened my door and saw people scurrying towards the staircase. It was an air-raid warning, an unusual happening for Hsinking, because the distance from the bases of the American Flying Fortresses was very great.

However, before long the throbbing of aero-engines could be heard in the sky. I went to wake Margherita and together we went down into the basement. The air-raid shelter in the Hotel Yamata was particularly solid, but its concrete walls were slimy with damp and I passed a strange night between Margherita, who was shivering in her dressing-gown, and a White Russian emigré who was soon telling me all about his life and misfortunes.

Explosions sounded dully, but occasionally they came closer and then the noise was ear-shattering. Towards five o'clock in the morning things were a little quieter and we left the shelter although the all-clear had not yet sounded.

We managed to get another hour's sleep and then we got ready and waited with impatience for the arrival of the representative of the Japanese Embassy who was to call for us at half-past eight, not knowing whether the damage done in the night would prevent our departure or not.

As soon as he came into the hall where we were waiting he declared:

'The Russians attacked in the night. It was their planes which bombed us.'

'Will the plane leave for Tokio just the same?' I asked anxiously.

'I don't know. Perhaps. We must wait and see.'

It was not a pleasant experience to wait for two or three hours on the first day of the war on an air field which had already been bombed and might be bombed again at any moment. We knew that if we missed the plane we might be cut off in Manchuria and have to take one of the overcrowded trains to Shanghai.

Towards midday an officer arrived and took us out on to the tarmac. There were numerous aeroplanes already in the sky, but no one seemed to know whether they were Russian or Japanese. The alert was still on.

Six Japanese officers were already seated in the small two-engine plane which was to take us to Tokio. We were the last passengers. The curtains were carefully drawn in the cabin and the cabin interior was quite dark. The air screws began to turn and in a moment or two the plane moved forward at a rapidly increasing speed. I was longing to feel that we had definitely left the ground because my first and very disagreeable impression was that we were hurtling forward into black nothingness.

Even when we were in the air our situation was far from reassuring; a chance meeting with a Russian or American plane might easily prove fatal. However, the lack of sleep the previous night and the darkness around us were stronger than my anxiety and I soon fell asleep.

Margherita woke me up two hours later and whispered in my ear:

'The blinds are not drawn in the lavatory.'

I took my map with me and went to the toilet. We were flying over the sea and I realized that we were now in all probability outside the radius of action of Russian planes. When I returned to the cabin I observed that the other passengers obviously thought the same thing for they were now engaged in chewing enormous sandwiches, judging, no doubt, that the one danger was safely past and the other not yet imminent.

An hour later a change in the sound of our flight made me suspect that we were flying over land. A quick glance behind the blind at my window showed me that we were flying over a wooded and very broken coastline. We were losing height rapidly and soon we landed on a very narrow air field.

'Tokio?'

'No. Toyama.'

We were on the west coast of Japan and we needed no more than an hour's flight to cross the whole island empire. The pilot inquired whether General Doolittle and his bombers were reported anywhere in the neighbourhood.

'The route is clear,' replied Tokio.

We did not learn until much later why the sky, which was usually crossed and re-crossed by planes, was so empty that evening.

The American air force had dropped only one bomb on Japan that day, but its explosive force was equivalent to the bomb-load of 2000 flying fortresses. It was the second atomic bomb and at 8.30 — just at the time we had learned of Russia's entry into the war — it had exploded in the air over Nagasaki.

The plane was flying low over the sea when we turned into Tokio Bay. On the horizon in the soft light of dusk the black outline of a very large town could be seen against the water. When we gained height before landing on the air field of Hanada between Tokio and Yokohama I could see nothing but burned out houses, collapsed walls, broken smoke-stacks and gutted hangars; a fantastic sweep of ash-coloured devastation merging into the night.

We stayed only one day in Tokio, August 10th, and in the evening, accompanied by our friends of the International Red Cross

Delegation, Angst, Bilfinger and Pestalozzi, we left for Karuisava.

A five-hour drive brought us to the charming place about 1800 feet above sea level where almost all foreign diplomats had sought refuge from the repeated bombing of the capital.

There were only two narrow streets in Karuisava with wooden houses on either side, which were all Japanese shops. The residential villas were dotted around in the near-by pine forest and reached by narrow paths through the undergrowth. One of these villas had been reserved for us. It was a real Japanese house with sliding doors and paper walls, and on the floors were the usual *tatamis* made of plaited straw. The two servants, Tie-san, a little Japanese woman with sparkling eyes who was to be our *amah*, and Li-san, the Chinese cook, had prepared us a very tasty meal.

The peace of the forest, the beautiful red and white striped lilies which graced the rooms, and the transparent moths which fluttered around the lamps created an atmosphere of peace and serenity which hardly seemed real after the fatigues and alarms of our journey.

In the morning the sun woke me at about nine, and I had to think for a moment or two before I could remember where I was: not in Paris or Berlin, not in London or Moscow, not in Cairo or Teheran, but in Karuisava.

The *amah* entered my room bringing a letter resting on the upturned palms of her hands which she proffered with a graceful bow.

It was a message from Kammerer, one of the secretaries of our delegation. I read it again and again. Every word of it filled my heart to overflowing with joy:

Dear Dr. Junod: The B.B.C. has broadcast Japan's acceptance of the Potsdam conditions. It is peace at last. Crowds are dancing in Trafalgar Square.

All the foreigners — French, Belgian, Swedes, Hungarians and Spaniards — who had taken refuge in Karuisava and the surrounding villas were now gathered in its two streets eagerly discussing the wonderful news.

I went at once to visit our Minister, M. Gorgé, who for four years had valiantly defended the interests of the allies in Japan, which had been entrusted to our Legation. He shared in our joy but he cautiously advised us not to be over confident.

'The Japanese have made no official announcement as yet. I know them very well by this time. No one can say what their reactions will be at the last moment. Apart from unconditional surrender the allies demand that the Emperor shall submit to their absolute control. We must know first whether the Emperor will agree, and secondly whether his generals will obey him if he does.'

'Do you think a revolution is possible, Your Excellency?'

'I should not like to say positively that it isn't,' he replied. 'If you had lived in Japan as long as I have you would know what violent fanaticism is hidden behind the outward stoicism of these people.'

The same day I got into touch with the Japanese Ministry for Foreign Affairs, which bears the sonorous name of Gaimucho. On August 12th Minister Susuki, who was in charge of all matters relating to prisoners of war, came to bring me a personal letter from the Minister for Foreign Affairs, Togo, who welcomed us to Japan and informed us that the Japanese Government proposed to make a considerable contribution to the International Red Cross.

I inquired of Susuki whether the Japanese Government had taken all possible steps to safeguard the prisoners of war in all circumstances and particularly if troubles arose between the time when the Emperor accepted the demands of the allies and the landing of American troops. It was obvious that he was anxious.

'You will have to go to Tokio as soon as the surrender becomes effective. I know no more than you what might happen.'

On August 15th, for the first time in history, the Emperor of Japan addressed his people and his speech was broadcast. The moment the Emperor began to speak our *amah* knelt down before the loud-speaker and then stretched herself out at full length, her forehead touching the floor. The Mikado announced the unconditional surrender. Tears flowed from the eyes of Tie-san. When the message was at an end she rose.

'The Emperor knows better than we do what should be done,' she said simply.

The following day disquieting rumours began to circulate. In Tokio the generals were said to be contemplating a seizure of power against the decision of the Emperor. Leaflets calling for the continuation of the war to the bitter end, the total destruction of the country and the death of the last soldier, had been dropped over Yokohama. Revolts had broken out in a number of towns in the south.

If the troubles became general what would be the fate of the prisoners?

In order to forestall and report to the Japanese Government, and perhaps to the Americans, the incidents we feared we decided that representatives of the International Red Cross Committee should go as soon as possible to all the most important prisoner-of-war centres; but there were seven of them and only four delegates. However, I managed to find three other Swiss who agreed to assist us, and together we held a short conference in our villa in Karuisava to decide the details and the zones to be entrusted to each delegate.

On August 17th, against the advice of the more prudent, we all arrived in Tokio by train. In order to find room for us the Japanese police emptied a compartment of its occupants, and this ruthless action aroused no protest whatever. At each stop curious faces appeared at the door of our compartment. No one showed us the slightest hostility though for the Japanese everyone white was vaguely a victorious enemy.

In Tokio we immediately got into touch with the authorities and a conference was arranged with representatives of the Gaimucho, the War Ministry, the Ministry of Communications and the Prisoners-of-War Department.

Above all we wanted to know exactly where the camps were. During the war the Japanese had informed us on a number of occasions that there were forty-three camps, but now we discovered that there were 103. We had also been told officially that the number of prisoners in Japanese hands on the mainland was 27,000; now they admitted to 34,000.

A plan for their evacuation was worked out. By wireless I informed General MacArthur, whose headquarters was still in Manila, that we were ready to establish liaison between him and the Japanese authorities in every port and at every air field where prisoners of war were in the neighbourhood. Manila had already issued instructions that huge letters 'P.W.' should be painted on the camps so that foodstuffs and other supplies could be parachuted in.

Tokio began to prepare itself to receive the conquerors. Companies of soldiers worked steadily to clear up the town, filling in craters and trenches, removing masses of scrap metal, barbed wire and fire-damaged wreckage from acres and acres of the town. Apart from modern buildings, almost all quarters of the town had been gutted, because the Flying Fortresses had dropped almost exclusively incendiaries. The flimsy Japanese houses had gone up like tinder. The only furniture which had resisted the fire was the safe installed to protect valuables and fragile goods in the event of earthquakes, and thus a strange feature of the devastated areas was the appearance of thousands of these safes standing out above the wreckage.

It was a tremendous job to obtain all the safe-conducts, the permits, the authorizations and so on which were essential for our delegates to fulfil their missions. The Japanese officials seemed more occupied in burning tons of papers, propaganda sheets and compromising documents.

At last, on August 24th, our delegates left Tokio on their various assignments, together with official Swiss representatives, who were the protecting power for American and British interests, and official Swedish representatives, who fulfilled the same office for the Belgians and the Dutch.

The revelation of the many camps whose existence had been previously concealed from us by the Japanese and the verification of the information given to us, often inaccurate or positively faked, led me to visit the camp at Omori on one of the small islands in Tokio Bay.

I was looking in particular for 200 airmen who were known to have baled out over Japan and about whose whereabouts we had never been able to discover anything in spite of repeated inquiries throughout the war.

The traditional Japanese reception in the officers' mess complete with cups of tea, small cakes and mandarines broken into quarters threatened to be every bit as long as the others, but I cut short the flowery discourses and asked Prince Shimasu, the Vice-President of the Japanese Red Cross Society, to make it clear to the Japanese commander of the camp that from now on the prisoners were not under his orders.

This was done, but we still had to listen to a last oration from him which was astonishing enough in the form and so typical of the spirit which reigned amongst Japanese officers at the time that its gist deserves to be recorded:

'Like all my comrades,' he informed me, 'I was determined to fight on to the last breath in my body. But since the speech of the Emperor all that has changed . . . I did my duty in commanding this camp. Now I will do my duty in liberating the prisoners under the best possible conditions.'

After that I was able to enter the huts where I was horrified to find amongst 1500 prisoners in a fairly reasonable state a group of men who were horribly emaciated, pale as ghosts, their limbs swollen with beri-beri, and hardly able to stand upright. Their eyes were staring and the pupils were very small and on their faces was an expression of heart-rending stupor. They were in the light of day for the first time for months, and some of them for years. These were the 200 airmen who had been taken out of the cellars of the Japanese General Headquarters in Tokio where they had been held incommunicado throughout the war.

They had been beaten and tortured, and the chief amusement of their jailers had been to chase them through the gloomy corridors of the basement which served as their prison. At least a quarter of these men were not ill, but dying. One of them, a major in the American naval air arm, could hardly speak when he tried to tell me his story. He was nothing but a skeleton with hardly strength left to stand on his feet.

'The war is over,' I said to him gently. 'Within a few days you will all be free.'

He could obviously not believe me and the tears ran down his sunken cheeks as though I were telling him some vain dream to console him in his sufferings.

On August 27th at nine o'clock in the morning the door bell rang in the little villa in the Torizaka quarter where we had found a lodging.

The *amah* came to announce that a Japanese naval officer wished to speak to me. I went out.

'Dr. Junod?'

'That's correct. What is it you want?'

'I have been instructed to inform you that Admiral Badger will expect you to come on board the *San Diego* in Sungami Bay at eleven o'clock tomorrow morning. We will send a car to fetch you at eight o'clock.'

So my message had reached Manila. The Americans were already informed that we were doing everything to return the prisoners to their homes. All day we had seen hundreds of American planes flying over Tokio in formation, but we did not know that American warships were so close behind them.

The following morning the car was there as arranged and we drove off towards Yokohama. An hour later we were in Yokosuka, one of the most important of Japan's naval bases.

I boarded a waiting launch together with about a dozen or more Japanese; including an admiral, five officers and a number of sailors carrying large rolls of documents. They were the plans of the defensive works of the naval base and of the mine-fields, which were to be handed over to the Americans. The Japanese were all unarmed and they carried out their mission with solemn dignity.

When the launch chugged out beyond the bay I saw the silhouettes of the American warships. Some of them seemed riding at anchor, but others were patrolling constantly up and down. We made our way towards the light cruiser *San Diego*. As we came near a score of reporters waiting along the rails raised their cameras.

Hundreds of sailors were visible on deck, some of them lining the rails, others sitting on the batteries and even on the gun barrels, watching the Japanese as they climbed up to the deck, small and stiff in their tight uniforms. Huge naval policemen searched them as they came on board and then conducted them to a cabin where they were locked in.

Someone called down to me from the bridge. I clambered up the ladder and was immediately introduced to Admiral Badger.

'I'm very happy to make your acquaintance,' he said with a warm handshake. 'What news have you for me?'

I described the situation to him as briefly as possible. He then introduced me to the Chief Surgeon of his squadron, Commodore Boone, and to Harold Stassen, the well-known leader of the Republican Party, who was serving his country in the navy. I told them that my chief anxiety was to secure the evacuation of the prisoners in the two camps in Tokio Bay, Omori and Shinagava, as soon as possible, as in Omori were 200 airmen in a parlous condition and many of them might still be saved if given immediate medical attention, whilst in Shinagava were gravely sick men who had been brought in from other camps, and in particular forty prisoners whose transfer I had secured quite recently from the terrible camp of Ofuna.

Harold Stassen went away and returned a few minutes later with a naval chart on which even the smallest detail was noted.

'Is that where the camps are?' he asked, pointing to the spot with his finger.

'That's right,' I replied. 'They are on very small islands which are connected with the mainland by wooden bridges.'

'And you think it's urgent to go and find them?'

'Beyond all question. Some of them are very near the end and we must do everything possible to give them a chance of survival. Blood transfusions, serum injections and penicillin could still work miracles.'

Unfortunately, it appeared, they had the strictest orders not to go ashore. So far only a few planes had landed at Atzugui, about two hours from Tokio.

'We must get into touch with Manila,' suggested Commodore Simpson.

Within the hour General MacArthur had granted permission.

'Will you come with me?' asked Commodore Boone.

I agreed and we were transferred to another vessel, the *San Juan*, which was lying in Tokio Bay. Motor landing boats with a square front and a sort of drawbridge arrangement for lowering on shore began to gather from all parts around the *San Juan*.

Boone, Stassen and I got into the first and the flotilla set off in the direction in which I believed the islands to lie, but after we had gone a mile or so I had lost my bearings and was beginning to feel rather ashamed of my vagueness.

'Don't worry,' said the Commodore. 'We'll call up the planes by wireless.'

A few minutes later four or five planes appeared and flying almost at sea level they showed us the way. After a while we came to a channel between piles driven into the sea bed, and then on either side hundreds of ragged figures appeared shouting with joy at the sight of us and the thought of their imminent deliverance. Some of them even plunged into the sea to meet us and others waved weakly to us with arms like matchsticks. In the centre of the island three large flags were hoisted on poles: 'Old Glory', the Union Jack and the Dutch tricolour.

Our boat crunched on the shore and we landed. My companions were immediately surrounded by happily gesticulating prisoners all talking at once and putting a hundred and one questions. When we made to penetrate into the interior of the camp a Japanese sentry lowered his rifle to bar our passage. Simpson frowned angrily. I intervened at once.

'Perhaps they have not been warned of our coming,' I said. 'It is best to avoid an incident if possible and go straight to the commander of the camp.'

Colonel Sakata, the Japanese commander, came forward surrounded by his officers. The usual ceremony in the mess was not at all to the taste of the Americans, and Commodore Simpson impatiently rejected the biscuits and the quartered mandarines.

'We are going to evacuate the camp at once,' he said bluntly.

Colonel Sakata passed his hand through his hair, bowed his head and smiled.

'Na . . . I have received no orders to that effect,' he observed.

'Well, take them now — from General MacArthur.'

At the sound of that magic name all difficulties disappeared. The news that the prisoners were to be evacuated at once went through the camp swiftly and an outburst of almost hysterical joy took place in which the prisoners danced and sang to the tune of a mechanical piano which they had dragged up from somewhere. Others were hastily gathering their poor things together in bundles together with one or two souvenirs of their exile. An airman supported himself against the door jamb of one of the huts. Tears poured down his worn and lined face. The emotion was too much for him. He fell to the ground and his emaciated body writhed in a kind of fit. He was taken away to the sick-bay.

'Nervous shock,' muttered the camp doctor, who had difficulty in standing up himself for sheer fatigue.

Whilst the evacuation of camp Omori proceeded Commodore Boone and I went off in a requisitioned car towards the hospital camp of Shinagava which was about a mile and a half away. It was six o'clock in the evening and we had to hurry. We passed on foot over a damaged wooden bridge to the island.

The first to receive us in Shinagava were three doctor prisoners who had been attached to the camp: Surgeon-Commander H. L. Cleave of the Royal Navy, a British captain named J. M. Warrack, and an American naval lieutenant M. L. Gottlieb. They immediately took Commodore Boone into the huts of this strange hospital camp for a rapid inspection and to choose the most urgent cases for evacuation.

The sick men were lying on thin mattresses on the ground and all the mattresses were verminous. Their eyes burned feverishly, but as they raised them towards us they were lit with a great joy. The worst cases were victims of under-nourishment and beri-beri. They were nothing but skin and bone, except that their limbs were horribly swollen with oedema. Two or three years of captivity had turned them into physical wrecks and they sobbed softly at the thought of their liberation.

Night had already fallen when the first landing boats set off with their human cargoes. Twenty-five sick men were lying in the bottom of each boat as it made its way seawards. The commanders picked their way towards the channel, trying not to destroy the fishermen's nets which were spanned from rock to rock. From time to time a dazzling searchlight flung a powerful beam of light across the water and was then suddenly extinguished.

Five miles off the coast waited the hospital ship *Benevolence*, the only ship of the squadron with all its lights on. It shone brilliantly and around it the water glistened like a halo.

It took the landing boats an hour to get to the *Benevolence* and transfer their passengers and then they turned about to return for others. In order to show them the way the prisoners had built a great bonfire at the nearest point of the island and its flames cast a fantastic light over the strange embarkation scenes.

Throughout the night the boats returned many times, and gradually the camp began to empty. The sick men, taken from their miserable palliasses, some of them barely conscious, awoke the next day in the luxurious surroundings of a modern floating hospital. It was a transformation scene indeed. At last they found real rest in a proper bed with clean white sheets, in an airy and silent ward with nurses always present to attend to their requirements and to give all the care which they might expect in the homes which awaited them and from the country which had found them again.

Within a few minutes of their arrival on board, the wireless had sent their names across the Pacific to the Kentish village or the Alabama town from which they came.

The bonfire on the beach at Omori gradually died down. When I left early in the morning with the last of the sick prisoners it was no more than a red glow which soon disappeared behind us as we put out to sea.

The sea had become rough in the meantime. A warm wind which came in gusts swept spray and mist before it.

The hospital ship *Benevolence* towered above us, its lights blazing. In order to lessen the waves around it the other ships manœuvred into position to form a sort of breakwater.

As soon as the last boats were within this artificial harbour they were picked out by the criss-crossing searchlights of the other vessels and followed until they transferred their cargoes in clouds of spray to the *Benevolence*.

The stretchers were gently drawn up by ropes against the lighted side of the hospital ship and deposited as gently on the wide stretch of peaceful deck beyond the rails.

CHAPTER IV

THE DEAD CITY

WHEN I returned from camp Omori I saw the first detachments of marines pouring out of the landing boats to occupy Japan. They assembled along the banks of Tokio Bay as though going on manœuvres. Their weapons glinted in the sun and the Japanese observed the scene with tranquil interest and showed no signs either of sadness or hostility. Indeed, they might have been watching the exercises of their own navy.

These people, who had counted it a supreme honour to have a member of their family amongst the dead, and who had been tremendously proud if a son or brother was amongst the *Kamikase* or suicide squads, as a suicide pilot or one-man torpedo crew, did not make a gesture or say a word against the invader. Had not the Emperor declared: 'The war is over.'

When a detachment of sailors passed before us preceded by their commandant I saw an old man in a grey kimono turn his head away almost unnoticeably. His narrow eyes became slits behind his gold-rimmed glasses and a polite smile crossed his closed lips. He was too moved not to smile. A white man would have wept.

I returned to the camp which we had emptied of its prisoners in the night. The gates were wide open and the forecourt was deserted. The mechanical piano stood there incongruously as though ready to play the songs of deliverance once again. An Alsatian dog trotted up and rubbed its head against my leg. It had been the mascot of Omori camp and now his masters were gone. Seeing the sailors he pricked his ears and made to follow them, daring yet uncertain, like a masterless dog.

In the forecourt, in the stores and in the deserted huts were many opened cases, some of which contained medical supplies, foodstuffs and clothing parachuted in by the Americans a fortnight previously, and now left behind by the prisoners. I had been authorized to collect it all for use in succouring not only the thousands of foreigners who were bombarding our delegation with requests for assistance but also the innumerable Japanese who had been bombed and burnt out of their homes and now faced the coming winter completely destitute.

At eleven o'clock planes arrived and began to fly in circles over the camp. They had come to parachute in further supplies although none of their men remained. White parcels began to fall from the air. Coloured parachutes unfolded above them like great flowers, blue, yellow, red and green, and the wind carried them towards the sea. Other parcels, thrown direct out of the planes, fell like bombs on the ground or smashed through the roofs of the huts. A big case containing two hundred pairs of boots burst only a few yards away from where I was standing. In fact I only just had time to dodge out of its way. Unfortunately a score or so of prisoners in various camps were killed by this rather summary method of providing them with supplies.

Japanese, who had themselves gone without many necessary things since the war, immediately hurried to obtain a share of this manna which came dropping from heaven, but as soon as they heard that it was now all to go to the Red Cross they helped with the loading of the lorries and not a single tin of meat or anything else was lost.

In the evening of August 31st I went to our office in the Maranuchi quarter to inquire if there was any news of our six delegates in the provinces who were organizing the collection of the prisoners and their transport in the same way as we were doing in Tokio. One of them, Bilfinger, had gone to the neighbourhood of Hiroshima, and I was awaiting news from him with particular anxiety.

Three weeks had passed since the two atomic bombs had been dropped on Hiroshima and Nagasaki but we still knew practically nothing about the fate of the devastated towns or of the innumerable victims. The American wireless had broadcast a very great deal about the preparations made for the use of the new weapon and about its extraordinary power, but information concerning the effects of atomic bombardment was limited to the horrible prophecy: 'for seventy years at least the radio-activity of the earth around the scene of the explosion will prevent all forms of life from existing there'.

The Americans I had met the evening before on board the *Benevolence* had all fallen silent the moment I had mentioned the word 'Hiroshima'. When they questioned me about Japan they carefully avoided all mention of it, and when I uttered the word I think we all felt an indefinable sense of discomfort. I knew that an American journalist had managed to get near Hiroshima in a plane, but his account had immediately been suppressed, and if military planes had flown over the town since the explosion their accounts of the terrible destruction had remained in the hands of the military and the scientists.

For different reasons the Japanese also maintained complete silence concerning the disaster which had brought about their sudden defeat. For a few days the Tokio newspapers had printed vivid descriptions of the effects of 'atomization' in order to prepare people's minds for the coming surrender, but since the surrender had become a fact not a single report had been published concerning the real extent of the disaster.

It was only through the verbal reports which went from one end of Japan to the other that we began to have some idea of what the sudden cataclysm had meant for the inhabitants of Hiroshima. One of our secretaries named Nohara, a half-Japanese, sometimes repeated to us more or less the gist of what was being rumoured amongst the Japanese. Many fugitives had fled from Hiroshima to seek safety with their families, and their first-hand descriptions of the horror were profoundly disquieting, the blinding light suddenly flashing out of a peaceful sky was a phenomenon much more terrible than an earthquake. It was a typhoon of glare, heat and wind which had swept suddenly over the earth and left a sea of fire behind it.

No one knew the total of the dead; 50,000 said some; 200,000 insisted others. And there were just as many wounded, or more. And of those who seemed at first to have escaped injury, thousands were dying every day with strange, new and inexplicable symptoms.

It was not until September 1st that the Gaimucho showed me some photographs taken in Hiroshima after the explosion of the bomb. Despite all we had already been told and all that we had already imagined, the greyish desert of broken earth was deeply moving. The death screams of those who died in Pompeii in a rain of incandescent cinders and red-hot lava had long since died away. Today in Hiroshima though there was no rain of incandescent cinders or flood of red-hot lava, the air had suddenly become heated to many thousands of degrees, and the Pompeian picture was repeated, but on a much vaster scale.

On September 2nd a Japanese policeman brought a copy of a telegram to our villa in Torizaka for which Tokio had not yet issued a censorship visa. Bilfinger had arrived at Hiroshima on August 30th and hurriedly sent off the following disjointed report:

Situation horrifying ... Ninety per cent of town razed ... All hospitals destroyed or severely damaged ... Have visited two provisional hospitals: conditions indescribable ... Bomb effects mysterious ... Many victims apparently recovering suddenly experience fatal relapse owing to degeneration of white corpuscles and other internal injuries ... Deaths still occurring in great numbers. More than 100,000 victims still in provisional hospitals in neighbourhood. Grave shortage material, bandages, medicaments ... Appeal allied high command asking supplies be parachuted immediately into centre of town. Urgently need large supplies bandages, cottonwool, ointment for burns, sulphamides, blood plasma and transfusion kits ... Immediate action necessary. ...

I took this telegram, and the photographs, which I still had in my possession, and went at once to the Yokohama Chamber of Commerce where General MacArthur had installed himself and his staff.

A few minutes after my arrival four high officers were bending over the table on which I had wordlessly placed the photos and the telegram: General Fitch, Chief of the U.S. Information Service; Colonel Marcus, of the Prisoners-of-War Department; Colonel

Webster, Chief of the Hospital Service; and Colonel Sams, who was in charge of assistance for the civilian population.

They were the first Americans to see photographs of Hiroshima taken on the ground after the fall of the atomic bomb. Their faces were grave and attentive, and their expressions were a trifle wry at the sight of those carbonized corpses, the skin hanging down in scorched strips from chests and backs, and the flesh often burnt away to the bone itself.

No one spoke. The photos went from hand to hand. General Fitch put on his glasses. He read the telegram twice and then he turned to me.

'What do you want us to do?'

What did I want them to do? Wasn't Bilfinger's telegram plain enough? There were 100,000 wounded people without proper attention. Bandages, sulphamides, blood plasma – Bilfinger had listed it all. I suggested that a rescue expedition should be organized at once.

The general turned to Colonel Sams:

'That's your department I think,' he said.

The four officers put their heads together. Then one of them picked up the photos and the telegram.

'Leave these with me,' he said. 'I want them to show General MacArthur.'

It was September 7th, five days later, before I heard anything further, and then Colonel Sams summoned me to Yokohama.

'It is impossible for the United States Army to organize any direct relief action,' he informed me, 'but General MacArthur is willing to let you have fifteen tons of medicaments and hospital material. They can be distributed under the control and responsibility of the Red Cross.'

And he added:

'A commission of inquiry is leaving for Hiroshima tomorrow. A seat has been reserved for you on board one of the planes.'

On the morning of September 8th six U.S. planes left Atzugui air field. In the plane in which I travelled were General Newman, Colonel Wilson and a physicist named Morrison, one of the technical experts who had been responsible for the construction of the bomb.

The bare cone of Fujiyama was just visible on the horizon as we flew over the 'inland sea' which lay beneath us like a lavender blue carpet picked out in green and yellow with its numerous promontories and wooded islands.

To our right was a long reddish grey smudge along the bank. It was the heap of rusty scrap iron and ashes to which a dozen or so miles of one of the most important industrial towns in Japan, Osaka-Kobé, had been reduced with its factories, docks and warehouses. Here and there one or two reinforced concrete buildings still stood upright amidst the ruins. They alone had escaped destruction in the rain of incendiary bombs.

I knew that Bilfinger must have established his camp somewhere in the neighbourhood over which we were flying, but I looked in vain for any sign of the Red Cross to indicate its position.

Towards midday a huge white patch appeared on the ground below us. This chalky desert, looking almost like ivory in the sun, surrounded by a crumble of twisted ironwork and ash heaps, was all that remained of Hiroshima.

In our plane the physicist Morrison was nervously going from one window to the other studying the scientific message the grim picture held for him. He compared photos he had with him with what he could see out of the windows, made hasty notes and sketched out a general plan. His nervousness and agitation contrasted with the rather shocked silence of General Newman. As for me, my feelings were very strange. I was less impressed with what I saw than with something I remembered: a picture of burnt and blasted Abyssinian huts and fleeing natives. Though flying above the remains of Hiroshima it was of Dessie I thought.

Our plane circled several times over the scene and then flew off to land about fifteen miles away at Ivakuni. The other five planes drew up alongside our own and soon the fifteen tons of medical supplies were being unloaded. Before leaving in a bus which was to take us to the military headquarters of the province of Hiroshima I entrusted the supplies to the care of a Japanese naval captain.

Then other Japanese officers led us to a ramshackle old bus and we set off. It was not long before the engine began to cough and splutter and finally it gave out altogether in the middle of a village.

The inhabitants came running up and when they saw the American uniforms they formed a silent circle around us. The district was not yet occupied and they saw Americans for the first time. None of us was armed and there were no Japanese soldiers escorting us. For a moment or two I felt some apprehension, imagining the reaction of the survivors of a European town which had been 'atomized' when the enemy sent a commission of inquiry so soon after the disaster to investigate the effects of its new weapon.

The circle became smaller and smaller, but the faces lightened with the same rather embarrassed and gentle smile which I had already seen on the face of the old man in the grey kimono at the sight of the American sailors on the shores of Omori. The children came closer, attracted by the packets of sweets the Americans were offering. There was not the slightest sign of resentment or hatred in the looks of any of the Japanese. They were intensely curious, that was all.

The break-down was prolonged and in the end a military lorry arrived to take us the rest of our journey and we arrived late in the afternoon at the Japanese headquarters, which was on an eminence about ten miles south of the town.

The place consisted only of a few wooden huts guarded by sentries who presented arms at our approach. We were received by a Japanese colonel surrounded by his officers, and their hand-shakes surprised me once again by their apparent cordiality. I knew perfectly well that these men were suffering in their hearts and that their pride had been bitterly humbled, but the order of their Emperor was enough to make them conceal their feelings and no one could have suspected in these polite and smiling men the mortification of defeat.

Maps were unrolled on tables and whilst orderlies passed round tea, biscuits and cigarettes arrangements were made for our visit to Hiroshima the next day.

As the sun went down we boarded a little steamer which took us to the island of Miyajima where the commission was to stay throughout its visit.

A little fishing village shaded by pine trees appeared around a creek of fine sand. It was dominated by the entrance to an old Buddhist temple, a shrine much visited by Japanese soldiers anxious to learn their fate. The priests would give them a written reply and they would carry it near their hearts to preserve them — not from death, but from lack of courage. If the presage were unfavourable they would pin it to one of the sacred trees near the temple in the hope that the gesture would avert the wrath of Buddha.

At the swimming pool, full of very hot water, at the little Japanese hotel where we were staying I met almost all the other members of the commission. Its head, General Farrel, was a physicist, and his immediate entourage consisted of three officers, Colonel Warren and Captains Flick and Nollen, and a Medical Corps colonel named Oughterson. They all observed the Japanese custom and dressed in kimonos, walking bare-footed on the carpeting of plaited rush.

The party was joined by two Japanese, a doctor of medicine named Motohashi, and one of the leading surgeons in Japan, Professor Tsusuki of the Imperial University of Tokio.

The professor was a highly emotional man of great intelligence. He spoke English and often his thoughts were expressed in short, almost vehement, phrases which he underlined with sudden gestures.

'Hiroshima — terrible. I saw it coming, over twenty years ago.'

He was not referring to Japanese research work into the splitting of the atom, which was far advanced in Tokio where the university possessed a cyclotron, but to a strange experience of his own which had not attracted much attention at the time.

'In 1923 I was a young doctor at the Imperial University,' he told us. 'We had just bought the first Coolidge tubes from America for the treatment of cancer. One evening when I had stayed behind in the laboratory after all the others had gone I suddenly had an idea. I took a rabbit and exposed it fully to the X-rays. I was interested to see what the effect of a full exposure to these new rays would be on a living body. I switched on the tube at nine o'clock. At half past nine the rabbit showed no signs of any effect whatever, and it was the same at ten o'clock. An hour later its reactions were still quite normal. By midnight I was bored with the whole thing because nothing whatever had happened and I switched off the current.

'I took the rabbit into my office and put it down on the carpet and lit a cigarette. Quite suddenly the rabbit went into convulsions and after one or two wild jumps it died before my eyes. I was deeply impressed and I tried to account for that delayed-action death. Rather disappointed and very much interested by the experiment I put the body of the rabbit into the refrigerator for examination later.

'The next day when I told the head of the clinic about it I had to accept a certain amount of half-humorous reproach and I was told that in some countries I might have been prosecuted for cruelty to animals. I put up with his chaff and said nothing. A few days later I made the autopsy on my rabbit, and to my astonishment I found that all its internal organs, the kidneys, the lungs, the heart, were suffused with blood from haemorrhages. Further experiments on a dozen or so other rabbits produced the same symptoms.'

Dr. Tsusuki took a document from his case. It was the report of his observations on the subject to the XXVII Congress of the American Radiological Society in Detroit in 1926. Dr. G. E. Pfahler of Philadelphia had commented with keen interest on his conclusions. The whole appeared later in New York in a leading medical publication under the title: 'Experimental Studies on the Biological Action of Hard Roentgen Rays.'

'Tomorrow when you go to Hiroshima you will see the upshot of my experiment,' said Professor Tsusuki, '80,000 dead and 100,000 wounded. The effects of the atomic bomb are almost exactly the same. The magnitude of the experiment is greater, far greater, but that's all.'

Early on September 9th the investigation commission left the island of Miyajima. From our hotel we walked along the shore to the little harbour. In the soft and diffused light of the early morning, the gilded pediments of the temple gate were lapped by the incoming tide. We boarded the boat which was to take us over the arm of sea which separated us from the main island.

A car was waiting for us there and I sat between two Japanese interpreters, a Miss Ito, who had been born in Canada, and a Japanese journalist who had spent twenty years in the United States. They both gave me a great deal of information about what Hiroshima had once been: its main activities and its geographical situation. I needed their accounts to compare the reality of yesterday, a busy prosperous town, with the reality of today: the desolating spectacle after its utter destruction by one flash of blinding searing light.

'Hiroshima,' explained the fragile Miss Ito in her blue kimono, 'means "the broad island". It was built on the delta of the river Ota which flows down from Mount Kamuri, and it was the seventh town in point of size in Japan. The seven arms of the Oto — seven rivers which pour their waters into the inland sea — enclose in an almost perfect triangle the harbour of the town, the factories, an arsenal, oil refineries and warehouses. Hiroshima had a population of 250,000 people and, in addition, there was a garrison of about 150,000 soldiers.'

The journalist described the main official buildings of the town, which were built of reinforced concrete and dominated a sea of low-roofed Japanese houses extending over six miles to the wooded hills I could see in the distance.

'The town was not much damaged,' he explained. 'It had suffered very little from bombing. There were only two minor raids, one on March 19th last by a squadron of American naval planes, and one on April 30th by a Flying Fortress.

'On August 6th there wasn't a cloud in the sky above Hiroshima, and a mild, hardly perceptible wind blew from the south. Visibility was almost perfect for ten or twelve miles.

'At nine minutes past seven in the morning an air-raid warning sounded and four American B.29 planes appeared. To the north of the town two of them turned and made off to the south and disappeared in the direction of the Shoho Sea. The other two, after having circled the neighbourhood of Shukai, flew off at high speed southwards in the direction of the Bingo Sea.

'At 7.31 the all-clear was given. Feeling themselves in safety people came out of their shelters and went about their affairs and the work of the day began.

'Suddenly a glaring whitish pinkish light appeared in the sky accompanied by an unnatural tremor which was followed almost immediately by a wave of suffocating heat and a wind which swept away everything in its path.

'Within a few seconds the thousands of people in the streets and the gardens in the centre of the town were scorched by a wave of searing heat. Many were killed instantly, others lay writhing on the ground screaming in agony from the intolerable pain of their burns. Everything standing upright in the way of the blast, walls, houses, factories and other buildings, was annihilated and the debris spun round in a whirlwind and was carried up into the air. Trams were picked up and tossed aside as though they had neither weight nor solidity. Trains were flung off the rails as though they were toys. Horses, dogs and cattle suffered the same fate as human beings. Every living thing was petrified in an attitude of indescribable suffering. Even the vegetation did not escape. Trees went up in flames, the rice plants lost their greenness, the grass burned on the ground like dry straw.

'Beyond the zone of utter death in which nothing remained alive houses collapsed in a whirl of beams, bricks and girders. Up to about three miles from the centre of the explosion lightly built houses were flattened as though they had been built of cardboard. Those who were inside were either killed or wounded. Those who managed to extricate themselves by some miracle found themselves surrounded by a ring of fire. And the few who succeeded in making their way to safety generally died twenty or thirty days later from the delayed effects of the deadly gamma rays. Some of the reinforced concrete or stone buildings remained standing but their interiors were completely gutted by the blast.

'About half an hour after the explosion whilst the sky all around Hiroshima was still cloudless a fine rain began to fall on the town and went on for about five minutes. It was caused by the sudden rise of over-heated air to a great height, where it condensed and fell back as rain. Then a violent wind rose and the fires extended with terrible rapidity, because most Japanese houses are built only of timber and straw.

'By the evening the fire began to die down and then it went out. There was nothing left to burn. Hiroshima had ceased to exist.'

The Japanese broke off and then pronounced one word with indescribable but restrained emotion:

'Look.'

We were then rather less than four miles away from the Aioi Bridge, which was immediately beneath the explosion, but already the roofs of the houses around us had lost their tiles and the grass was yellow along the roadside. At three miles from the centre of the devastation the houses were already destroyed, their roofs had fallen in and the beams jutted out from the wreckage of their walls. But so far it was only the usual spectacle presented by towns damaged by ordinary high explosives.

About two and a half miles from the centre of the town all the buildings had been burnt out and destroyed. Only traces of the foundations and piles of debris and rusty charred ironwork were left. This zone was like the devastated areas of Tokio, Osaka and Kobé after the mass fall of incendiaries.

At three-quarters of a mile from the centre of the explosion nothing at all was left. Everything had disappeared. It was a stony waste littered with debris and twisted girders. The incandescent breath of the fire had swept away every obstacle and all that remained upright were one or two fragments of stone walls and a few stoves which had remained incongruously on their base.

We got out of the car and made our way slowly through the ruins into the centre of the dead city. Absolute silence reigned in the whole necropolis. There was not even a survivor searching in the ruins, though some distance away a group of soldiers were clearing a passage through the debris. Here and there a little grass was beginning to sprout amidst the ruins, but there was not a bird or an animal to be seen anywhere.

Professor Tsusuki led the way and spoke in a loud voice so that we could all hear what he said. His sentences came to us disjointed as though by deep excitement and emotion.

'We must open our minds ... We must try to understand everything.'

He pointed to the remnants of a wall, the base of which ran for perhaps six or seven yards.

'There was a hospital here, gentlemen. Two hundred beds, eight doctors, twenty nurses. Every single one and all the patients were killed. Never mind. What does it matter. That's what an atomic bomb does.'

Sometimes I could catch only the last words of a sentence:

'. . . open our minds . . . so much to say. Let's go on to other things.

'Here's a half-destroyed bank. Employees from another town came here two days after the explosion. They spent the night in a room which had a metal curtain rail and silk curtains. They are both down with pernicious anaemia. . . .'

Whilst the American physicists took notes and used their detecting instruments to make quite certain that all radiation had ceased Dr. Tsusuki led his fellow doctors to the hospitals. It was there that the most terrible sights of all awaited us.

These 'hospitals' had been set up on the outskirts of the town in the rare buildings which had escaped complete destruction and were regarded as 'less damaged'. Even if there was no roof and only the walls standing, scores and sometimes even hundreds of wounded had been carried there. There were no beds, no water, no medical supplies and no proper medical attention.

The first of these places visited was installed in a former school which had been only partly demolished. Eighty patients were stretched out on the bare floor and there was nothing to protect them from the rain or the chill air of the nights. In many cases their wounds were still unbound and clouds of flies had settled on them. A few pots of ointment were ranged on a shelf. Substitute bandages had been made out of some coarse material. That was all the medical attention half a dozen nurses assisted by perhaps a dozen or so girls whose ages ranged from twelve to fifteen, could give their patients.

Professor Tsusuki was now talking of the patients as he had previously talked of the ruins. He pointed to one woman, who was only semi-conscious. The flames had disfigured her face.

'Infection of the blood,' he observed dryly. 'White corpuscles almost entirely destroyed. Gamma rays. Nothing to be done about it. She'll be dead this evening or tomorrow. That's what an atomic bomb does.'

We visited dozens of such improvised hospitals as well as the hospital of the Japanese Red Cross Society, which was ultra-modern. It had no glass in any of its windows now and all its laboratory apparatus had been put out of commission. Six hundred out of a thousand patients had died in the first few days and been buried somehow in the neighbourhood of the hospital.

One could go on indefinitely describing the horror of it all; the thousands of helpless, suffering bodies stretched out on the ground; the thousands of swollen charred faces; the ulcerated backs; the suppurating arms raised up in order to avoid contact with any covering.

And each one of those human beings represented an infinity of suffering. Those disfigured masks would always retain the horror of what they had witnessed. What must they have been thinking when they saw the neat American uniforms passing through their ranks?

Professor Tsusuki had no time for discretion and he continued to talk loudly:

'All these people here,' and he indicated them with a wave of his arm, 'are lost. Condemned to death. This one has angina necrosis. That one has leucopaenia. In many cases it is impossible to administer blood transfusions; the vessels burst.'

We went into a shed away at the bottom of a garden. The fumes of formol made the eyes smart. Tsusuki raised a sheet under which two almost carbonized bodies were lying.

'We must open our minds,' he said.

To listen to him one would have thought that we were in a giant laboratory, operating with thousands and thousands of human beings instead of guinea pigs, and it was in this spirit of passionate scientific interest that he showed us dissected members, histological cuts and tables of statistics drawn up according to his clinical and pathological anatomical investigations.

'Under the microscope you can see every possible aspect from advanced hyperaemia to muscular atrophy and degeneration. It seems that the cause of death is severe aplastic anaemia with leuco-paenia and all the usual complications: infection, septicaemia. . . .'

He turned to me holding a dissected brain congested and suffused with blood, and in a peremptory voice he said bluntly:

'Yesterday it was rabbits; today it's Japanese.'

The Commission of Investigation went on to Nagasaki to con-tinue its study of the effects of the bomb there and I stayed behind to supervise the distribution of the medical supplies we had brought with us.

A young Japanese doctor accompanied me to the train when I left to return to Tokio.

On what remained of the station façade the hands of the clock had been stopped by the fire at 8.15.

It was perhaps the first time in the history of humanity that the birth of a new era was recorded on the face of a clock.

CHAPTER V

THE MURDER OF DR. VISCHER

By September all the Americans who had been prisoners of war in Japan were repatriated.

Our delegation in Tokio now had different tasks. We began to assist, feed and clothe the thousands of foreigners who had been caught in Japan at the beginning of the war and who had lived there throughout the war, often in very miserable circumstances. Amongst them were many priests, French and Italian missionaries, and nuns who had lived behind their convent walls for three years, cut off from the outside world. There were also hundreds of Jews, many of them Germans who had been expelled from the Nazi colony and sometimes imprisoned and tortured by the Japanese.

Fortunately the foodstuffs and the clothing handed over to us by the Americans represented quite a considerable stock. From all the 103 camps into which they had parachuted supplies we obtained something like 400,000 dollars worth.

We also co-operated, wherever our assistance and our mediation was of some service, in that vast movement of withdrawal which during the course of about a year brought back 9 million Japanese to their own narrow territory, the already greatly over-populated Japanese mainland.

In addition to those 9 million returned Japanese there were 9 million others who had lost their homes as a result of the bombings. Extreme privation prevailed in most Japanese homes, in all the devastated towns, and in all the idle factories, but the Japanese suffered in disciplined silence. Their obedience to the behests of their Emperor was as absolute in defeat as it had been fourteen years before when they had set out to conquer the Asiatic continent. On board the Liberty ships which the Americans had handed over to them they returned home from China, Malaya and Burma until soon the only Japanese prisoners left were in Russian hands, the men of the Manchurian army.

The delegates of the International Committee of the Red Cross, some of whom had not been heard of for two or three years, now began to get into touch with Geneva again from Batavia, Singapore, Manilla and Hong-Kong or Shanghai. One only did not re-appear. That was Dr. Vischer, who had been stationed at Bandjermasin in Dutch Borneo at the time of the Japanese invasion.

And yet a month before when I had given the Gaimucho a list of our delegates in the Far East and asked that my instructions should be forwarded to them the name of Vischer had aroused no comment.

'We will do so,' was all the head of the Prisoner-of-War Department had said.

Vischer had not acknowledged the receipt of my instructions.

I began to press Tokio to find out the reason for his silence, and in the end the same official informed me laconically:

'Dr. Vischer is dead.'

'When did he die?'

'In December 1943.'

'Why wasn't I told before?'

'Our Navy Department will be able to give you an explanation.'

But when I pursued my inquiries at the Japanese Navy Department I was met with evasions.

'All the documents in the case were burnt during the fire at the ministry.'

'What documents in what case?'

'Dr. Vischer and his wife were tried and convicted by a Japanese naval court.'

I sprang to my feet indignantly.

'Why were they tried? If the documents are missing then I want to have the witnesses and the members of the court found.'

The officer hesitated and then promised that inquiries would be made. Three weeks later I found myself face to face with the Naval prosecutor of Bandjermasin, a young and more than usually stolid lieutenant.

'I conducted the investigations in the case,' he observed tonelessly.

I kept my anger under control; I wanted to learn all the details.

'What offence were they charged with?' I asked.

'Dr. Vischer was in possession of a revolver.'

'What of it? Everyone goes armed in Borneo, if only for protection against jackals.'

'We also think that he tried to get into touch by wireless with enemy submarines.'

'Did he have a wireless broadcasting station in his hospital then?'

'No, it was kept in the hut of a native.'

'So I suppose the native was tried as well?'

'No, only Dr. Vischer.'

'What information had he been transmitting?'

'Information concerning prisoners of war and interned Dutch civilians.'

'If the Japanese Government had applied the provisions of the Geneva Convention as it promised to do it would have transmitted such information, not prevented it.'

'He was in receipt of money from abroad.'

'Of course he was: the money came from the Swiss Legation through the medium of your government to help carry on his work.'

'He was also accused of more serious things.'

'What, for instance?'

'He tried to get into touch with the internees themselves.'

'Of course he did; that was his duty.'

I tried to master the poignant emotion I felt at the tragic deaths of a brave man and his wife.

The Japanese did not understand in the slightest degree what I felt or what I was thinking. He was quite sure that he had brought home to me the guilt of the man whose head he had demanded, and obtained, and he added as though to clinch the matter:

'Dr. Vischer and his wife admitted everything and they confessed to having taken part in a great anti-Japanese plot.'

I wanted to hear no more and I asked for a written report.

'The records of the court have been destroyed,' the fellow replied.

'Then use your memory to reconstruct the case,' I demanded.

Four days later I had the original text of the indictment in my hands. I had only to read between the lines to realize the sufferings Vischer and his wife must have endured. I could see their crushed fingers as they were 'examined'. I could see the sordid prison in which the 'Kempetei' examiners manhandled and flogged them in order to extort the 'confession'. At the trial itself Japanese was the only language allowed. There was no interpreter and no defending counsel. Any defence was impossible. Dr. Vischer and his wife were probably unaware that sentence of death had been passed on them when they were taken out to the place of execution and be-headed together with the twenty-six hostages whose lives they had tried to save.

And the man who had demanded and obtained the slaughter stood before me, without remorse, impassive. Perhaps he was right from his standpoint. I knew as well as he did that Vischer had been guilty of doing his duty to the last; guilty of having tried to learn the names of the hostages; guilty of having informed them — by what acts of complicity and with what dangers to himself, his wife and his friends! — that he would do his best to plead their cause with the Japanese authorities; and guilty of having tried to assist them, and perhaps of having succeeded in assisting them; guilty of having smuggled news to them, or simply that food more precious than bread, that water more precious than the clearest spring — hope.

There was no need for me to read the record of the trial. I could only tell the impassive faced man who had decided that they had committed a crime what Vischer's instructions as a delegate of the Red Cross had been.

I knew that Vischer was guilty of having done everything in his power for the prisoners — out of 700 allied internees in Borneo only six were still alive on the day of liberation.

I knew that Vischer was guilty of having done everything in his power to make known their fate, even to the extent of using a clandestine broadcasting station. If he had actually sent messages in this way I knew who it was he was trying to reach in his efforts to secure help: Geneva.

I knew that Vischer and his wife were guilty of a plot — not an anti-Japanese plot, but a world-wide plot — to bring aid to suffering humanity under a white flag bearing a red cross.

And I knew that Vischer would have seen that flag flying in his mind's eye even when the sabre whistled through the air to end his life.

Four months had passed since my plane had touched down on Hanayo air field and my mission in Japan was approaching its end.

Before returning to Europe I was to go to China and Malaya to get into touch with our delegates in the Far East. Separated from each other by thousands of miles, fifteen or sixteen Swiss, doctors, missionaries, merchants and business men, went about the affairs of the International Committee of the Red Cross in Asia. With Egli and Jost in Shanghai I should meet Senn from Chunking, Zindel from Hong-Kong and Bessmer from Manilla. With Schweizer at Singapore I should meet Hurlimann of Saigon, Lüthy of Sumatra, Helbling of Batavia and Salzmann of Bangkok.

Each of them would tell me his story, and I could only hope that one day those stories might appear in print to show the world the battle these men had fought — often in the face of wounds and humiliations — to defend the defenceless and to save even a little of their threatened existence.

A few days before I left Tokio, on the morning of Thanksgiving Day, Brigadier-General Baker, one of the American officers in charge of foreign relations, informed me that General MacArthur wished to receive the delegation of the International Red Cross.

I went to the reception together with Margherita Straehler and our comrades Angst and Pestalozzi, who had spent the whole of the war in Japan, standing up to the bombings and doing everything they could to alleviate the lot of the allied prisoners.

General MacArthur received us in his light and airy office on the top floor of the Daiichi building. He was wearing the ordinary service uniform of the U.S. Army and the only indication of his high rank were five stars on each shoulder strap. Leaving his desk he came towards us, a very upright man with a slim, pale face in which two piercing eyes glowed under thick brows.

He invited us all to sit down near the window, which gave on to the grounds of the Imperial Palace, and sitting down with us and smoking his traditional corncob pipe he talked to us freely.

He thanked us for the work we had done on behalf of the imprisoned Americans, but we could feel that his thoughts went even further than the fate of his own men. He was thinking of everyone who had been assisted and protected by the Red Cross, of all those who in their exile and humiliation had no other hope of assistance.

'The supreme value of human life and human blood has been forgotten,' he said, 'and human dignity too.'

In a firm voice, emphasizing each word, he went on:

'Force is not a solution for man's problems. Force on its own is nothing. It never has the last word. Perhaps you find it strange that I, a professional soldier, should say that to you.'

The chief architect of victory in the Pacific did not conceal his opinion that peace still lay far ahead in the future. When his glance turned towards the south could he still see the monstrous column of smoke which marked the final hecatomb of five years of war?

'Even with our present weapons,' he went on, 'not including those still to be developed, a new war would leave nothing behind worthy of mention.'

And in even more precise terms he sketched the danger of death and destruction which still hung over the world.

'Too much has been destroyed in this war, and the physical exhaustion is too great, for there to be another war during the next twenty or twenty-five years. But what will happen after that? What will happen unless between now and then we do everything possible to save mankind from itself?'

His voice took on an aggressive tone when he spoke of the 'crackpots' who disturbed and misled public opinion whilst that terrible question, the only real question, still remained unanswered.

'What disinterested voices are there today?' he asked. 'The Churches can no longer make themselves heard. They raise their voices only once a week whilst the crackpots pour out their insane propaganda on the wireless every day.'

And suddenly he turned to us:

'Who can unite sufficient voices everywhere to speak clearly, no longer in the name of force, but in the name of the spirit?'

There was a moment's silence.

'Perhaps the Red Cross could do it,' he added.

He had already twice sent away an officer who had come in to remind him that urgent matters awaited his attention. He had been speaking for twenty minutes and now his voice became more urgent:

'The Red Cross is too modest,' he insisted. 'It has hidden its light under a bushel. It should not confine its activities to succouring the physically wounded and organizing material assistance. Its aims are too limited. It should go further.

'It holds a unique position in the world. It enjoys universal confidence. Its flag is respected by all peoples and by all nations. And now its value should be utilized to the full. It should be concentrated on the very heart of the problem. . . .'

And his sense of realism dictated his final words:

'It is only a question of finding out if you can mobilize sufficient means to defend those ideas and propagate that faith. Have you the money? Have you the men?'

CHAPTER VI

THE THIRD COMBATANT

THE International Committee of the Red Cross is now permanently installed in one of the big Geneva hotels which was placed at its disposal during the war. Intense activity is going on in the one-time Carlton Hotel over which the Red Cross flag now flies. Here at last is the great building I imagined as housing the Red Cross when, in the sanatorium at Hasenrein, I first received the invitation of the International Committee to take part in its work.

But it was to the Villa Moynier that I returned one evening. In its peaceful grounds the little house from which I had set out twelve years before for Abyssinia on my first mission was now abandoned. I stood alone in the deserted hall; only the big oval table with its green top was still there.

But on the wall there still hung a picture, depicting the gesture which gave birth to the Red Cross, less than a hundred years before: it was the evening of the battle of Solferino, June 24th, 1859. The army of Franz Joseph had fled leaving the French victorious on the field. The picture showed them burying their dead and tending their wounded. The Austrian wounded had no help to expect. Even defeated, disarmed and bleeding they were still enemies. But a man who belonged neither to the camp of the victors nor to that of the vanquished, a man who knew neither friend nor enemy amongst all these soldiers, and who refused to make any distinction between their uniforms, approached the stricken men and attended to their wounds.

His gesture had such repercussions that today it has become natural not only for the 80 million people who today belong to the various national Red Cross societies, but to all men and all combatants everywhere.

The child who draws a red cross with his crayon in his exercise book knows the meaning of the emblem he sees everywhere: on a parcel of bandages or medicaments, on the side of an ambulance and on the flag flying over a hospital. There is not a man, or a woman or a child who has not at some time or the other been given assistance in its name. In all languages all over the world the word 'aid' summons up the emblem of the Red Cross.

For us of the Red Cross that picture of the battlefield of Solferino does not represent a victory gained by one side and a defeat suffered by the other. It is the symbol of a victory gained by man over himself, a victory which makes him see the sufferings of his enemies as well as of his friends.

But that victory will not be complete until the same protection is assured to every human being who has been robbed of his means of defence; victim of the bullet which hits him or of the idea which he serves. In both cases the victor accepts the same sacrifice. As the victor no longer fires at a wounded enemy so he must contain himself equally towards his disarmed enemy, who still has the right to the highest thing of all: his own integrity. The Red Cross upholds these two demands, which merge into one: respect for the human being whether he is victor or vanquished.

It was this idea which inspired the two Conventions to which all the nations of the world were invited to subscribe. Every day the experience of their limitations and their defects serves to make them more accurate and more embracing. In the future they must be extended still further as the threat which brought them into being in the first place becomes more terrifying and more universal. The same spirit must prevail above the exigencies of totalitarian warfare and above the bloody intolerance of civil war, whilst the obvious excesses committed even in times of peace must not be excluded from its beneficial sphere.

The texts of these two Conventions merely regulate the application of that principle of humanity of which the Red Cross is the symbol. And it was in this spirit that they were first drawn up. No one can be certain that this principle and this spirit will not disappear from the world if the organization which has arisen to preserve them ceases to keep the flame burning clearly.

No matter what their intrinsic value and significance, texts rely for their application on the action of men.

Again and again on the missions which took me to many theatres of war I have had the lively impression that I too was a combatant engaged in battle.

A battle must be waged against all those who violate, or neglect, or know nothing of, the provisions of these Conventions. A battle must be waged for their proper application and for their extension. And if the texts should prove imperfect then a battle must be waged to secure recognition for their spirit.

Whoever accepts such a mission is in no way exempt from the risks of battle, but he must become blind and deaf to the reasons why it is being waged.

There are never more than two adversaries engaged in battle. But these adversaries are apt to find that suddenly in their midst is a third combatant — a warrior without weapons.

He fights for everything which human combat spoils and destroys. He appears wherever a human being is left, under no matter what form, at the mercy of his enemy. His only aim is to prevent the victor, whoever he may be, from relentlessly persecuting the vanquished.

To intervene on behalf of the victims — often enough that means no more than to recall their very existence (even when they are held out of sight) to the authorities who have power over them, and to make the reality of their sufferings appreciated.

To fulfil its mission in all theatres of war and on all continents the International Committee of the Red Cross had no more than 150 delegates even at the height of the struggle. Sixteen of them were in the Far East and twelve in the whole of occupied Europe.

We were a handful of Swiss, and millions of men turned to us for help in their distress: a letter from a dear one, a sign of life from a beloved family, a reminder to their jailers of the principles of humanity, a visit to their prison camps bringing them a breath of a free but lost world, food to stay their hunger and save them from a terrible death.

It was difficult not to be depressed by the defeats we suffered, and discouraged at the paucity of our human resources which often prevented us from besieging and forcing open the forbidden gates, from being always present, and from being present everywhere our help was needed. How could we not have felt the tragic hiatus between our weak powers and the magnitude of the drama unleashed all around us?

Once we had crossed the frontiers of a belligerent country we often felt terribly alone and isolated in our work.

Where were the 80 million supporters of the principle which was born at Solferino? Were they quite blinded by the great issues at stake, by the hatred which arose in their breasts at the spectacle of their own devastated towns, their own dead and wounded?

How should we not fear the day when there is no longer a single country not directly engaged in the conflict, when no single country is any longer in a position to offer the guarantee of its neutrality to the belligerents?

However, even in a world dominated by fear and violence we sometimes found men who were not neutral but whose ideas were so near to our own that they accepted us in their midst to tend their enemies despite their own sufferings — or perhaps because of them. And they did not hesitate to brave the intransigence of authority to serve our cause.

Let us hope that in every country and in every community there will continue to be men like that, prepared to place their honour as third combatants even above their own battle.

I write this now at a table where all wars, all human drama and all human distress have found an echo. I feel their presence around me now. They seem to converge on this unique spot where so many poignant appeals have been, and are still being, heard.

In the shadows around me I seem to divine all those suffering bodies, all those anxious faces lined with pain, which haunted me during the twelve years of my long journey on their behalf.

I can see the walking skeletons along the tracks of Sidamo and the Abyssinians seared by the burns of mustard gas helplessly crying

'Abiet!' to their Emperor in the heavy night of the Abyssinian jungle. I can see the Italian Semprebene in his cell fearfully awaiting the morning of his execution, and the children of Bilbao stretching out their arms to Maria Olazabal. I can see thousands of children suffering the pangs of hunger — in Poland as well as in Greece. I see the civilian internees of Larissa, and the Russian prisoners of war under the whip of the German *Feldwebel*. I see the camp at Mukden with the bowed backs of its slaves, and the camp at Omori with the American airmen blinded by the unaccustomed light of day. And I see the horror rising from the white desert which was once the thriving town of Hiroshima.

All these pictures are not merely out of the past. They are still with us all today and they will be with us still more tomorrow. Those wounded men and those pitiful captives are not things in a nightmare; they are near us now. Their fate is in our care. Let us place no reliance on the slender hope which lawyers have aroused by devising a form of words to place a check on violence. There will never be too many volunteers to answer so many cries of pain, to answer so many half-stifled appeals from the depths of prison and prison camp.

Those who call for help are many. It is you they are calling.

INDEX

INDEX

INDEX

316